The Anatomy of Error

The

Anatomy of Error

Ancient Military Disasters and Their Lessons for Modern Strategists

Barry S. Strauss
and Josiah Ober

St. Martin's Press
New York

Production Editor: David Stanford Burr

Design by Judy C. Dannecker

Library of Congress Cataloging-in-Publication Data

Strauss, Barry S.
    The anatomy of error : ancient military disasters and their
lessons for modern strategists / Barry S. Strauss and Josiah Ober.
        p.   cm.
    "A Thomas Dunne book."
    Includes index.
    ISBN 0-312-07628-2
    1. Military art and science—History.   2. Military history,
Ancient.   I. Ober, Josiah.   II. Title.
U29.S77   1992
355'.009—dc20   92-3448
                                                            CIP

10 9 8 7 6 5 4 3 2

To the ASCSA, 1978–79

Contents

PREFACE   ix

INTRODUCTION   1

CHAPTER ONE
Xerxes of Persia and the Greek Wars: Why the Big
Battalions Lost   17

CHAPTER TWO
The Alcibiades Syndrome: Why Athens Lost the
Peloponnesian War   45

CHAPTER THREE
Lysander and Agesilaus: The Spartans Who
Defeated Themselves   75

CHAPTER FOUR
Darius III of Persia: Why He Lost and Made
Alexander Great   103

CHAPTER FIVE
Hannibal Versus Rome: How to Win Battles and
Lose a War   133

CHAPTER SIX
Jugurtha Versus Rome: How Both Sides Can Lose   163

CHAPTER SEVEN
Mark Antony: The Man Who Would Be Caesar   189

CHAPTER EIGHT
No Second Alexander: Why Julian's Persian
Expedition Failed   217

CONCLUSIONS   245

FURTHER READING   249

INDEX   263

Preface

WE BEGIN WITH TWO WORDS—ancient history—and a paradox. This book means to speak to today's strategic dilemmas, and yet its subject matter is described by the two words that, in colloquial speech, mean out-of-date and irrelevant: "oh, but all that's just ancient history now." Some may doubt that "ancient" and "relevant" can coexist in a single volume. Yet a look at the world around us confirms our belief that trying to understand the distant past can still offer vital lessons in the present.

The international world appeared very different a few years ago, when we began this book. The Cold War was still pretty frigid; German reunification seemed a fantasy; South African apartheid seemed permanently entrenched. All this and much more has changed radically, and other great changes are no doubt in store. The resulting world order looks new and it may be brave, but it is hardly novel. History is full of revolutionary and unexpected changes, and these changes have always offered both threats and opportunities. In times such as ours, the need for studying history, for seeking models, examples, and cautionary tales in the record of the distant past, is even more pressing than in periods of apparent stability.

In times of flux, the danger of repeating old errors is greater than ever and as a result, the subject of strategic error should assume greater prominence. Today's strategists should be wondering about false steps and roads not taken, about the pitfalls of sending and receiving false signals, about the links between international affairs and the domestic political order. In the chapters that follow we discuss the reasons why we believe that the lessons of errors past are important for modern strategic planning and we explain why ancient military history seems particularly relevant today.

The translations of ancient Greek and Latin texts are either our own or are adapted from translations in the Loeb Classical Library or the Penguin Classics. The issue of how to spell proper Greek names crops up in every book on Greek history, and scholars in the field have pretty much given up trying to achieve standardization. Thus some of our spellings will not agree with those readers may come across in other books. Among the most common differences will be "k" for "c" (Alkibiades versus Alcibiades), "kh" for "ch" (Khios versus Chios), "os" for "us" (Agesilaos versus Agesilaus).

We hope to offer our readers some original insights and interpretations, but we are deeply indebted to previous, political, work by ancient and military historians. Some of the books and articles which have influenced our thinking can be found at the end of this volume, in the Further Reading section. We would never have begun this project were it not for the opportunity we have had to lecture and conduct seminars on ancient strategy at the U.S. Naval War College in Newport, Rhode Island. We would like to thank the faculty of the NWC Strategy Department—and particularly its former Chairman, Alvin Bernstein—for their collegiality and encouragement over the years.

We owe a different sort of debt to another venerable institution: the American School of Classical Studies at Athens, where we first met as students in 1978. The School is a unique place that nourishes the interdisciplinary study of archaeology, history, and literature. In our experience (maybe there was something special in the air during that year in Athens) it also nourishes lasting friendships. While at work on this book we lost two of the friends and teachers we were lucky enough to meet at the School, Colin Edmonson and Eugene Vanderpool. We miss them.

We have incurred many other debts of gratitude: Susan Zilber provided advice from the book's inception; Thomas Olofson skillfully guided the book through production. Barbara Mayor provided type for the maps. Friends and colleagues in Ithaca, Bozeman, and elsewhere have been very supportive, among them Ned Lebow, David Mc-Culough, John Najemy, Richard Polenberg, Margaret Washington, Thomas Kelly, David Large, David Quammen, and Gerald Olson. We have benefited from the wisdom of our teachers, including Donald Kagan's course on the comparative origins of war, Chester Starr's seminar on ancient sea power, Walter LeFeber's memorable lectures on "Great Losers in American History," Ramsay MacMullen's course in the Later Roman Empire, and John Eadie's seminar on the frontier provinces of the Roman Empire. Our greatest debt is to Marcia Strauss and Adrienne Mayor. They drew the maps, corrected our prose, and helped us to avoid errors of our own.

April 1990

Wisdom is better than weapons of war, and one mistake can undo many things done well.

—Ecclesiastes 9:18

The Anatomy of Error

Introduction

THIS IS A BOOK ABOUT ERROR and failure but it is not a book about born losers. Indeed, we begin with the premise that military planners who fail are seldom foredoomed. Unsuccessful generals are not necessarily victims or duds. On the contrary, they are often highly talented men with long records of success. The fail not because they are "born to lose" but because they choose the wrong strategy—because their plan for victory turns out to be fatally flawed. An anatomy of catastrophic strategic and policy errors should not be overly concerned with the psychology of losers, nor is it particularly a subject for persons who see themselves as unsuccessful. Rather, our assessment of military failure is a study of talent gone astray, of good intentions undone, of best-laid plans not coming to fruition: in short, it is a meditation on the many and subtle snares that war sets for all warriors.

Our emphasis on error rather than success is as much a pedagogical decision as it is a product of sympathy for the underdog. Strategic failure is a complex subject. The student of military disaster must be simultaneously unsentimental and awake to the irony and mutability of the fortunes of war. But by the same token, the lessons of defeat are often both more poignant, further-reaching, and more clear-cut than those of victory. Strategic failure should, therefore, be as important a concern to the citizens and leaders of successful and powerful states as to the heads of defeated and weak ones. By studying failure with respect and sympathy, decision makers guard against the twin dangers of idealizing the past and looking down on it.

From the outset, we have been guided by three methodological decisions. First, we have chosen to emphasize strategy and policy rather than tactics and battle. Second, we have focused on the interplay between military factors and the larger realm of the political, personal, social, and cultural forces—in a word, the ideology—that inevitably shapes every commander's strategy. Third, we have elected to write about several of the great cultures of the ancient Mediterranean world, primarily classical Greece and Rome, but also Persia and North Africa. Each of these decisions needs to be explained.

STRATEGY

"No one starts a war—or rather, no one in his senses ought to do so—without first being clear in his mind what he intends to achieve by that war and how he intends to conduct it." So wrote Clausewitz in *On War*, one of the classics of military thinking.

The national goal, what the nation hopes to gain or defend in starting a war, is *policy*. The overall approach to winning the war, the central game plan that determines the conduct and timing of individual engagements, is *strategy*. The link between policy and strategy is what usually decides the outcome of a war. Generals have often won big battles but have then gone on to lose the war because their strategy was defective—because it was not properly anchored to a rational and coherent national policy. Of course, having a good strategy does not in and of itself spell victory, since poor execution can ruin the best strategic plan. But, assuming that the fighting ability of an army is roughly predictable (and this prediction must always be part of strategic assessment), then strategy becomes the crucial variable in the calculus of victory and defeat.

A strategist must take into account the strengths and weaknesses of his own forces and those of his enemy. He must have an intimate and accurate knowledge of the variables of manpower, distances, terrain, and supply— no mean feat in antiquity given the generally poor quality of communications and military intelligence. Clausewitz put it elegantly when he wrote that a strategist should act with utmost concentration of force and with utmost speed, and that he should attack the hub of the enemy's strength—his "center of gravity." A good strategist must resist the temptation to make showy short-term gains that do not contribute to the long-term policy goal. Instead he should harbor his resources for the final victory; he might even have to be willing to endure short-term losses or a temporary retreat in order to position himself for an ultimate win.

Given Clausewitz's popularity among serious military thinkers, all this is fairly well known. Much of it might be obvious, upon reflection, to anyone who has ever been in a schoolyard fight. Yet Clausewitz's most basic point has sometimes escaped attention: *a strategist must understand politics*. Not "office politics" or bickering in back rooms (although such knowledge may be a precondition of success) but rather the great policy aims of states and how these are formulated and translated into action.

If strategy dictates tactics, then policy dictates strategy. For example, a brilliant defensive strategy will do no good if a state's overall policy is to be aggressive, or vice versa. In Clausewitz's famous phrase, "war is merely the continuation of policy by other means." Hence, sound *military strategy* presupposes the mastery of an overarching *grand strategy*. A strategist must have a clear idea not only of *how* he plans to fight particular battles, but also of *why* he is fighting the war. States have sometimes failed in war not so much because they had an incompetent army or incompetent battlefield commanders, but because they chose to fight at the wrong time, or fought the wrong enemy, or were unsure how victory should be defined.

OPERATIONAL TACTICS

Our focus on policy and strategy intends no disrespect to the important subjects of tactical maneuvers, battlefield realities, or combat training. These topics are crucial to a proper understanding of warfare, ancient or modern. If we touch on them only briefly here, it is because excellent work on these subjects has appeared in recent years. John Keegan's *The Face of Battle* brought the subject of what it feels like to be in a battle to a new level of vividness and sympathy. Victor Hanson, who writes about ancient warfare in the Keegan tradition, has recently provided in *The Western Way of War* a graphic picture of that long-obscure subject, the experience of the heavily armed infantryman in classical Greece. In his *Alexander the Great and the Logistics of the Macedonian Army*, Donald Engels elucidated how an ancient army was fed and how it moved. A spate of work on ancient military operations (see Further Reading) has clarified many issues of ancient tactics. Archaeologists have played a very important role by uncovering ancient weaponry and armor, detailing the chronology and function of fortifications, providing clues to the sites of ancient battlefields, and, most dramatically, making possible the reconstruction of a full-scale working model of a classical Greek warship.

Among the fundamental operational realities of Greco-Roman land warfare was the dominance of heavy infantry. Both Greek hoplites and Roman legionaries were infantrymen who wore helmets and body armor, carried massive shields, and fought in close formation. Lighter-armored skirmishers, who used the javelin, the bow, or the sling, were sometimes deployed in harassment operations. Occasionally, given the right terrain and the right

general, light battalions using these weapons could be decisive. But relatively few classical battles were decided by
projectile barrage. Cavalry was also generally light, used
to guard the wings of the infantry formation and for pursuit of the defeated after one side's line had broken.
Among the ancient warriors considered here, only the
Macedonians and the Parthians successfully used heavy
cavalry to assault infantry drawn up in formation. The ancient equivalents of modern tanks, elephants and scythed
chariots, were relatively ineffective against well-trained infantry. Field artillery, in the form of catapults, was used
by the Romans, but unknown to Greek armies until the
time of Philip of Macedon (mid-fourth century B.C.) and
rarely employed even then.

The typical ancient battle was therefore decided by
hand-to-hand fighting. The key weapons were the thrust-
ing spear (for Greek hoplites) or the short sword (for Roman legionaries). The ancient warrior was thus able to
deploy force, to inflict punishment on his opponents, only
at very close range: the length of his arm and his weapon.
In terms of tactical deployment, this meant that ancient
generals tended to concentrate on encirclement and flank-
ing maneuvers. The goal was always to maximize the
number of one's own men who were able to reach the
enemy with their hand-weapons, and to minimize the
number of the enemy's troops who were able to engage.
This is why Hannibal's encirclement of the Roman legions
at Cannae was so deadly: when the maneuver was completed virtually all of the Carthaginians were engaged,
while the great bulk of the Roman troops were helpless to
reach anyone with their swords—other than their fellow
Romans.

Classical naval tactics were closely analogous to those
used on land. Ancient warships were oared galleys,
powered by the arms and shoulders of several hundred
rowers (almost invariably free men; the use of slaves as
oarsmen was the rare exception, popular belief notwithstanding). The main weapon was usually a bronze ram on
the ship's prow; the combat goal of an ancient warship

captain was to ram the ships of the enemy and avoid having his own ship rammed. Like infantry, classical naval squadrons tended to confront the enemy drawn up in battle lines. Thus, as in land battles, the fighting was close up—prow to prow, if not hand to hand. Unlike modern warships, ancient galleys could not carry much in the way of supplies (their speed and maneuverability depended on minimizing the ship's displacement), nor were there sleeping quarters on board. Thus, if the crew were to drink, eat, and rest, the warship had to beach each night and this meant that ancient navies were not suitable for blockades or the extended blue-water patrols typical of modern war at sea.

In general, it is fair to say that the pace of ancient warfare was somewhat slower than that of modern "Blitzkrieg" operations. Classical armies could not move faster than a man could march. Greek armies were usually encumbered with extensive baggage trains (of carts or pack animals); beginning at about the time of the Jugurthine War (late second century B.C.) Roman legionaries carried most of their equipment on their backs. In any case, communication between army (or navy) groups and between field commanders and the central command was very slow and easily interrupted. Intelligence gathering was typically spotty, and intelligence failures were frequent. All of these factors limited the operational potential for tactical innovation. And thus, strategic sense was all the more important.

IDEOLOGY, PARADIGMS, MODELS

In *The Art of War*, the great Chinese strategist Sun Tzu admonishes his reader to "know the enemy and know yourself; in a hundred battles you will never be in peril." Of course he is absolutely right, but by the same token self-knowledge is much easier to recommend than to achieve.

Sun Tzu's concise statement introduces the issue of ideology, by which we mean the matrix of unexamined assumptions, opinions, and prejudices that every human being brings to the decision-making process. As we have defined the term, ideology is not something that one can escape from; it is not possible to think, much less to act, without taking some postulates for granted. And Sun Tzu knows this. He does not advise ridding oneself of presuppositions, but rather admonishes the strategist to be aware of the premises that underlie his own decision-making processes. Such awareness is regrettably rare. Many strategists prefer to assume that their "common sense" is to be equated with perfect rationality, and so they imagine that common sense will allow them to muddle through. Sun Tzu reminds us that sense is usually idiosyncratic and seldom crosses cultural lines. To know the many ideological factors affecting both one's own thinking (on a personal and national level) and that of the enemy is the most difficult task that faces the strategic analyst.

Rather than rely on common sense, we suggest that policymakers and strategists should develop working models (explanations of how and why things happen) and build these models into a flexible paradigm (a coherent and self-consciously formulated decision-making system) that will be the basis of strategic decision making. The paradigm must be not only flexible but multifaceted. It must take into account social, cultural, political, and economic factors—in both one's own and in one's enemies' societies. The ideal strategist is thus a master not only of maneuver and logistics but of the human sciences. He must certainly have a grasp of such technical matters as deploying men in various types of terrain, but he also must understand a multiplicity of subjects not found in a field manual—for example, the roots of the willingness of his own troops and those of the enemy to risk their lives in the trial of combat. He must be aware of the impact the war will have on *both* sides' political, economic, and social systems. Military security policy cannot be made in a vacuum and there is no advantage to a victory in the field that is won at the expense of every value that one's society holds dear.

Where is the strategist to find the models of human behavior that he will use in constructing his paradigm? The usual answer is in his personal observations of the world immediately around him and his own experience of the short-term historical past. These sources are not to be despised; personal experience will always be a basis for understanding larger strategic situations. But if personal experience and short-term history alone are allowed to dominate the model-building process, the resulting paradigm will be very limited. The error of policymakers and strategists who insist on trying to "fight the last war" is a phenomenon all too well known to students of military history. The tragic consequences entailed by this error could often have been avoided, if the relevant decision makers had bothered to go outside the framework of their own personal experience in constructing a strategic paradigm.

We believe that the study of ancient policy and strategy failures is among the most fruitful sources for policy/strategy model building. While case studies from every age can teach the strategist valuable lessons, the military history of the ancient world offers some unique advantages in this regard. The ancient world is distant in time and hence the analyst is not drawn into the emotion-laden game of cheering for the good guys and booing the villains. Because the issue of whether Carthage or Rome won the Second Punic War is a matter of relative indifference to most of us today, the model of strategic action suggested by that war can be pondered more or less dispassionately and adapted according to the paradigm-building needs of the individual.

Thus, while the strategist cannot get outside ideology, he can consider the implications of conflicts fought by nations whose cultural, political, economic, and social traditions are radically different from his own. A better understanding of how ideological factors invisible to the participants led to strategic errors allows the modern policymaker to challenge his own inbred prejudices. If, as we believe, there can be no such thing as a perfectly "realistic" vision of the world "as it really is"—an understanding of the multiplicity of factors that played into past failure can nonetheless allow the strategist an oblique glimpse at the size and contours of his own cultural blinders and he can correct for what the blinders cover up by consideration of historical case studies. In short, history can be the window that will allow us to "know the enemy and know ourselves."

WHY ANTIQUITY?

Even granted that chronological distance may yield a certain impartiality of perspective, the reader may still wonder whether this book's focus on antiquity is fully warranted. Can modern policymakers really derive lessons from ancient warfare? In the defense of the usefulness of studying the classical past, one might, of course, quote tags like "all philosophy is a postscript to Plato"; or conjure up such images as Napoleon on campaign in Egypt, listening as his secretary read aloud from an ancient history of Alexander the Great; or summon the ghost of U.S. Secretary of State George C. Marshall, who said in 1947 that to understand the emerging U.S.-Soviet conflict one had first to read Thucydides. If none of these witnesses are authoritative, perhaps they can at least persuade the skeptic to pause for a moment and consider the possibility that antiquity offers lessons worth pondering.

All very fine and well, our skeptical interlocutor might reply, but after all, have not the art and science of war changed enormously in an age of mass armies and revolutionary ideologies, in an era of air power, submarines, and nuclear weapons? Of course. These and other changes cannot and should not be minimized, but the advent of modern technology has in no way lessened the strategist's need to adapt his military plan to social and political realities. The second half of the twentieth century has seen a series of startling defeats handed to great powers by warriors whose strategic insight made up for their inferior weapons. Algeria, Vietnam, and Afghanistan are cases in point. Evidently, technology has not replaced strategy as the determining factor in military success. We believe that it is precisely the technologically low level of ancient warfare that makes it so valuable an object of modern study.

Twentieth-century thinkers have often complained that we live in an era in which things are in the saddle and ride men. This is all too often the case with military planning. It is a supremely dangerous error to suppose that technology is a solution for the problems of war. A strategy devised by technocrats, based solely on superiority in weaponry is no strategy at all. Machines do not win wars. A new weapon may indeed give one side a battlefield advantage, but only if that weapon is deployed within a proper strategic framework. Strategic planning takes time and thought—attributes that are often pushed into the background by the race to find the next high-priced technological fix to the eternal dilemmas of national security. We believe that one way to correct for this problem is to study the achievements and failings of earlier, less technologically advanced civilizations. While the ancient Mediterranean world was far less industrialized than ours, its best strategists were hardly less sophisticated.

Our own country's recent and wrenching experience in Vietnam is a brief for the usefulness of reexamining ancient models. Consider for a moment the errors in American strategy in Vietnam. American policymakers underestimated the enemy's resolve and overestimated the strength and viability of allies in South Vietnam. More fundamentally, the U.S. government failed to realize the difficulty of marshaling its citizens behind a war fought for an abstract principle rather than for any direct or tangible gain. When American policymakers decided to escalate the nation's role in the Vietnam conflict, their aim was in large part to use military force to make a psychological point. They hoped to demonstrate to the world the iron nature of American resolve by proving the seriousness of the U.S. commitment to South Vietnam. Such a demonstration would strengthen America everywhere, it was felt, because it would show a willingness to respond to a challenge anywhere.

Obviously this approach failed badly, and the failure was a product of the strategic decision to deploy military force to demonstrate resolve. Why was America's resolve such an important issue to American policymakers in the mid-1960s? The answer is complex, and includes such factors as their conception of how states operate, previous confrontations with Communist powers, domestic political experience and, no doubt, even personal psychology. Among the reasons that policymakers themselves most frequently adduced at the time, however, was the model of Munich. Many of the men who planned American strategy in 1965 remembered the Munich crisis of 1938, and Munich seems to have become a central paradigm for American policymakers on the eve of escalating the Vietnam War.

The word that best sums up the perceived lesson of Munich is appeasement. Britain and France had appeased Hitler by surrendering Czechoslovakia's strategic northwest territories to Germany in order to avoid fighting a war. The war was averted, all right, but Hitler's appetite had been whetted. When war came a year later in 1939, Nazi Germany was stronger than it would have been had it been forced to fight in 1938. Furthermore, the irresolution of the Western allies, especially the flimsiness of France's prior guarantees to Czechoslovakia, had been exposed.

American policymakers of the mid-1960s applied the Munich model directly to the Vietnam situation. They were determined that, unlike Britain and France in 1938, they would stand up to aggression and thus prevent a worse crisis later on. However laudable their intentions, the result was disastrous. America fought long and hard in Vietnam, but its resolve was the last thing that was demonstrated. As critics have pointed out since, America's leaders had chosen the wrong model. South Vietnam was not Czechoslovakia, and North Vietnam was not Nazi Germany. North Vietnam *was* arguably analogous to North Korea, an ally of the Soviet Union, and the American public had been willing to fight in Korea just a decade previously. But by the mid-1960s the Communist menace was not what it had been in the American mind in 1950, and in any case the Korean War had been settled in three years. The American public might have bought a three-year war in Vietnam, but when it came to a protracted conflict, Americans of the 1960s and early 1970s became increasingly skeptical about the gains to be accrued by fighting in faraway southeast Asia. In short, because American policymakers had chosen the wrong model they lost the support of the citizenry, and so lost the war.

American leaders made other mistakes and miscalculations in Vietnam—both in strategy and tactics—besides an overreliance on the Munich analogy. Nor was the extent of American failure in Vietnam a certainty in 1965; various midcourse corrections might have led to different outcomes. Finally, Munich was not the *only* model Americans had in mind; models of counterinsurgency campaigns in the Third World, especially the British success against Communist guerrillas in Malaya and the Philippine government's success against the Communist-led Hukbalahap rebels, were also of great importance. Nevertheless, the prominence of the Munich model is an example of how significant the lessons of the recent past are for contemporary policymakers. So we return to the subject of ancient strategists.

It is easy to second-guess failure, harder to learn from it. Still, it seems fair to say that American leaders on the eve of Vietnam would have done better if they had cast their nets more widely and not leaned so hard on the model of Munich. They might have reflected on the difficulty and expense of putting down a popular revolutionary movement thousands of miles from home. A cogent example was close at hand, as the late Barbara Tuchman suggested, in the failure of the British government to sup press the American Revolution in the eighteenth century. But the strategists of the 1960s did not often look to the 1770s for wisdom, much less the fifth century B.C. Had they done so, they would have found themselves forced to confront cultures and ideologies far removed from their own. The result might have been a fresh look at their own assumptions and the policies based on those assumptions. Many of the case studies in this book could have reminded them of the dangers inherent in underestimating one's enemy (Xerxes on Athens, Hannibal on the Italian Confederacy, Antony on Octavian). Reading about Athens' disastrous invasion of Sicily is to be reminded of the danger of following a young, charismatic leader's flattering and seductive evocation of the nation and its ideals—whether that leader be Alcibiades or John F. Kennedy. Hannibal's invasion of Roman Italy demonstrates that it is quite possible to win big battles and still lose a war.

Each of the cases presented in the following pages shows how difficult it is for strategists and policymakers to escape from the web of unexamined assumptions and cherished ideals. The ancient case studies also demonstrate how tight domestic political constraints usually are on the making of foreign policy. There is no guarantee that a study of these or other classical examples would have led to a different American strategy in Vietnam, but such a study certainly would have led to a strategy whose context and consequences were better understood.

CHOICE OF CASE STUDIES

This book emphasizes the civilizations of classical Greece and Italy but it also includes two important neighbors, western Asia and North Africa: places where the Greeks and Romans traded goods, technology, and culture, and with whose people they fought. In two chapters, the central subjects are Persian kings: Xerxes and Darius III. Hannibal of Carthage is the focus of a third chapter, and Jugurtha, King of Numidia, shares the spotlight with several Roman generals in a fourth. Two other chapters concern Greeks: Alcibiades of Athens in one, and Lysander and Agesilaus of Sparta in another. Two chapters focus on Romans: Mark Antony in one and the emperor Julian "the Apostate" in the other. Geographically and chronologically, the first four chapters are set in Greece and Persia of the classical period—the fifth and fourth centuries B.C. The next three are set in Rome and North Africa in the era of the middle and late Roman Republic—from the third to the first centuries B.C. The eighth and final chapter is a kind of epilogue; it is set in the later Roman Empire of the fourth century A.D. and harks back to two of the most important themes of the earlier chapters: the clash of Persia with the Greco-Roman world and the flawed leadership of a young, brilliant, and overconfident leader.

All historians have to decide not only what to include but also what to exclude, and we have left out many famous and noteworthy instances of strategic failure in the Greco-Roman world (for example, Athens versus Philip II, the First Punic War between Rome and Carthage, Pompey versus Caesar). Moreover, anyone familiar with ancient Mediterranean history will notice that we make little or no reference to numerous major ancient civilizations: those of the Assyrians, Babylonians, Celts, Egyptians, Hittites, Israelites, and Sumerians, among others. This omission is no comment on the importance or greatness of these civilizations but, rather, an index of the limitations of time and space, and of our own specialized knowledge.

If our case studies cannot be comprehensive, neither were they chosen at random. One guiding principle in our selection was the desire to provide a variety of strategic decision-making environments. The cases cover a wide range of political regimes: a democracy (Athens), republics governed by narrow elites (Sparta, Carthage, Rome), and monarchies (Persia, imperial Rome). The leaders examined are young (Julian) and old (Agesilaus), born to the purple (Xerxes) and self-made (Jugurtha), patriots (Hannibal) and scoundrels (Alcibiades).

Above all, the cases illustrate a variety of problems in fitting strategy to policy in light of ideological considerations. Chapter 1 shows the problems that arise when policy is a direct product of an imperial ideology and a political leader's sense of personal legitimacy becomes involved in strategic planning. In Chapter 2, we investigate the suicidal policy that resulted when a charismatic general played upon a democratic society's vision of its own greatness. Chapter 3 considers the irony of an elite that was so thoroughly indoctrinated in the myth of its own military invincibility that it fell victim to its own self-deception and propaganda. The illusions of another elite, this one too proud, greedy, and hidebound in the face of invasion to adopt an unconventional retreat and scorched-earth policy, is the subject of Chapter 4. In Chapter 5 we assess what happens when a tactically brilliant general who loves to fight builds a strategy on a falsely optimistic view of the instability of the enemy's alliance system. Chapter 6 concerns the terrible social toll exacted from a state that allows its policy and strategy alike to become enmeshed in the selfish political ambitions of a narrow ruling clique. In Chapter 7 a politician's use of image projection, cultural myth manipulation, and negative propaganda lead to the fall of a masterful field commander. Image leads to error again in Chapter 8, in which an emperor launches a war to enhance his image with his own subjects and loses it because of a disastrous delusion of his own grandeur.

In each case study, we see a failure by policymakers and strategists to know themselves, to know their enemies, or both. In none of the cases is the lack of knowledge just a psychological quirk—as we stated at the outset, this is not a study of born losers. To know oneself is to look outward as well as inward. Each of the failures presented here resulted from someone's or some group's fatal misapprehension regarding the natures and needs of (at least) one of the societies involved in the conflict. It is in the field of the policymaker's vision of social and political reality that the most dangerous strategic errors lie.

Greece and Anatolia in the early fifth century B.C.

Chapter 1

Xerxes of Persia and the Greek Wars: Why the Big Battalions Lost

IN THE BRONZE AGE of the second millennium B.C., Greece was run by a network of petty warlord kings, who organized their states along the lines of ancient Near Eastern palace economies. But this "Mycenaean" world collapsed by around 1100 B.C., probably as a result of invasion, and Greece entered a long Dark Age. The glorious warrior kings of the Bronze Age were remembered only in epic stories sung by traveling bards. Eventually these legends crystallized in the great poems we know as the *Iliad* and the *Odyssey* of Homer. By about 750 B.C. large-scale contact with the older civilizations of the Near East was reestablished by the Greeks and an alphabetic system of writing adopted. In the course of the next quarter-millennium, a unique system of government, the *polis* or city-state, evolved in southern and central Greece.

A polis was a smallish territory (Athens was regarded as huge with 1,000 square miles) with a smallish population (never more than a few hundred thousand persons, generally very many fewer than this). The polis was characterized by the intense civic/political life of its citizens, and by its fierce sense of independence. By 500 B.C. there were hundreds of independent poleis on mainland Greece, the Aegean Islands, southern Italy, Sicily, and the west coast of Anatolia (an area also called Asia Minor: roughly modern Turkey), most of them quite tiny. While the Greeks shared a common language and some aspects of culture, each of these poleis was, in principle, a completely independent nation, with its own political system, its own educational and religious traditions, and its own history. A typical Greek polis tended to fight its neighbor poleis frequently. The system of warfare—using heavily armored citizen infantries—had become quite formalized: a single battle usually solved interpolis disputes, at least for a while.

By 500 B.C. the most powerful polis in the Greek world was undoubtedly Sparta, a highly militaristic city-state that had brought almost all the poleis of the Peloponnesos (mainland Greece south of the Isthmus of Corinth) under its sway. In central Greece, the large and populous polis of Athens had recently embarked on the startling political experiment that was to lead to democracy. These two states were natural leaders of the mainland Greeks, but there was no love lost between Athens and Sparta. Moreover, many other mainland Greeks, for their part, were not eager to be led. It would take an overwhelming external threat to convince the independent poleis of Greece that they should unite even temporarily. That threat eventually materialized in the person of King Xerxes.

THE BATTLE OF SALAMIS

Early one September morning in 480 B.C. Xerxes, King of Persia, Great King, King of the Universe, absolute monarch of the largest and most powerful empire the world had ever seen, sat on a Greek hillside overlooking the straits of Salamis. Xerxes had commanded his portable throne to be set up there in order to obtain a panoramic view of what promised to be an exciting and enjoyable spectacle: the decisive battle of his ambitious invasion of Greece. He intended to pay close attention to the details of the individual actions, so that afterward he could reward the bravest and most successful of his captains—and punish any slackers. Xerxes was a man who appreciated the value of the symbolic gesture. Generous rewards and horrendous punishments were the carrot and stick by which the king kept his subjects in line.

The narrow straits that were the focus of Xerxes' attention separated the island of Salamis from the mainland territory of Athens, a city his army had recently sacked and burned. Many Athenians who had escaped the rampage were encamped on Salamis, and the combined Greek navy was holed up in the straits. The Persian fleet, with its core of crack Phoenician triremes (three-banked oared warships), was poised to move into the straits and engage the Greek ships. The superior size of the Persian navy and the superior seamanship of the Phoenician oarsmen gave Xerxes a clear edge. Furthermore, a Greek traitor named Themistocles had conveniently disclosed to the Great King the Greeks' position and had pointed out that a quick attack would catch their fleet in the straits before the individual city-state contingents could disperse to their home ports. From Xerxes' point of view that was one of the nicest things about fighting Greeks—there was always a traitor around when you needed one.

According to Xerxes' strategic plan, a decisive victory in the battle of Salamis would break effective Greek resistance. With the Greek war fleet smashed, Xerxes' overseas supply lines back to the Persian Empire would be secure. This meant that his gigantic land army could be resupplied in Greece during the winter. Many Greeks would presumably see the light and surrender. Xerxes' massive army would have no difficulty in sweeping away what was left of the Greek opposition by next spring—even the frighteningly well-disciplined Spartans could be beaten if the odds were right. Thus, the naval battle about to be fought promised to determine the outcome of the war. Everything pointed to a victory that would be the crowning achievement of Xerxes' career as king.

The Great King must have felt a surge of pride and excitement at the majestic sight of his approaching warships slicing through the calm waters of the straits. The long, sleek triremes advanced in orderly lines, their stately advance the product of years of training on the part of the oarsmen and their captains. Soon only the little islet of Psytallia stood between the Persian fleet and the Greek ships, who were deployed in a line at the other end of the strait. The drama was about to commence, and Xerxes, as befitted his rank, had the best seat in the house.

When the curtain rang down at the end of the day, Xerxes' expectations had been shattered. His ships were sunk or in disarray, while the victorious Greek fleet commanded the sea. As a result, the Persian supply lines were fatally threatened. The food convoys from the empire, necessary to feed the huge army, were now liable to attack by the Greek warships. It was unthinkable, but instead of making preparations for the final conquest of Greece, Xerxes hurriedly began planning for the withdrawal of most of his men back to Asia. The combined forces of the most powerful empire in the world had proved unable to beat a ragtag coalition of a few dozen mutually suspicious Greek towns. What went wrong?

THE PERSIAN EMPIRE

The origins of Xerxes' failure to defeat the city-states of central and southern Greece can be traced back to the conditions of the foundation of the Persian Empire, more than a half-century before the battle of Salamis. The Persians had not always been an imperial power. In the late seventh century, in the waning days of the mighty Assyrian Empire, the Persians were a vassal tribe, virtually unknown outside their homeland in the Iranian highlands. These highlanders were great fighters; hence Persian units constituted an important element in the army of their overlords, the Medes. Persian units helped to topple the Assyrians, yet the Persians, lacking the Medes' organizational skills, remained in vassalage through the early sixth century. But as their masters squabbled with the Babylonians over control of lands formerly ruled by the Assyrians, the Persians were about to find the charismatic hero who would lead them to world dominion.

Cyrus, son of a Persian chieftain, was born early in the sixth century B.C. The legends that grew up around him claim that as a boy Cyrus showed such remarkable leadership ability that the king of the Medes plotted to have him killed. The plot failed—according to a legend kindly shepherds took in the boy after he had been exposed on a hillside by the Median king's minions. Cyrus claimed his inheritance and became vassal king of the Persians and commander of the Persian forces in the Median army (559 B.C.). Once he had gained the loyalty of his troops, Cyrus organized a successful military coup. In 550 B.C. the Medes were pushed into vassalage by their former subjects, and the Persian Empire was founded. But this was just the beginning of one of the most remarkable careers in military history.

Cyrus ranks with Alexander the Great and Genghis Khan as a conqueror, but he was more successful than either of the others in the long term. Cyrus not only marched his armies over huge territories and defeated diverse peoples, he created a coherent empire. From his base in Iran he led his Persian troops on a wave of conquest that soon encompassed all of the old Assyrian Empire and more. By the time of Cyrus's death in battle in 529 B.C., the Persians claimed most of western Asia from the Aegean to the Himalayas, from the Indian Ocean to the Caspian Sea. Moreover, the rudiments of an efficient administrative system had been laid. The Persian Empire was already among the largest and most internally stable political entities the world had ever seen. But despite his genius for both conquest and administration, Cyrus unwittingly sowed the seeds of Xerxes' disastrous Greek expedition.

Cyrus's immensely successful career of military conquest set an impossible standard for his royal successors. As founder-hero of the empire, Cyrus's grave in holy Pasargadae became a national shrine. His descendants (real and pretended) had to cast themselves in his mold. In practice this meant that the Persian king must be a conqueror. The Persian people expected to be ruled, and the army expected to be led, by a man of proven battlefield ability, a conqueror who had added territory to the already unthinkably huge empire.

Cyrus's son and immediate successor, Cambyses, fulfilled the unspoken mandate by invading Egypt. The operation went well and the conquest was complete by 525 B.C., but the young king did not live for long after the final victory. The Egyptians claimed that their gods had taken revenge for Cambyses' killing of a sacred Egyptian bull; in any event, Cambyses' death was sudden, and there was no provision for a successor. The result was several years of civil war, characterized by a chaotic series of coups and countercoups. The ultimate winner of these internecine struggles was Darius, son of a Persian nobleman. The successful usurper linked himself to the old royal family by marrying Cyrus's daughter, Atossa.

Many noble Persians knew that Darius had no blood claim to the throne. This knowledge stimulated the new king's desire to establish his own legitimacy in the eyes of the rest of his imperial subjects. He publicly proclaimed his right to the kingship in an official autobiography, sent out in clay-tablet form to the major cities of the empire. This autobiography is an important document, because it demonstrates very clearly the ideology of Persian royal legitimacy.

The best preserved version of Darius's autobiography was carved into the face of an Iranian cliff, the Rock of Behistun. The Behistun inscription proclaims that Darius is the legitimate king, and links him with the royal succession from Cyrus. Legitimacy comes from noble ancestry and military success, as the inscription emphasizes. These written claims are given visual expression in an accom-

panying relief sculpture depicting the mighty king dominating a number of his pathetic, defeated enemies who
are either bound at the neck or being crushed under the
king's feet. These enemies are referred to in the inscription as revolutionaries, who were successfully put down
by the armed might of the king.

The other main figure in the Behistun relief is a god:
Ahuramazda, Divine Lord of Light and Truth. The
prophet Zarathustra had converted the Persian nobility to
the worship of Ahuramazda; the central belief of the new
religion was an emphasis on the absolute dichotomy between Ahuramazda's realm of Truth/Light and an utterly
evil realm of Lie/Darkness. For Persian followers of
Zarathustra's teachings the world was conceived as an
eternal struggle between Truth and Lie; thus dishonesty
was regarded not only as immoral, but as an attack on the
good half of a divine order. Liars showed themselves to
be allied with the forces of Darkness, so they had to be
crushed in the name of Truth and Light. The king sym-
bolically received his crown from Ahuramazda; he was
the earthly guardian of Truth. All pawns of the Lie were
by definition the king's enemies—and vice versa. It was
the king's religious duty to punish his opponents
ruthlessly.

The Behistun inscription and relief neatly sum up the
ideology of the Persian king: his legitimacy as king is
based on his connection to a line of noble ancestors, on
his military prowess, on his demonstrated loyalty to
Ahuramazda's Truth and his vigorous punishment of followers of the Lie. Loyalty to family (including imaginary
ancestors), success in warfare, and the defense of Truth
were central to the Persian view of the role the king was
expected to play in the empire. Because the king's authority in Persia was in principle absolute, the ideology of
kingship was a major factor in determining the empire's
foreign policy. All three of the central ideological factors—
family, military prowess, and Truth worship—were key
elements in Xerxes' war against the Greeks.

GREEKS AND PERSIANS

Another major factor in the origins of Xerxes' war was the complicated history of Greek-Persian relations from the mid-sixth to the early fifth century B.C. Before Cyrus's conquests, few Greeks were even aware of the existence of the Persians as a separate people. Indeed, Greek writers stubbornly persisted in calling Persians "Medes" long after the Medes' power had been overthrown, and cooperation with the Persians was later commonly called "medism."

The Persians became a major issue for the Greeks in the 540s, when Cyrus's imperialistic campaign brought him to the western coast of Anatolia, the region known as Ionia by the Greeks. Ionia had been settled by Greeks from the mainland around 1000 B.C.; by the sixth century it was the home of some of the largest, richest, and most culturally advanced city-states in the Greek world—including the famous towns of Miletos and Ephesos. The Ionian Greek city-states did their best to resist Cyrus's advance, but to no avail. By 540 B.C. all the city-states of Ionia and some of those on the nearby islands had been forced into submission; Ionia was incorporated into a satrapy (province) of the Persian Empire.

Some Greeks living on mainland Greece may have watched the growth of Persian power with concern, but most of the mainlanders were too involved with their own problems to worry much about their cousins on the Anatolian coast. Warfare among the mainland Greek city-states was incessant throughout the period of Cyrus's and Cambyses' conquests, so the mainlanders had little energy left to worry about what their cousins across the Aegean were suffering. During the second half of the sixth century the crack hoplites (infantrymen) of Sparta defeated the city-states of southern Greece (Peloponnesos) one by one. The Peloponnesian cities retained internal autonomy, but were forced into a league dominated by Sparta which in turn became the most powerful city-state of the mainland.

Meanwhile, in the central Greek city-state of Athens, an

apparently unrelated chain of events was unfolding which would eventually help draw Persian armies into the Greek mainland. Athens had been taken over in 546 B.C. by a populist tyrant (the word in Greek means "ruler," not "dictator") named Pisistratus. In order to consolidate his position, the tyrant attacked the power of the old aristocratic elite that had run Athens for generations. Because they hoped to break the hold of the aristocrats on the hearts and minds of the ordinary citizens, Pisistratus and his sons successfully encouraged the Athenians to become more self-consciously patriotic: Athens, they proclaimed, was for all Athenians, and was the greatest city of the Greek world. The intense patriotism the tyrants stirred up in the Athenians outlasted the popularity of the tyrants themselves. In 510 B.C. the Spartan army invaded Athens and drove out Hippias, Pisistratus's last son.

And now the link was forged between Athenian internal politics and Persian foreign policy: defeated by the Spartans, Hippias fled from Greece to the court of the Persian king—which had become the residence of choice among deposed tyrants from throughout the Greek world. The Persians were quite willing to offer sanctuary for these exiles because they might come in handy someday. The deposed tyrants languishing in Persia dreamed of a return to power and provided their hosts with useful (if self-interested) intelligence on the internal affairs of Greece.

Meanwhile, in Greece, the Spartans expected the Athenians to be grateful for their intervention against Hippias, and they pressed Athens to join Sparta's Peloponnesian League. But the highly patriotic Athenians were uninterested in dancing to Sparta's tune. They rose up against their "liberators" in 508 B.C. and threw a Spartan garrison out of their city. This revolt led to a series of political reforms that were eventually to transform Athens into a democracy. But, meanwhile, Athens' big problem was the inevitable Spartan counterattack.

Some Athenians were convinced that they had no hope of holding out against Sparta and its numerous allies for long. These pessimists figured that Athens needed an alliance with a state so powerful that even the angry and arrogant Spartans would be willing to leave Athens in peace. Persia was the obvious choice, and a delegation of Athenian ambassadors set out to seek the alliance. King Darius (acting through his envoy, the satrap of western Anatolia) was quite willing to make a treaty on the usual terms: the Athenian ambassadors were regarded as plenipotentiaries and were required to give over a handful of Athenian soil and a measure of water from an Athenian spring. This offering of "earth and water" symbolized the submission of the Athenians to the Persians; in essence the ambassadors had "given" Athens to the king. In Darius's mind, the ambassadors' act was binding and Athens was now his possession regardless of whether or not he chose to do anything further about the place.

But back in Athens, things were changing fast. The new regime fielded a large and high-spirited army that astounded the Greek world with its successes. An attempted Spartan attack fizzled, and in 506 B.C. the Athenian army smashed invasions launched on Athenian territory by Spartan proxies. Suddenly, Athens had no need of protection from Darius or anyone else. The ambassadors' action in offering earth and water became a distinct embarrassment. After all, who had told them they had the right to accept such an unequal alliance? The government had been in revolutionary ferment since 510— were the ambassadors even officially accredited? After their recent battlefield successes the Athenians decided that the ambassadors had acted wrongfully, without appropriate authorization. For Athens, the Persian alliance was null and void. Anyway, the king was a long way away, and what would he care?

From a Persian perspective this unilateral action on the Athenians' part was simply not acceptable. The Athenians had offered earth and water, and now they refused to acknowledge the meaning of their action. They had given their word, and now they were going back on their word. They were liars. Liars must be punished.

Darius's duty was clear. But the king's agenda was very full and had been since his accession to the throne in 521 B.C. Egypt had revolted and now had to be reconquered. There were flickerings of local nationalism in Palestine which needed to be snuffed out. The king's armies were striving to expand the empire into the Indus valley in the east, and, in the west, against the nomadic Scythians of southern Russia. This last campaign did not go well at all. The Scythian horsemen used scorched-earth and guerrilla tactics to good advantage against the slower-moving Persian infantry. The Persian invading army finally had to withdraw from Scythian territory in disarray.

The poor showing of the Persian army against the Scythians gave impetus to a rebellious sentiment among the Greeks of Ionia. To be sure, many Ionian Greeks were probably quite happy to be subjects of the Persian Empire. Persian rule was not harsh. The Persians maintained internal peace, allowed limited self-government, exercised religious toleration, and promoted trade throughout their empire. Taxation was reasonable by ancient standards. But there were reasons for discontent, too. The Greek ideals of autonomy and independence had not been extinguished by a generation of Persian rule. Some Persian satrapal governors were not as sensitive to Greek concerns as they might have been, and some leaders of the pro-Persian puppet-governments in the city-states were unpopular. There were those among the Ionian Greeks who had political ambitions that could not be accommodated within the context of Persian authority.

The result was a plot by several Ionian Greeks against Persian rule. The conspirators kept their plans secret for as long as possible, sending each other coded messages tattooed on the shaved skulls of slaves (the messages, presumably not terribly urgent, were dispatched when the hair had grown back). The plotters were ultimately successful in gaining widespread support, and several Ionian Greek cities openly revolted against Persia in 500 B.C.

The revolutionaries realized that they could not hope to hold off the Persian imperial armies for long without help from the outside. They turned hopefully to their fellow Greeks across the Aegean. But the Ionian ambassadors who went seeking military support for their revolt soon found that most of the mainland Greeks were not very keen. Before condemning the ancient Greeks for their lack of sympathy with their fellow Greeks, we must remember that Greek city-states were independent nations. While many mainlanders may have had sentimental feelings for "fellow Hellenes" across the Aegean in Ionia, most of them were sensible enough to realize that sentiment and war with the Persian Empire were two very different things.

The Ionians' best hope was Sparta. One of the kings of Sparta actually expressed preliminary interest in the Ionians' ambitious plan to topple the Persian Empire. But then he learned that it was a three-month march inland from the Ionian coast to Susa, the nearest major Persian city. The Spartans liked their campaigns short and sweet. A three-month march just to get to the enemy's homeland was unthinkable and the Ionian ambassador was sent on his way empty-handed. In the end only two city-states sent contingents to help the revolutionaries: Eretria, a town on the island of Euboea, sent five ships; Athens, by now the largest city-state of the Greek mainland, sent twenty.

The Ionian revolters, with only paltry aid from their mainland kinsmen, needed a quick and showy success to make the revolt appear viable. This might spread revolutionary fervor through western Turkey. They chose as their target the town of Sardis, a satrapal capital that lay only a few days' march from the coast. The Greek raid on Sardis was successful in that the town burned to the ground, but the approach of Persian forces required that the raiders retreat back to the coast. The revolutionaries' record, therefore, was mixed. The Athenians and Eretrians went home. They apparently realized that the Ionian plan to topple the empire—or even to sustain the revolt—was chimerical in light of the military forces the Persians could bring to bear. On the other hand, the revolt did spread, and it took several years for the Persians to put it down completely.

THE BATTLE OF MARATHON

By 490 B.C. Darius had gotten his agenda cleared. Everything now pointed to an expedition against mainland Greece and especially against Athens: the deposed tyrant Hippias was still knocking around the Persian court and agitating for a campaign against his native city. The Athenians had proved themselves evil liars when they broke the good-faith alliance their ambassadors had contracted with Persia. To add injury to insult, Athens had aided and abetted the revolt of the king's Ionian subjects. The Scythian debacle had left a strain on Darius's military reputation, which the usurper-king could not afford to allow to remain. Unlike the nomadic Scythian cavalrymen, the Athenian hoplites could be expected to stand up and fight for their agricultural lands, and the odds would be right. A quick, clean, overwhelmingly successful campaign against Athens would set Darius's ledger straight. Hippias could be established as puppet-ruler of Athens and the city itself then could be used as a staging area for the takeover of the rest of mainland Greece.

Darius decided that the quickest way to accomplish these desirable goals was a naval expedition. In the summer of 490 the Persian navy, commanded by Darius's admiral, Datis, and with Hippias along as adviser, began island-hopping across the Aegean, taking over the Cycladic Islands' city-states one by one. When the expeditionary force reached the island of Euboea, the Eretrians retreated into their walled city. A potentially time-consuming siege was avoided when two Eretrian traitors secretly let the Persian troops into the city. Eretria was burned in retaliation for the burning of Sardis, and the populace was enslaved.

Viewed from a Persian perspective, the campaign was going splendidly. Eretria was only a short sail from Marathon, a little coastal plain twenty-six miles northeast of the city of Athens. The Persians landed their army of some 25,000 men and established a beachhead on the north end of the plain of Marathon. Meanwhile, the Athenians had decided to fight it out in the open field. The Athenian hoplite army—some 10,000 men strong— marched north to Marathon and camped at the southern end of the plain. Neither side was in a hurry to begin the battle: the Athenians were badly outnumbered and hoped that the Spartans might show up to help fight the common enemy. The Persians, for their part, hoped that Hippias's friends in the city would pull off a pro-Persian coup while the Athenian army was out of town. After a few days of indecisive maneuvering, the Athenian commanders realized that with the enemy in their territory they would have to take the offensive. They formed up their phalanx, marched into the center of the plain, and charged.

The outcome must have surprised everyone. The heavily armored Athenian hoplites, densely packed in close-ordered ranks and fighting for their lives and their homes, made short work of the more lightly armored Persian infantrymen. The Persian ranks faltered and broke, and their retreat became a rout when they ran into a swampy marsh that slowed them down long enough to give the pursuing Athenians a chance to catch up. Later legend claimed that the ghosts of Athenian heroes joined in the pursuit, goading forward their mortal descendants. The swamp became a blood-soaked killing-ground; by the end of the day some 6,400 Persians lay dead, compared to only 192 Athenians.

The rest of the Persian army successfully embarked their ships, despite the best attempts of the Athenians to detain them—one of the Athenian casualties was a warrior whose arm was hacked off as he attempted to board a Persian ship. Marathon had been a debacle, but Datis still hoped to take Athens by surprise. He sailed the fleet around Cape Sounion, planning to make a sudden landing outside the city of Athens while the Athenian army was still celebrating at Marathon. But the city was ready for them: a mighty runner had covered the twenty-six miles back to the city in record time (the original "Marathon run") and announced the victory. The rest of the Athenian hoplites also overcame their battle fatigue and marched in double time back to the city. When Datis's ships neared the shore they were met by the grim spectacle of their recent conquerors waiting for them.

Datis and Hippias realized the campaign was over. Despite their successes in the Cyclades and against Eretria the expedition's leaders would face Darius's displeasure. Datis's fate is unknown; Hippias had the good sense to die on the return voyage. The stain left on Darius's career by the lying and revolt-abetting of the Athenians had been made blacker by the defeat at Marathon. Lest the King of the Universe lose sight of the need for revenge, he delegated to a slave the single chore of frequently whispering into his ear "Remember the Athenians"—or at least so said the rumors that floated back to Greece. Yet Darius never got his revenge. He died four years after the battle of Marathon, before a new expedition could be launched. The duty of wiping out the stain was thereby passed on as a legacy to his son and heir, Xerxes.

XERXES' INVASION OF GREECE

When Xerxes came to the Persian throne in 486 B.C., the campaign against Athens must have been a high priority. Like his predecessors, Xerxes inherited Cyrus's legacy of the need for legitimation through conquest. Indeed, because he was a direct lineal grandson of Cyrus (his mother was Atossa, Cyrus's daughter), the expectation that he would be a great military leader must have been especially high. Greece was an obvious military target: the Ionian revolt had already demonstrated that the Greeks within the empire would always be restive as long as their kinsmen were free. Xerxes' duty to his father was also clear. The Athenians had lied and had attacked the empire but had not been properly punished. The loss at Marathon was humiliating on several levels: liars should not win victories over the agents of Truth. Persians should not be beaten by miserable bronze-clad barbarians, especially not when Persians had the weight of numbers on their side. Puny little towns like Athens should not be able to cause problems for the mighty Persian Empire. Yet all these things had happened. So, despite the sensible advice of Xerxes' "realist" advisers simply to ignore the Greeks—despite the tiny significance of a place like Athens in the bigger picture of the Persian Empire— the plan to invade Greece was personally important to Xerxes. He would win this one for glory, god, and family honor. The Greeks thought he was driven by a diabolical divine force to launch his attack, but Xerxes' demons were only those that drove every Persian ruler in the line of Cyrus.

As usual, it took a while to get the expedition ready to go. There was another tiresome Egyptian revolt to put down, and there was the Grand Army to gather. Grand Army indeed: Xerxes intended to lead this campaign himself and to make it a project of the entire empire. The army would not be limited to Persian soldiers—on the contrary, there were to be units from every part of Persia's empire; the Greek historian Herodotus, our best source for the war, lists 46 different ethnic units. There was no standard uniform: each soldier would use his own nation's accustomed weaponry and armor. There could be no standard system of communication; the expeditionary force was a polyglot mix of dozens of dialects and languages. The command structure was a crazy-maze of complexity, as interpreters attempted to convey the orders of the royal commander-in-chief—and his 6 field marshals, 30 general officers, and uncounted junior officers—to regiments differing radically in size, equipment, weaponry, military tradition, and internal organization.

Accompanying the Persian battle-army was a second army, at least as big, of porters, camp followers, and assorted hangers-on. Sailing along with the Grand Army, in close coordination with the marching route, was a huge fleet of merchantmen—essential for conveying the food that the soldiers and their dependents would eat along the way. The size of the Grand Army made it impossible for the Persians to live off the land; indeed, even finding enough drinking water was a major logistical problem—wild rumors claimed that the army was drinking major rivers dry. Protecting the merchantmen was a second fleet, of warships. Like the land army, the navy and merchant marine were drawn from a broad spectrum of subject peoples.

The total size of the Persian expeditionary force was staggering, literally unimaginable at the time. Ancient Greek writers estimated the total at several millions. Modern authorities have generally preferred considerably smaller totals, but on most estimates Xerxes' troops numbered in the hundreds of thousands. It was probably one of the largest armies the world had ever seen. And this leads the modern strategic analyst to ask "Why so big, Xerxes?" If Cyrus had conquered the bulk of the empire with a much smaller force made up primarily of ethnic Persians, why did Xerxes choose to create a multinational army whose linguistic diversity alone would lead to logistical nightmares? The Greeks supposed that the gods had filled Xerxes with hubris—overwhelming arrogance combined with self-destructive pride. How else was one to explain the actions of a man who had his slaves whip the Hellespont straits (the Dardanelles) to punish that naughty body of water for churning up a storm and breaking Xerxes' pontoon bridge?

But, hubris and gods aside, gathering together the Grand Army made sense in terms of the Persian Empire's need for a form of self-representation. In other words, it made political sense, if not military sense. There was no way for anyone—even the Great King—to visualize the empire as a whole. It was simply too big, too diverse, too complex to be conceived of in abstract terms. But if no one could conceive of it, how could the empire survive? How long would people remain loyal to something they simply could not imagine?

The solution to this dilemma was to represent the empire through its military might. Gathering the warriors of the empire into a single Grand Army was a way to display the empire in concrete form. It must have been a mightily satisfying experience for the king himself to watch his empire parading before him; but it was also good propaganda. The soldiers who marched to Greece would never forget their role in the Grand Army. When they went home they would tell their people about it. The unimaginable power and glory of the Persian Empire was thus made thinkable in the body of the army itself. Imperial subjects who saw it, participated in it, or heard about it would learn that the empire was real and really powerful. They would be suitably impressed and encouraged to be good, loyal taxpayers. They would not be seduced into following the Lie by an inability to comprehend the system they were part of.

Gathering the army was also a way of testing the loyalty of Xerxes' subjects. Any subject people who did not send the appropriate levy would be marked out as potential troublemakers; meanwhile the men they did send would be not only soldiers of the king but hostages for the good behavior of those who stayed at home. Persian noblemen, potential rivals if civil war should ever break out, were also tested. An unwillingness to serve or a desire to withhold one's sons from service showed a lack of faith in the king's invincibility. One Persian noble, for example, attempted to persuade Xerxes that his youngest son should be exempted from the draft. Xerxes was unamused. He left the boy on Persian soil all right—cut in two halves so that the entire army could march between his remains. The bloody object lesson was intended to encourage the rest of Xerxes' subjects to identify their interests unswervingly with those of the king. When the king marched, everyone marched.

In sum then, the Grand Army was as much symbol as fighting machine. Its symbolic and military roles were often at odds, however, and this led to real troubles for Xerxes.

Back in Greece there was uncertainty and fear. Some of the Greek states of the northern mainland had already given earth and water to the Persians; others now hastened to follow their sensible example. Even the Greek gods seemed pessimistic. Apollo's famous oracle at Delphi, among the most important religious institutions in the Greek world, counseled the Athenians to "flee to the ends of the earth." Indeed, it looked especially bad for the Athenians; they could not expect lenient treatment even if they did beg forgiveness. They decided, therefore, to fight it out to the end. A handful of other central Greek states also decided to oppose the invaders, but the centerpiece of the Greek resistance was the Peloponnesian League, home of the greatest infantrymen of Greece. The Spartans saw that a Persian victory would mean the end of their own hegemony in southern Greece and of their unique way of life. They would fight to the death to save their peculiar sociopolitical system. Most Peloponnesian states had to follow Sparta's lead, like it or not. In the end only thirty-one (out of several hundred) Greek city-states joined the Hellenic League that was formed to resist the invasion.

Although Sparta was its acknowledged military leader, the Hellenic League did not have a very tight command structure. Strategic decisions had to be made in council and were the subject of endless squabbling based on local self-interest, old national rivalries, and personal animosity. In the end the decision was made to take a stand with the land army at Thermopylae, a narrow pass halfway up the eastern Greek coast between sea and mountain. Meanwhile the Greek navy would take up a position at nearby Artemisium on the northern tip of Euboea.

In early 480 b.c. Xerxes mustered the Grand Army in Ionia and marched north to the Hellespont. The invasion plan was much more ambitious than that of Darius's naval expedition of 490. Xerxes intended to take all of Greece—the punishment of the Athenians would be only one aspect (albeit a particularly gratifying one) of a much greater campaign of conquest intended to extend Persian domains far to the west.

After the initial difficulties that led to the water-whipping incident, the Hellespont was successfully bridged. The Grand Army crossed into Thrace and marched down through Macedon and Thessaly. There was little fighting to do yet; most of the states in this northern Greek region had already seen the wisdom of accommodation. The Persian army stuck close to the coast whenever possible. This route facilitated the resupply by the merchant fleet—a logistical sine qua non for the survival of the troops.

Meanwhile, the land army was ensuring that the triremes of the Persian battle fleet had secure beaches to pull up on every night. Unlike modern "blue-water" naval squadrons, triremes were linked logistically to the coasts. There were no sleeping quarters on board, and the light ships could not carry much food. Thus, the Persian ships were beached every night, so that the oarsmen could eat and sleep in relative comfort. Owing to these logistical factors, the Grand Army and the Persian navy were mutually supportive and could not operate independently of each other. The army needed the food carried by the merchant marine, the merchant marine needed the protection of the battle fleet, and the battle fleet needed the secure beachheads established by the army. This web of interdependence was a major weakness of the Persian strategic plan: not only did it limit the tactical maneuverability of the various branches, but it meant that even a temporary collapse in the operational effectiveness of any one of the branches would fatally compromise the goals of the entire expedition.

When Xerxes arrived at the pass of Thermopylae, he found it held by the Greeks. He sent his men forward in waves, but they made no headway. When fired from a distance, Persian arrows did little good against the heavily armored Greeks; when the Persians closed the gap, they were at a disadvantage in hand-to-hand battle owing to their lighter armor. Their superior numbers were meaningless in the narrow confines of the pass. Absurd as it seemed, Xerxes and his Grand Army were apparently stymied by a few thousand men. But, as Datis had learned at Eretria, when fighting Greeks there's always a traitor around when you need one (or at least someone who conceives of his own and his state's interest in terms of cooperation with invaders). In due course, a resident of the Thermopylae area came forward to tell Xerxes about a back way around the main pass. Xerxes sent his crack Persian "Immortals" to turn the pass.

The Greek position was now untenable. Only the willingness of a few Greek units, including a 300-man Spartan contingent, to fight a suicidal rear-guard action allowed the rest of the Greek army to be evacuated safely. The Spartan troops earned eternal renown for their inhuman coolness before the final battle and their valor during the battle itself. Xerxes was learning why everyone in Greece feared Spartan battle discipline and his army suffered heavy casualties. But the Greek rear guard was inevitably overwhelmed and Xerxes' way was now open to central Greece and Athens.

While the land troops were fighting at Thermopylae, the Persian battle fleet engaged the Greeks at Artemisium. The Greeks were driven back, after inflicting some losses. The Persian fleet did not pursue the retreating enemy; the oarsmen recognized their duty to remain with the main army in order to protect the logistically vital merchant ships. The delay in sailing south was costly, however. The Greek navy was safely in port near Athens when a violent northerly storm came up, which caught the Persian navy unprepared and destroyed a significant number of the Persian ships. The Greeks were elated, and offered grateful sacrifices to the god North Wind. The Persians still had a big numerical advantage in terms of their battle fleet, but the advantage was not so overwhelming as it had been before the storm. Yet there was surely no reason for real concern on Xerxes' part. Even if the numbers had been even, the tactical skills, superior speed, and maneuverability of the Phoenician triremes gave them a great advantage over their Greek opponents.

The Grand Army moved south, through Phocis and Boeotia and across the hills into the territory of Athens. This should have been the highpoint of the invasion: a chance to grind the hated Athenians beneath the Persian boot; Xerxes would now repay Athens with fire and sword for his father's humiliation. Fire there was, and plenty. The temples and sacred places of the city and its surrounding countryside were sacked and torched. But there was not as much work for the Persian swords as Xerxes might have hoped. After the turning of Thermopylae the Athenians had evacuated their territory en masse. Some of the refugees went to the Peloponnesos, others camped out close to home on the offshore island of Salamis. They hoped against hope that the allied navy, which had withdrawn to Athenian harbors, would be able to save them from the Persians. Only a few dozen old men remained on the holy Acropolis, behind improvised barricades, victims of the Delphic oracle's ambiguous comment that "a wooden wall" might yet save the Athenians. The Persian archers and assault troops made light work of them, but the bloodletting was hardly the revenge Xerxes had dreamed of.

By late summer of 480 the prospects for Greek success looked very dim indeed. Only the allied navy stood between the Persians and the Athenians on Salamis, and the Peloponnesian admirals were not eager to stay for long in this vicinity. The Spartans urged withdrawal, with regrouping for a stand at the Isthmus of Corinth. They had already begun to build a wall across the narrow neck of the isthmus to that end. The Athenians, understandably, were not eager to see their occupied territory permanently abandoned, and their commanders were not sanguine about the long-term chances for the isthmus-wall strategy. The Athenians threatened to pull out of the allied command. Only the fact that Athenian ships made up a plurality of the Greek navy, and the recognition that a divided naval command would eliminate any chances of victory at sea, kept the rest of the Greek admirals in the harbors of Salamis. But that logic would not keep them away from their home ports for long.

From Xerxes' perspective, the campaign was going well, but not quite well enough. He had achieved half of his objectives: he had conquered half of Greece and had half punished the Athenians. The long-term prospects for final victory looked good, but a long campaign was less than ideal. If the war dragged on it might appear—to his army and to those at home—that the king had to work hard to subdue the barbarian Greeks. Perhaps, too, he remembered that the revolt which had brought his father to the throne had broken out while the Persian army was on an extended campaign in distant Egypt. The longer Xerxes and the Grand Army were off in the west, the better the chances that some Persian noble would attempt a coup or some subject nation would revolt.

Many of the anticipated benefits of representing the empire through the medium of the Grand Army would be lost if final victory were delayed for too long—it would begin to look as if a gigantic sledgehammer army was a stupid tool to swat a Greek gadfly. And the hammer's royal wielder would lose the prestige that the campaign was designed to gain him. Imagine, then, Xerxes' pleasure when his men announced that a messenger had been secretly sent to him by Themistocles, the most prominent general of the Athenians and a leading light in the Greek high command. There was always a traitor. . . .

Themistocles' slave-messenger told the king a tale that was music to Xerxes' ears. Themistocles had seen the futility of the Greek cause and was eager to be the king's friend after his inevitable victory. The Athenians would drop out of the war and the coordinated Greek effort would collapse as soon as the navy was destroyed. And the Greek navy was bunched up in the straits, waiting to be plucked like a ripe fruit. But Xerxes needed to hurry—the various Peloponnesian contingents were about to disperse, and the Athenians would go with them. If he did not catch the Greeks now, the campaign must surely grind on for another season, maybe much longer.

There was no time to lose: the Phoenician galleys were ordered into position and Xerxes' portable throne was established on the hillside overlooking Salamis. The Persian fleet sailed into the straits of Salamis—and into the jaws of a trap. As Themistocles had realized, the straits were too narrow for ships to maneuver, so the seamanship of the Persians never came into play. The little islet of Psytallia disrupted the Persian ships' line, and just then a favoring wind sprang up (as it did most mornings, as Themistocles knew) behind the Greek ships. The Greek rowers bent to their oars and their ships surged forward. The engagement soon became completely chaotic, with the mass of long ships resembling a logjam. The Phoenicians were unable to execute any of the fancy maneuvers that made them so deadly in open water. Greek marines swarmed onto the encumbered Persian ships and slaughtered the unarmed rowers. The Persian fleet was unable to disengage, and had fatally lost its momentum.

The battle of Salamis was a naval analog of Marathon ten year earlier, and as unexpected. But it was even more decisive in its impact. With the loss of so many ships at Salamis Xerxes no longer enjoyed seapower superiority. One more serious naval defeat and his merchantmen would be sitting ducks. And that could mean a military disaster unequaled in Persian history: the entire Grand Army could disintegrate if supply lines were disrupted. Suddenly, the limitless possibilities for the Grand Army had evaporated. The only option was withdrawal of most of the Persian forces. Xerxes began the march back—humiliating enough in itself, but made worse by his position, at the head of an army of men who, except for a few at Thermopylae, had never engaged the enemy. Xerxes got over the Hellespont bridge before the winter storms, happy to salvage even an orderly retreat from the debacle. A relatively small elite force was left behind in Greece. Xerxes hoped these men might yet save his face.

What little we know of Xerxes' subsequent career suggests that the king never really recovered from his failure. His forces left behind in Greece were beaten by Greek hoplites the next year in a hard battle outside the Boeotian town of Plataea. The Greek navy followed up its victory at Salamis by making a landing on the Ionian coast and catching the remnants of Xerxes' battlefleet on the shore at Mycale. The northern Greek mainland, the Greek islands, and Ionia revolted against Persia. Their revolt was supported by an Athenian-led naval confederation that swept the Aegean clear of Persian warships. Xerxes was finally killed in a palace revolt/harem intrigue in 465 B.C.

THE LESSON

In retrospect, Xerxes' strategic errors were manifold, and it is not really so miraculous that the Greeks beat him. The goals of the expedition were vague, contradictory, and poorly motivated. Xerxes was trying to do too much. His planning was driven by his desire for personal ideological legitimacy, rather than by any rational assessment of the long-term strategic needs of the empire. Xerxes hoped that the Grand Army would be a fine symbol and also an effective fighting force. It could not be both. He wanted to punish the Athenians and conquer Greece. But the focus on Athens and revenge led him to overlook diplomatic opportunities (for example, the neutrality of Peloponnesian Argos—a potentially devastating weakness in the Peloponnesian League) that might have helped him to conquer Greece.

Xerxes made a basic error that Clausewitz warned against: he did not fit his use of appropriate military force to a clearly articulated goal. The Grand Army was a completely inappropriate tool for fighting in Greece. Its grandiose size would have been an advantage only if it could have been deployed in battle in a geographical setting in which a high percentage of the Persian troops could be engaged. Since the Greeks were smart enough to realize that they would be outflanked and overwhelmed in battle on an open plain, they changed their usual open-field tactics accordingly. When the Grand Army could not be effectively deployed, it became a liability. The hundreds of thousands of Persian soldiers and their supernumeraries did Xerxes no good, but they still had to be fed. This obvious fact led Themistocles to realize that defeating the Persian navy would set up the end of the war.

Xerxes' ideological blinders tricked him into a foolish imperialistic campaign and then into dependence on traitors. The Greeks Xerxes was used to dealing with were not a very good analog to the men he would meet in battle. The failed tyrants, obsequious ambassadors, and other toadies who infested the Persian court learned quickly to tell the king what they supposed he wanted to hear—or what would benefit their personal political agendas. Xerxes' experience with Greeks, in Persia and on the road to Athens, set him up for Themistocles' ploy.* In the end, then, Xerxes lost because he allowed himself to be a pawn of his own preconceptions: about the nature of the empire; about the nature of the king's responsibilities to glory, god, and family; about the nature of his enemy.

Xerxes thought that a Great King had to be a great conqueror, and he suffered the consequences. He apparently forgot about the second half of his grandfather's genius. Cyrus had been not only a conqueror but a fine diplomat who took over Babylon without a fight and (uniquely for a

---

*Assuming, of course, that it was a ploy and not a clever double game. Themistocles himself ended up in the Persian court when the Athenians kicked him out for excessive political ambitiousness!

pagan of this period) earned the praise of the Jews for his equitable treatment of religious minorities. The Persian Empire survived for a century and a half after Xerxes' ill-conceived invasion of Greece because later Great Kings remembered the diplomatic side of Cyrus's legacy and learned from Xerxes' errors.

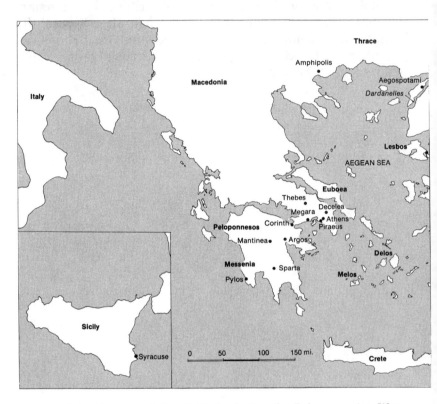

Greece, Asia Minor, and (inset) Sicily during the Peloponnesian War, 431–404 B.C.

Chapter 2

The Alcibiades Syndrome:
Why Athens Lost
the Peloponnesian War

The map on the left shows:

to the Ukraine

Asia Minor

tilene

rginusae Is. • Sardis

• Notium

amos

A COALITION OF GREEK states led by Athens and Sparta defeated Persia, but Athens emerged in the next generation as the big winner. The Greek Islands and the newly liberated Greek city-states on the Asia Minor coast wanted a permanent alliance to prevent Persia from returning. Sparta turned down a role in the alliance, since most Spartans wanted no part of military entanglements hundreds of miles from home. Athens, on the other hand, with its new fleet and burgeoning pride, accepted the leadership. In 477 B.C., Athens became the head of the Delian League, a military alliance of some 150 Greek city-states. An annual tribute collected from the members built up the league's war chest.

Over the next fifty years, the Delian League grew to a membership of an estimated 250 city-states, and Athens changed its status from first among equals to that of imperial power. Athenian foreign policy was league policy. In the league army and navy, most of the men and virtually all the commanders were Athenians. Athens controlled the league treasury, and did not scruple to use it to fi-

nance ambitious public-works projects at home. The Delian League became an Athenian empire.

Ironically, the same forces that made Athens an empire
also made it a democracy. The empire rested on the Athenian fleet, which rested in turn on the rowers, who represented the poorest men in society. By about the year 450,
they had transformed their military power into political
power, too. The state embraced a democratic ideology emphasizing freedom, equality, and participation. Through
such institutions as a popular assembly and jury courts, a
direct democracy—limited to be sure, to the citizen elite,
and excluding women, resident aliens, and slaves—was
put into effect. Political leaders, of whom Pericles was the
most successful, were directly accountable to the people
and constantly had to put their proposals before the assembly.

Athens was the dominant naval power in Greece—indeed, in the eastern Mediterranean—and the Persian
threat, though still imaginable, had receded far below the
horizon. On the other hand, Athenian power was challenged by Sparta and its allies in the Peloponnesian
League. The Peloponnesians were jealous of Athenian
success and feared that Athenian dynamism would challenge their power abroad and their conservative regimes
at home.

Athenians and Peloponnesians fought an on-again, off-
again war on several fronts between about 460 and 445. At
one point, the Athenians gained control of the territories
of Megara and Boeotia to their north and west, but they
had overextended themselves in an ambitious and ultimately unsuccessful attempt to drive Persia out of Egypt.
The Peloponnesians forced Athenian armies home from
Megara and Boeotia. In 445, the two sides made an uneasy peace in which they recognized each other's power,
but many in each camp expected to fight again another
day. The years from 435 to 431 were marked by a tense
escalation of local crises.

By 431, the stage was set for the Peloponnesian War, a
conflict between dynamic, democratic Athens with its

naval empire, and the conservative, narrowly governed Peloponnesian states with their formidable armies.

A STRANGE DEFEAT

At the end of the autumn of 431 B.C., the first year of war between Athens and Sparta, the great Athenian leader Pericles delivered a solemn oration at the public funeral of the dead. Speaking in Athens' main cemetery, surrounded by symbols of family and fatherland—with the Acropolis itself as backdrop—Pericles compared the Athenian state to a parent burying his own children. A man in his sixties, Pericles himself had become a father figure to the people of Athens.

Sixteen years later, in the spring of 415, Pericles was dead, the war was still going on (after a brief truce), and a very different speaker got up to address the Athenians. He spoke not at a funeral, but at a boisterous and controversial assembly meeting. Although he was the former ward of the late Pericles, the speaker could hardly have adopted a more different public persona. He was young, iconoclastic, and far from a father figure—in fact, he was virtually the embodiment of youth in rebellion. His name was Alcibiades, and the difference between him and Pericles epitomizes the reason why Athens lost the Peloponnesian War.

To be sure, Pericles was hardly the Nestor that his many admirers have discerned. As a strategist he was a failure, and deserves a share of the blame for Athens' great defeat. But the lack of foresight that was only a surface flaw in the father became a consuming illness in the foster son. Moreover, Alcibiades was no isolated case. He exerted a fatal attraction on others of his generation. To a remarkable degree, Alcibiades sums up the ills of an entire country, and helps us to understand why internal conflicts rather than external defeats ultimately cost Athens the war.

At the start of the Peloponnesian War, in 431, few people expected Athens to suffer a crushing defeat. Imperial mistress of the Aegean, economic center of Greece, and the most populous Greek city-state, Athens was also the foremost democracy of the day, propelled by a popular ideology of civic equality. In 431, the Greek future seemed to be Athens'.

To be sure, Sparta and its allies in the Peloponnesian League outnumbered and outclassed Athens in heavy infantry: they were supreme on land. But the Athenians ruled the waves, and as long as they did, Sparta could annoy Athens but not inflict any long-term damage. In 431, Athens had a superb navy, with more than 300 seaworthy triremes. The city had a magnificent fortified harbor at Piraeus, a rich infrastructure of dockyards and shipsheds, and access to raw materials for shipbuilding. Athens had enormous and liquid financial resources in gold and silver. The Athenian people were a resource in themselves: skilled rowers and seamen, they were patriotic and knowledgeable and hence likely to make informed decisions in the assembly. Finally, Athenian naval strength guaranteed Athens' food supply, in the form of grain imported from the Ukraine, even if Sparta invaded Athenian territory. By contrast, the Peloponnesian navy was deficient in size, strength, experience, and finances, and the Peloponnesian peoples knew relatively little about naval warfare.

Yet, despite these Athenian advantages, the Peloponnesian War of 431–404 ended in total Athenian collapse. In the terrible, twenty-seven-year-long war against Sparta, Athens suffered an immense defeat, comparable to Germany's or Japan's in 1945. Athens lost about half of its manpower and wealth, as well as its chief fortifications, all but a skeleton fleet, and its entire empire. Sparta was now the strongest power in Greece, and Persia was once more a key player in Greek affairs.

How are we to account for this stunning reversal? Thucydides, the great historian of the Peloponnesian War and himself an Athenian general, gives a clear answer. Sparta did not win the war, he says, Athens lost it, and mainly because of selfish politicians, who put private ambition and profit before the public good. "In the end," Thucydides writes, "it was only because they had destroyed themselves by their own private quarrels that finally they were forced to surrender." He was skeptical about democracy in general, believing that it could at any time turn into mob rule and suffer Athens' fate.

Thucydides' history is a brilliant, enduring analysis of the nature of war and politics. But Thucydides was a contemporary, and like all contemporaries, he sees things a little too close-up. Athens' problem in the Peloponnesian War was neither selfish leaders nor democracy; Athens' problem lay in being a Greek city-state. This may sound flippant, but it is not. As a city-state, Athens was relatively homogeneous and unified, but also relatively fragile. Athens could not fight a twenty-seven-year war without suffering terrible cracks in the foundation of its society. No city-state could. Sparta was an oligarchy and won the Peloponnesian War, but Sparta was soon destroyed by its "victory." Rome, also an oligarchy, did much better in its long imperial wars, but only temporarily; Rome too eventually paid the price, in the coin of one hundred years of civil war and the destruction of its republican political system.

As Greeks, Athenians had another problem. In times of very great stress, Greeks tended to put personal interest ahead of the public good. Worse still, Greek culture had a strain of heroizing and romanticizing the loner whose lodestar was his own glory rather than his country's. This tendency goes as far back as Achilles, the young hero of the epic *Iliad*, a warrior who was as great as he was utterly selfish. When the leader of the Greek army to Troy took away Achilles' girl—his "prize"—Achilles retaliated by withdrawing from battle and sulking in his tent while the Greeks suffered defeats without him. Moreover, stubbornness and the Greek emphasis on saving face made it all the more difficult for Achilles to admit error when once embarked on the road of selfishness. At the time of the Peloponnesian War, Achilles was still a Greek hero and dubious role model.

As a Greek city-state, therefore, Athens could ill afford a long and drawn-out war, because of the unbearable strains war would place on its society, its political system, and its national character. Ultimately, these strains caused Athens' defeat. After the war, Athenians debated why they had lost, but most would have agreed that the human symbol of breakdown and failure was Alcibiades, the Achilles of their generation.

When he appeared on the public stage in 420 at about the age of thirty, Alcibiades seemed to embody the Achilles fantasy, the young prince who can take on the world. This is a Greek instance of a perennial myth, from David to Parsifal to Henry V to John F. Kennedy. Alcibiades was youthful, supremely talented, and well-born: his guardian, the famous Pericles, had dominated Athenian politics for a generation. Alcibiades was also remarkably handsome, an athletic entrepreneur—his chariots raced and won at Olympia—intellectually brilliant, a superb speaker, and limitlessly ambitious. In 415, he urged Athens on to the invasion of Sicily. Even after the invasion ended in disaster, even after thousands of casualties, even after Alcibiades himself had been twice exiled, Aristophanes could still say in 405, referring to the city's feeling for Alcibiades: "It longs for him, it detests him, but it wants to have him" (*The Frogs*).

Alcibiades and the Athenians engaged in a ritual dance of adulation and exile. To the people, Alcibiades represented everything they both admired and feared. Although they knew he was bad for them, they couldn't resist paying attention to him. Perhaps they thought that by taking Alcibiades in small doses, they could build up an immunity. If so, they were mistaken: by war's end the Athenian people had become, at least temporarily, as selfish, unstable, and treacherous as Alcibiades himself.

The subject of this chapter, then, is what we call the Alcibiades syndrome. The symptoms are easy to distinguish: on the one hand, extraordinary talent—ambition, charm, persuasiveness combining both charisma and flimflam; on the other hand, extraordinary egotism. The ultimate goal of life is supreme political power, and everything—friendship, love, sex, education, sports, politics, and warfare—becomes subordinated to that goal. Sometimes the victim of the syndrome is able to achieve great success, but usually, as with Alcibiades himself, his arrogance gets in the way. Alcibiades' scandalous behavior in the bedroom and at the altar—he flaunted his sexual escapades and his contempt for religion—hurt rather than advanced his political career and ultimately cost him the trust of the Athenian people.

So much for the symptoms of the Alcibiades syndrome. Our task in the following pages is to trace its workings in the unfolding of Athenian strategy in the Peloponnesian War. Before Alcibiades rose to prominence, three men dominated Athenian politics in turn—Pericles, Cleon, and Nicias—and each shows signs of a partial case of the syndrome. With Alcibiades' rise to power, we see for the first time a full-blown case; afterward, the disease became a generalized problem of the Athenian body politic, and the corresponding decline of Athens as a political and military power was predictable.

LEADERSHIP AND STRATEGY BEFORE ALCIBIADES

Historians usually divide the Peloponnesian War into four periods. First comes the Archidamian War of 431–421, named for King Archidamus of Sparta, commander in chief of the Peloponnesian forces. In both military and political terms, this first phase of the war was inconclusive. Neither side acquired a clear advantage over the other, and both remained suspicious and unsatisfied. Next comes a period of uneasy peace, the so-called Peace of Nicias of 421–415. In the third period, 415–413, Athens launched and lost the vast armada of its Sicilian expedition: a great defeat with enormous casualties. The fourth and final phase, the Iono-Decelean War of 413–404, saw important struggles, mainly at sea, and was finally decided in the Dardanelles.

Pericles

Pericles dominates the strategic thinking of the first part of the Archidamian War, just as he dominated Athenian politics until his death in 429. A superb speaker and a leader of the democratic movement, Pericles nonetheless was an aloof and frosty aristocrat who won the nickname of "the Olympian" or "Zeus." As a democrat, he might have affected the common touch, but he preferred instead to cut a distant, patriarchal figure—all the better to get the people to follow his advice. By projecting this image successfully, by winning a series of political battles, and by keeping a finger on the popular pulse, Pericles managed to promote democratization without losing his personal prominence. By 431, at the age of about sixty-five and after thirty years as a major political figure, Pericles was Athens' grand statesman, well able to forge a consensus behind his policies.

Because of his clout, Pericles was able to impose a politically costly and unpopular strategy on Athens. Although his plan failed, its daring and originality are still impressive. Pericles saw that Athens had to find a way not only to play its strong card, its navy, but to trump the strong card of the Peloponnesians, their army. The solution was for Athens to become an "island" fortress, supplied by sea through the nearby port of Piraeus, to which it was connected by the Long Walls. The rural population would move into this fortress during the summer months of enemy invasion. In a world in which the failure to come out and fight an invading army was considered unmanly (at best), Pericles' plan was revolutionary and controversial.

Pericles was willing to counter enemy invasions of Attica with sea-launched Athenian attacks on the Peloponnesos. In truth, however, Pericles expected to win the war psychologically, not by invading the Peloponnesos, but by letting the Peloponnesians see how fruitless their invasions of Attica were. In short, he planned to wage a defensive war—or at least a mainly defensive war. Pericles also had the Athenian army invade and ravage its western neighbor Megara, a Spartan ally. The hope was either to bully Megara out of the Peloponnesian League, or at least frighten the Spartans with that possibility.

In the first year of the war, Pericles raided Peloponnesian territory by land and sea. Little damage was done (except in Megara), but that was probably the plan: not to enrage the enemy, but to persuade Sparta's allies that the war was not only unwinnable, but would be a constant irritation—if not at once, then in a year or two. The Peloponnesians' war plan was simpler. Knowing that they could not defeat Athens at sea, they intended to invade Attica, which they expected would bring Athens to its knees, if not at once, then in a year or two. The Peloponnesians expected the Athenians to come out and fight fair (and get beat), and were no doubt shocked when they did not do so. As it turned out, both plans proved ineffective.

In the second year of the war, the Peloponnesians stayed in Attica over a month and did considerable damage to Athenian agriculture, but far from enough to bring Athens down. Infinitely more serious, however, was the epidemic that broke out in Athens in the spring of 430. This epidemic (the precise disease is unknown) would last for several years, and ultimately killed between one fourth and one third of the population of Athens. In the wake of this disaster, Athenian morale plunged. Pericles was driven from office, and the assembly sued for peace. Sparta's price was too high, however; not even an epidemic could make the Athenians surrender their empire. Pericles was restored to office, only to succumb to the epidemic himself in 429.

Students of the war have often wondered why Pericles didn't employ a bolder and more aggressive strategy. The answer has to do in part with his sober assessment of Athens' weakness on land against the Peloponnesian army, but also with his fundamental war aims. Although Pericles had not shrunk from war with Sparta, he had not provoked war either. The cause of the war, rather, was Sparta's fear of Athens' ever-growing power, and Spartan desire to stop that power before it was too late. Sparta's professed war aim was to "free the Greeks," that is, to dismantle the Athenian empire, which was quite a tall order. Pericles might have liked to destroy Sparta's power in turn, but he had no need to go after such a big and expensive prize. Rather, all he needed to do was to blunt Sparta's attack on Athens, which required only a limited war. Pericles knew that a powerful faction in Sparta had opposed the war. By showing Athenian restraint, perhaps he aimed at driving a wedge between Sparta's doves and hawks.

Or perhaps, as Thucydides suggests, Pericles had another reason for his mainly defensive strategy: fear that all-out war would unleash what we call the Alcibiades syndrome. Thucydides wrote with hindsight, however, after the war's end. It is more convincing to see Pericles, for all his virtues, as someone who opened the door a crack wider for Alcibiades' eventual entrance. Pericles proclaimed the superiority of Athenians to all other human beings, and he emphasized Athenians' intellectual gifts. But what Athenians needed was not so much praise as warnings about the dangers of oversophistication and clever con men. Pericles encouraged dangerous notions of an all-powerful people led by an Olympian leader. His own strategy for the war was the epitome of cleverness and sophistication—some would say of oversophistication and of being too clever by half. Pericles neither won the war nor inoculated Athens against the Alcibiades syndrome.

Cleon

By 427, events, and perhaps also Athens' hawks, made impossible any return to Pericles' defensive policy. A leading hawk, Cleon, was now the man of the hour. He has received a bad press from most commentators, both ancient and modern. The ancients disliked Cleon because, unlike Pericles, he was not an aristocrat: his grandfather had made a fortune in the tanning business. Because he adopted populist rhetoric and gestured broadly when making his speeches in a way that appealed to the man in the street but offended the snobs, he has been branded a demagogue. Many modern scholars have condemned Cleon's aggressive war policy as mindless, emotional, and unsuccessful.

The truth is, Cleon was both a hawk and a patriot. Cleon actively courted the people where Pericles had claimed to stand above them. Like a modern populist, Cleon praised common sense and derided the speechifying intellectuals whom the Athenian upper classes adored. But he was neither mindless nor a demagogue in the modern sense of the term. In fact, in one important category he scores higher than Pericles: Cleon warned Athenians against the dangers of oversophistication and of overly clever rhetoric—precisely the dangers that Alcibiades was to represent. Cleon may have been common and anti-intellectual, but he was a straight shooter in this regard.

On the other hand, Cleon did exhibit one symptom of the Alcibiades syndrome: a more than healthy ambition to expand his country's power in various directions. In policy terms, Cleon abandoned significant aspects of the Periclean strategy. Until 425 there was no way to stop the Peloponnesian invasions of Attica, so the "city-island" element of strategy was retained. No longer, however, would Athens attempt to win the war by passively accepting Peloponnesian invasions of Attica and demonstrating their futility. Instead, Athens would move to take the offensive on several fronts, intervening in Sicily (unsuccessfully); on the island of Lesbos, where the Athenians brutally put down a pro-Peloponnesian rebellion; and in northwest Greece, where they denied the enemy control of a strategically important region. Cleon's finest hour, though, came in the southwestern Peloponnesos, at a rocky, uninhabited promontory called Pylos, which Athens seized and fortified in spring 425.

Pylos is in Messenia, a territory the Spartans had controlled for centuries and whose inhabitants, the so-called helots, they had reduced to serfdom. Any fort there might be a refuge for runaway helots, and was as frightening to Sparta as John Brown's Harpers Ferry base for runaway slaves was to white Southerners in 1859. In short, fortifying Pylos was an inexpensive way for Athens to hurt Sparta psychologically and materially. As a result of a blundering Spartan counterattack, Athens trapped some 400 Spartan soldiers on an island off Pylos, including sons of the first families of Sparta. Sparta sued for peace, but Cleon considered the terms ungenerous, and persuaded the people to continue the war. He has been criticized for rejecting a reasonable offer, but Cleon knew that Athens was about to have the Spartans where Athens wanted them, and should not give up. He promised to succeed where other Athenian generals had failed: to storm the island and capture the Spartans. Succeed he did: with the help of knowledgeable locals, Cleon surrounded the Spartans and took 290 alive. With these hostages in hand, Athens was able to continue the war free from the inconvenience of Spartan invasions—by threatening the lives of the hostages Athens prevented Sparta from invading Athenian territory.

Unfortunately for Athens, Cleon's aggressive strategy saw no further successes. Athenian attempts in 424 to invade Boeotia, a Spartan ally on Athens' northern border, failed and entailed very heavy casualties. The same year, a young Spartan general, Brasidas, led a daring overland expedition through several hundred miles of hostile territory, toward Thrace, the only part of the Athenian empire accessible to Sparta because it was on the Greek mainland. Through diplomacy and force, he won over several important Athenian allies in eastern Macedon, above all, the strategic Athenian colony of Amphipolis. This city was important to Athens in many ways: as a military port, as a base on the grain-import route, as a linchpin in the imperial administration, and most particularly for its access to a hinterland rich in shipbuilding timber. The loss of Amphipolis was a major disaster, and it is not surprising that the Athenian commander of the region, who failed to bring relief to Amphipolis in time, was cashiered. He was none other than the historian Thucydides, who went into exile for the rest of the Peloponnesian War.

The loss of Amphipolis brought a one-year truce between Athens and Sparta in 423. The next year, Cleon himself sailed north to try and recapture the city, but he both failed and died trying—and Brasidas died on the battlefield with him. With the deaths of these two men, the "mortar and pestle of war," as a contemporary called them, it was time for the diplomats.

From the perspective of the Alcibiades syndrome, Cleon is a study in paradox. He was neither young, dashing, nor aristocratic; he hated intellectuals and they responded in kind; his rhetoric was rough and gruff rather than smooth and outwardly clever (though, needless to say, Cleon did not choose his words carelessly). In all these ways, he was an antidote to the syndrome. On the other hand, he would probably have agreed with Alcibiades that Athens' destiny lay in expansion. Cleon may have been right to press on until he had captured the Spartans on the island, but he then should have quit while Athens was ahead. Cleon's strategy failed because he underestimated the resourcefulness of his opponents and overestimated the limits of Athenian power and patience. In retrospect, the pity is that his failure wasn't worse—it might have taught Athens a lesson and prevented the disasters of the following years.

Nicias

The leadership of Athens now fell to Cleon's long-standing rival, Nicias. Nicias was no more of an aristocrat than Cleon; his considerable fortune came from huge gangs of slaves that worked in the Athenian silver mines. Even so,

Nicias was much more acceptable to ancient opinion makers than Cleon had been, because Nicias returned to Pericles' calm and aristocratic rhetorical style. The people liked him too: although Nicias lacked Cleon's ability to give a crowd-pleasing speech, he made up for it by sponsoring lavish and spectacular plays, sports events, and religious festivals. A general as well as a politician (most Athenian leaders of this period were both), he had a reputation for winning. But was this reputation deserved? Maybe he did win the battles he fought, but if Thucydides is to be believed, Nicias was so concerned about keeping this reputation that he usually preferred to avoid battle altogether! More a tragicomic than a heroic character, Nicias can be accused by no one of representing the dangerous allure of Alcibiades. On the other hand, his reluctance to fight battles lest he risk his reputation does suggest a key symptom of the Alcibiades syndrome: a preference for his own rather than the public good.

In 421, Nicias was the peacemaker. He led the Athenian negotiating team, and the peace treaty that was eventually struck is usually referred to by his name. Unfortunately, the Peace of Nicias was unlikely to satisfy anyone. Although it called for fifty years of peace, the arbitration of differences, and the restoration of prisoners of war and of captured places, it satisfied neither side's original war aims. Sparta had neither destroyed the Athenian empire nor freed its subjects. Athens had won recognition of its empire from Sparta, but it had failed to take Megara and had lost face because of its defeats in the northeast. Furthermore, there were problems with implementing the treaty. The two major Peloponnesian allies, Corinth and Boeotia, refused to ratify the peace. Nor was Athens able to regain Amphipolis, because the Amphipolitans themselves would not hear of it. A miffed Athens in turn refused to give back Pylos, although the Spartan hostages were sent back home. The Peace of Nicias was virtually a dead letter from the start.

The next six years witnessed a series of shifting alliances and complex, Borgia-like plots and counterplots.

For a time, it looked as if Athenian diplomacy might break up the Peloponnesian League with a new anti-Spartan coalition. Sparta, however, won a decisive victory and restored its dominant position in the Peloponnesos at the battle of Mantinea in 418. All Athens could do in return was bully the small Aegean island of Melos into submission. The islanders put up stiff resistance before Athens captured their main town. As punishment for Melian recalcitrance, Athens stooped to an atrocity, killing all the Melian men and enslaving all the women and children. War, as Thucydides remarks on another occasion, is a harsh teacher.

ALCIBIADES: THE SOWER OF DISCORD

The proponent of this draconian punishment was Alcibiades. About thirty-five years old in 415, he had entered Athenian politics five years before with all the force of one of his victorious Olympic stallions—or was he rather a Trojan horse? A skillful democratic politician, Alcibiades was an aristocrat who would later express contempt for democracy; many were convinced that his real goal was tyranny. An anecdote about his childhood tells a lot about how the Greeks viewed his character. According to the biographer Plutarch, young Alcibiades once came upon his guardian, Pericles, preparing his accounts to deliver to the people after his year in the general's office. Alcibiades supposedly advised Pericles that he would be better off devising a scheme to avoid having to render his accounts.

In 415, Alcibiades revealed another of his basic traits: the tendency to attract enemies. The factional winds of the 420s were blowing strong by 415, and Alcibiades was in the eye of the storm. He had played a key role in the breakdown of the Spartan-Athenian rapprochement following the Peace of Nicias; indeed he had almost single-handedly scotched the peace in 420 by deliberately lying to a deputation of Spartan ambassadors. The ambassadors believed Alcibiades' misinformation and unwittingly insulted the Athenian assembly. If this gambit stiffened Athenian resolve, opened the way for an Athenian alliance with the formerly neutral state of Argos (an important military power), and led to the creation of the new anti-Spartan coalition of 418, it also had its price. Alcibiades made a deadly personal enemy of Nicias. Nicias and his faction were not strong enough to save their peace with Sparta, but they could and did block Alcibiades' policy of renewed war in the Peloponnesos. Hence, the Athenian contingent arrived too late to play a role at the important battle of Mantinea in 418.

With Spartan power on the rise again and peace unraveling, Athens could ill afford the politics of personal animosity, but Nicias and Alcibiades both reveled in it. To Nicias's personal reasons for preferring peace we may add Alcibiades' personal reasons for seeking war: when he attempted to initiate a rapprochement with Sparta after Pylos in 425, the age-conscious Spartans had rebuffed him on account of his youth. In 415, it all came out in the wash: personal resentment, youth versus age, war versus peace, glory versus security. The occasion was the Athenian assembly's debate over Alcibiades' plan to reopen the war in a new venue: Sicily.

It is not entirely clear just what Athens expected to gain by invading Sicily. Success would certainly bring glory and tribute and new opportunities abroad, but these things would not defeat Sparta's land army. It is possible that Alcibiades saw the Sicilian Expedition as only the first step in the conquest of Carthage and southern Italy, which would bring access to tough mercenary fighters for use against Sparta—but this was a long shot. In any case, Alcibiades initially planned to send only a medium-sized expedition to Sicily: 60 ships, the same number Athens had sent on a previous expedition there in the 420s. Alcibiades is certainly guilty of distracting Athenian energies from the conflict with Sparta, a distraction meant to enhance his own glory. He does not, however, bear sole responsibility for leading Athens into a quagmire. *That* disaster only came about because the Alcibiades syndrome had spread more widely among Athens' leaders.

At first, the Athenian assembly voted to send the 60-ship fleet to Sicily. Within a week, however, the issue was forced back open and the assembly was reconvened. Nicias went on the political warpath; in a speech to the assembly he highlighted the dangers of opening a front in Sicily, with Greece still unsettled, and bitterly attacked the proponent of the expedition, his rival Alcibiades. Nicias called him a young man in a hurry, accused him of inexperience and personal extravagance, and blamed him for harboring selfish motives. Then he castigated Alcibiades for stirring up intergenerational conflict and for encouraging the young to browbeat the old into war. In other words, Nicias spoke like a scolding parent.

Alcibiades was probably gleeful at the chance to respond to such charges, for poor Nicias had played right into his hands. Did Nicias call Alcibiades a golden boy who swept away all before him with vigor and charm? Did he say that Alcibiades represented overabundant youthful energy that had to find new worlds to conquer or else stagnate? Guilty as charged! Alcibiades knew his audience; he knew just how very willing they were to rally to the banner of a young hero. Finally, as for intergenerational conflict, Alcibiades knew how to blunt Nicias's attack by appealing for harmony between young and old, "just as our fathers" enjoyed.

Nicias was beaten, but he employed the final trick of a scare tactic, demanding that the Athenians almost double the size of the expeditionary force. The tactic backfired, however, as the assembly, far from being scared, eagerly agreed to the bigger force. Athens was now committed to a huge armada of over 100 warships, at least 5,000 infantrymen and additional light-armed troops. And all because of the personal rivalry between Nicias and Alcibiades. Worse still, in order to forestall further political bickering, the assembly divided the command of the expedition between the two rivals, adding for good measure the general Lamachus (more of a military man than a politician). It was doubtful whether so bitterly divided a command could accomplish much. Finally, there is the problem of the expedition itself. Victory in Sicily could not defeat Sparta, but failure could do serious damage to Athens, especially now that so large a force was at risk. Having spread discord, Alcibiades proceeded to lead the Athenian people down the garden path.

He had underestimated his opposition, however. Although his debating tactics had failed, Nicias had poisoned the well of public opinion sufficiently to put Alcibiades in a difficult position when a scandal broke soon afterward. The notorious Affair of the Herms began one night in June 415, just before the sailing of the fleet. On that night most of the Herms, busts of the god Hermes which stood before many Athenian houses and in sacred places, were mysteriously mutilated. Since the Herms were both religious and patriotic symbols, and since Hermes was the god of travel, people suspected a plot against the Sicilian Expedition. Although he was the chief proponent of the expedition, Alcibiades became a major suspect.

The reasons were his notorious private life and his famous ambition. As Thucydides writes: "Most people became frightened at a quality in him which was beyond the normal and showed itself both in the lawlessness of his private life and habits and in the spirit in which he acted on all occasions. They thought that he wanted to become a tyrant, and so they turned against him."

The Affair of the Herms turned into a McCarthyesque witch-hunt, eventually exposing Alcibiades' participation in a parody of the solemn religious ritual of the Eleusinian mysteries—a black mass, if you will. Although almost certainly innocent of mutilating the Herms, Alcibiades' record was nonetheless stained. The mystery of the Herms has never been solved completely satisfactorily, but the likeliest culprit was a group of young, wealthy, pro-Peloponnesian Athenians who admired Sparta and its oligarchic government.

Alcibiades' enemies were legion: not only Nicias, but

many other politicians had been offended by him. They now tried to bring him to trial immediately—which would have kept him from leading the Sicilian Expedition—but his support among the young Athenian men who manned the soon-to-sail armada was too great. What happened next is, in many ways, a microcosm of Athenian disunity and a foretaste of the problems that would, within a decade, cost Athens the war. First, once the fleet and the bulk of Alcibiades' supporters had sailed, his enemies seized the moment to indict him; they recalled him from Sicily to stand trial. At first Alcibiades went along quietly, but when the ship to Athens docked in Italy, he bolted and hid until he could catch a ship for the Peloponnesos and, eventually, Sparta.

Far from lying low there, Alcibiades engaged in overt treason. His silver-tongued voice described grand Athenian plans of conquest in the west, and thereby nudged Sparta into action. On Alcibiades' advice, Sparta sent an officer to direct the defense of Athens' main target in Sicily, the city of Syracuse, and sent troops to build a fortified garrison at Decelea in the hills above Athens—a base for raiding Athenian territory year-round. Both were important contributions to Athens' ultimate defeat.

With the recall of Alcibiades and his treachery at Sparta, we see the clearest symptoms of the Alcibiades syndrome. Neither Alcibiades nor any of his opponents were willing to place the national interest above personal advantage. They were unable to separate military from political reasoning. To deprive the Athenian expeditionary force of its most popular leader was military madness; to spite domestic enemies by helping the enemy was worse. The Alcibiades syndrome was in full swing.

SICILY

Whatever its defects as a strategy to win the Peloponnesian War for Athens, the Sicilian Expedition should have been winnable as an operation in and of itself. The divided command structure hamstrung things from the first, however, and the recall of Alcibiades both deprived the force of its most vigorous leader and hurt morale. Even had he stayed on, though, Alcibiades would certainly have had problems, because he had passed up the best military plan. The key to Athenian victory was speed. The third commanding general, Lamachus, recognized this, and urged an immediate attack on an unprepared and frightened Syracuse. Alcibiades, however, pressed for and got a slower, step-by-step plan of winning allies and supplies in Sicily before attacking Syracuse.

By the time Athens attacked Syracuse, Alcibiades was gone and the Syracusans had gained time and confidence. Worse still, Lamachus was soon killed in battle, leaving the Athenian army in the hands of a general who would have preferred not to be there: Nicias. Under his leadership, the campaign turned into a quagmire, a long, costly, and frustrating siege of Syracuse by land and sea.

Just as the Alcibiades syndrome explained the Athenian decision to launch the Sicilian Expedition and the elimination of Alcibiades as its commander, so it explains the disastrous collapse of the expedition. Left by default as commander, Nicias proved unable to separate military and political reasoning. Long a conservative general, he now became a defeatist, jeopardizing the safety of his men to save his own political neck—in effect letting the ship sink slowly in the perverse hope that he, as captain, would not have to go down with it. In two years of campaigning, the Athenians failed to take Syracuse. By 413, morale had declined considerably, and the ships, their hulls rotting in the stagnant waters of the harbor, their crews inactive for over a year, had passed their peak of readiness. Syracuse's walls were as impregnable to Athenian troops as Athens' city walls had been to the Spartans, and the Athenian infantry failed to control Syracusan territory. Athenian reinforcements arrived, but to no avail; Athens suffered defeats on land and sea.

When his fellow general urged a withdrawal while there was still time, Nicias refused at first, on the grounds that the Athenian assembly would blame him. To quote Thucydides:

> He said, too, that many, in fact most of the soldiers in Sicily who were now crying out so loudly about their terrible position, would, as soon as they got to Athens, cry out the opposite and would say that the generals had been bribed to betray them and return. For his own part, therefore, knowing the Athenian character as he did, rather than be put to death on a disgraceful charge, and by an unjust verdict of the Athenians, he preferred to take his chance, and if it must be, to meet his own death himself at the hands of the enemy.

Nicias got his wish. The army stayed until it was too late to retreat safely, the men were slaughtered, and he was executed by his Syracusan captors.

Selfish as Nicias's actions were, he nonetheless deserves some sympathy. The Athenian assembly did have a tendency to kill the messenger who bore them bad news, even if he was a general. Nicias should have been willing to take a political risk on behalf of his men, but his fears were well founded.

The defeat in Sicily was a disaster for Athens, which suffered major losses in ships, manpower, prestige, and morale. Sicily was the signal for revolts up and down the Athenian empire, and it opened the way for an alliance between Sparta and the Persian king, who was itching to overthrow Athenian seapower in the Aegean. Nevertheless, in spite of all, Athens was able to hold out for another nine years, in the last phase of the war, the Iono-Decelean War (413–404). Not only to hold out: Athens won four major naval victories against Sparta, and twice drove Sparta to sue for peace. In purely military terms, Athens was strong enough to survive Sicily as an imperial power. The main reason that the Athenians lost the Peloponnesian War in the end—as Thucydides recognized—was political, not military.

ATHENIAN POLITICS IN DISARRAY

The narrative of the Peloponnesian War after Sicily is very complex. We shall briefly trace only two themes of the 413–404 period: Athens' continuing political crisis and the fate of Alcibiades.

Two years after Sicily, Athens came close to civil war. In 411, a narrowly based oligarchy (the so-called Four Hundred) seized on dissatisfaction with the government's prosecution of the war and, using tactics of terrorism and assassination, overthrew the democratic government. The oligarchs ran afoul of popular opposition and their own divisions, however. In desperation they plotted to turn Athens over to the Spartans to save their own necks; once again, personal ambition took precedence over patriotism. The plot leaked out, however, and was foiled by patriotic Athenian infantrymen.

In the aftermath of their aborted act of treason, the Four Hundred were overthrown, and democracy was restored. In the meantime, Alcibiades had reentered the Athenian political stage. Last seen in Sparta, he had left in a hurry when he was revealed as the lover of Sparta's Queen Timaia, who allegedly bore his son. He supposedly remarked that his motive was neither lust nor scorn, rather it was the desire that his descendants rule Sparta—but typically, he supposedly said this in a sarcastic tone. Cynic, opportunist, and hustler, Alcibiades laughed at everything and used everyone. His next stop after Sparta was Persia, where he was welcomed as a double defector with unique insight into the strategic plans of both sides. But Alcibiades wanted to go home, and he intrigued with the commanders of the Athenian fleet on the island of Samos, off the coast of Asia Minor. He promised them Persian financial and military support, which he could not possibly deliver, but that hardly mattered to him—nor, as it turned out, to the Athenians. After Sicily, Athenians were ready for a hero again; proving that hope springs eternal, they embraced Alcibiades gladly. They had learned little; he had lost none of his old eloquence or mystique, and now he was also a nostalgic symbol of better days. So Alcibiades became admiral of the fleet; under his command and that of his supporters, Athens won brilliant victories over Sparta in the next few years.

Alcibiades returned in triumph to Athens in 407, but his triumph was ephemeral. Soon afterward, one of his lieutenants lost 22 ships to a Peloponnesian force at Notium, off the Asia Minor coast, while Alcibiades was on a scouting expedition. Notably he had delegated authority for the fleet not to the next in command, but to a petty officer, who blundered in the ensuing battle. Why? Alcibiades was seeking not military competence but personal loyalty: the petty officer was a close friend of his. Once again, political calculation (and faulty political calculation at that) outweighed military reasoning. The Athenians blamed Alcibiades for his lieutenant's failure and exiled him—the charismatic politician was finally caught by the double edge of the sword of a career based on personality and personal interest.

The absolute nadir of political maneuvering was reached a year later, after the battle of Arginusae in 406. By now, Sparta had found a virtually bottomless source of funding in Persia, who built its new ally fleet after fleet: each time Athens destroyed one, Persia supplied another. Persia's plan was simple: by funding a fratricidal Greek war, it would clear the field for Persian reentry into the Aegean power game. Sparta promised to surrender the Greeks of Asia Minor as the price for help against Athens.

Although defeated at Notium, Athens had rallied to win three great victories between 411 and 407, but they were indecisive strategically and left the city exhausted. Nevertheless, when a new threat arose in 406 from yet another Spartan fleet, Athens mustered an enormous effort and manned a new fleet. At the battle of Arginusae in the northeastern Aegean, Athens crushed the Peloponnesians yet again. Of some 275 ships in the battle, the Peloponnesians lost 69, Athens only 25. Because of a sudden storm, however, the Athenian survivors could not be saved, and 5,000 lives were tragically lost.

Athens had won a smashing victory, but at a price. Stirred up by crusading politicians, an angry assembly blamed the casualties not on the storm but on the Athenian admirals, who were arrested. An inquest followed, leading to an unseemly exchange of charges and countercharges between various officers who had been in the battle. As each player sought to save his own neck by sacrificing his subordinates, superiors, and the public interest generally, it was the Affair of the Herms all over again.

Although the procedure was flagrantly unconstitutional, the assembly voted to try the six generals as a group rather than individually. They were condemned and executed. Among them were some of Athens' best military commanders, including Pericles, son of the great Pericles.

It was a low moment in Athenian history. Popular passion and political maneuvering had wiped out military common sense. You do not win wars by killing your own generals. The Athenians needed to present a united front; instead, they turned on themselves. The fear of retribution at home now became a major constraint on the remaining commanders. Alcibiades was gone, but the Alcibiades syndrome destroyed what the Athenian fleet had achieved.

The stage was now set for disaster. First came a political error. After Arginusae, Sparta again offered peace terms: the status quo, plus the evacuation of its garrison in the hills above Athens. With some of the empire still in revolt, the terms were not perfect, but they offered Athens the best hope of a needed respite. Why then, did the Athenians refuse the offer? The answer is probably the Alcibiades syndrome. Any politician who accepted the deal would be pounced on by rivals, branded as a defeatist, and hauled off. So the war went on.

In late summer 405, Sparta returned to the attack with a new fleet of about 175 ships, paid for by Persia and led by the brilliant and ruthless commander Lysander. Lysander captured a key city on the Dardanelles, which threatened to cut Athens' grain lifeline to the Ukraine. An Athenian fleet of 180 ships hurried to the rescue, bent on retaking the city and defeating Lysander.

A trireme fleet generally based itself in a city's harbor, where the men could find food and supplies. In order to pressure the Peloponnesians into fighting, however, the Athenians landed at a beach near the village of Aegospotami ("Goat Rivers"), which was opposite the enemy on the other shore of the Dardanelles. On several mornings, the Athenians offered battle to the enemy, but Lysander refused to take on his skilled opponent. Each afternoon, the Athenian fleet rowed back to Aegospotami, and the men scavenged for food or napped. The Peloponnesians observed from spy ships.

On the fourth afternoon, the Athenians had an unexpected visitor, an exile who happened to live in a nearby fortress: Alcibiades. His presence on the eve of the last battle of the war seems a Hollywood touch, but the sources confirm it. Alcibiades urged the Athenians to withdraw to the nearby town of Sestos, where their fleet would not be exposed each afternoon to the enemy. For once, Alcibiades was offering sound advice: good generalship dictated a tactical retreat, or at least extreme caution. But his countrymen refused to listen. They were contemptuous of the enemy, and besides, they had to consider the adviser. Like the boy who cried wolf, Alcibiades was no longer credible. The irony of the Alcibiades syndrome is that even when its namesake may have been acting disinterestedly, the waters had become too muddied for anyone to take him at face value. After the charges and countercharges of the Arginusae affair, which general wanted responsibility for retreating from the enemy? Which general wanted to be known as a follower of the disgraced Alcibiades?

The fleet stayed. The next day, after the Athenians had returned to Aegospotami in the afternoon, Lysander struck, capturing virtually the entire Athenian fleet—apparently only about a dozen ships escaped.

The war was over. It still remained for Lysander to execute 3–4,000 Athenian prisoners, for a Spartan army to lay siege to Athens for several months, and for the Peloponnesian fleet to sail into Piraeus. However dramatic, these events were secondary. The war was decided at Aegospotami.

As for Alcibiades, his fate had also been sealed at Aegospotami. He was dead within a year of the war's end. At the time, he was living in a village in central Anatolia with his current mistress. Hired assassins set fire to his house and shot him dead with javelins and arrows when he ran out to escape. The sources disagree about who had engaged the killers. One version says it was the Spartans, eager to rid themselves of a potential leader of a revived Athens. Another has it that it was his mistress's brothers, who wanted vengeance for the girl's seduction. Alcibiades, a man who once paraded through Athens with a golden Cupid emblazoned on his shield, might have appreciated this version. In either case his death was a product of the way he had lived his life. It was no hero's death, but Alcibiades was no hero. He had made his way by brilliance, seduction, and betrayal. Ultimately, he died of complications caused by the syndrome we have named after him.

THE LESSON

Athens lost the Peloponnesian War at sea, but in the last analysis, its defeat was more political than military. Sicily was the turning point in Athens' fortunes, and the Sicilian Expedition would never have been bungled, or even attempted, had Athens enjoyed unified and unselfish political leadership. Without the failure of the Sicilian Expedition, Persia could never have dared to intervene on Sparta's side; and without massive and continuous Persian aid, Sparta could never have defeated Athens. Even after Sicily, even with Persia helping Sparta, Athens was still strong enough in military terms to win a decent peace that left most of its empire intact and Athens itself strong enough to regain the rest in due time. Once again, it was disunity, suspicion, and selfishness at home more than failure in the field that lost Athens the war.

As the war dragged on, the Athenians became increasingly prone to what we have called the Alcibiades syndrome. Rooted in the deepest level of Greek culture and in the experience of city-states, this syndrome has several primary manifestations. It affects both individuals and entire societies. On the individual level, the afflicted are both brilliant and arrogant. They are convinced of their superior genius, they weave grandiose and fantastic plots of aggression, and they tend to put their own private ambition before the public interest. Their considerable charm and eloquence makes them particularly dangerous. On the societal level, the syndrome turns selfishness and factionalism into generalized problems. It also makes the citizenry extremely susceptible to the allure of a leader like Alcibiades.

Alcibiades cut a splendid figure in the Athenian assembly on the eve of the Sicilian Expedition. He was as brilliant and as blue-blooded as Pericles, as bold and as aggressive as Cleon, and equal to both in rhetorical talent. If he was also as selfish as Nicias, he knew how to turn this potential flaw into an attraction by portraying his personal triumphs (alliances created, horse races won) as propaganda victories for all Athens. Best of all, he was the embodiment of youth. He showed his countrymen the flattering self-portrait of endless vigor and self-confidence, of Achilles as Everyman—and they bought it gladly. In peacetime, they might have appraised him more coolly and soberly, but in the pressure of war, Athenians let themselves be hustled.

But every Achilles has his heel. Alcibiades forgot that his countrymen expected some limits on his youthful exuberance, and if he failed to observe limits, that they could treat him as selfishly as he treated them. Hence, his scandalous personal life led to exile at the peak of his power. Although he was able to survive the stigma of collaborating with the enemy and to come home again, it would never be the same. Thanks in large part to his own pernicious influence, Athenian political culture as a whole had become thoroughly infected by the last years of the war. Squabbling, refusing responsibility, and scapegoating had become the order of the day; the execution of generals, cronyism, and treason were becoming commonplace. Not even Alcibiades could survive in an Athens in which the Alcibiades syndrome was raging. Athens lost the war at Aegospotami, but the disarray of Athenian politics for several years previously had made something like Aegospotami all but inevitable.

Athens' overwhelming strength at the start of the Peloponnesian War was a bitter irony to Thucydides, who lived to see the terrible outcome. Although Athens lacked the land army needed to destroy Spartan power completely, its naval hegemony should have prevented Sparta from inflicting serious damage on Athens. Thucydides' implicit argument to the contrary, the reason for Athens' ultimate failure was not democracy. Rather, the reason was war, twenty-seven years of it. Most previous conflicts in Greece had been solved by a single battle—Greek political culture was simply not designed to withstand the strains of generation-long conflicts. Sparta is an interesting counterexample and confirmation. If Sparta won the Peloponnesian War, it was only thanks to the Persian alliance, paid for by the freedom of the Asia Minor Greeks. Moreover, Spartan generals like Brasidas and Lysander demonstrated, in their own ways, symptoms of the Alcibiades syndrome: ambition, egotism, rhetorical flair, personal empire-building. Winning the war and succeeding Athens as the leader of Greece put unbearable strains on the Spartan social and political system: thirty-five years after Aegospotami Sparta suffered a total collapse, from which it never recovered.

No Greek city-state society could have withstood the strains Athens faced and won the war, at least not without an ally like Persia. After Sicily, the Athenians should have jumped at the chance to make peace with Sparta.

Their failure to do so bespeaks a political climate in which no one is willing to take the rap for a difficult decision, in which private interests take precedence over the public good, in which people are blinded by the illusion of salvation by a young hero: in short, a full-blown case of the Alcibiades syndrome.

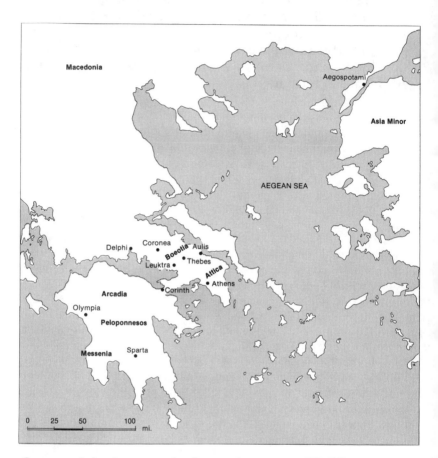

Greece and the Aegean under Spartan hegemony, 405–371 B.C.

Chapter 3

Lysander and Agesilaus: The Spartans Who Defeated Themselves

THE SPARTANS MARCHED OFF to the war in 431 B.C. under the banner of liberating the Greeks. When they finally defeated Athens twenty-seven years later, it was time for Sparta to put its money where its mouth was. But in 404, the world looked very different than it had in 431. The more the Spartans got involved in Greek politics outside the Peloponnesos, the more interested they became in staying out there. So, after evicting the Athenians from the city-states of their former empire, Sparta did not leave those city-states free, but rather moved in with governors and tribute collectors of its own. The admiral Lysander, who defeated the Athenian fleet for good in 405, championed this imperial policy, while other factions in Sparta called for a return to traditional isolationism.

To complicate the picture, in order to conquer Athens, Sparta had been forced to make a deal with its hereditary enemy, Persia—an act as shocking in its day as, say, the Nazi-Soviet Pact of 1939 or Richard Nixon's opening to China in 1972. Persia supplied the fleets and money needed to drive Athens from the sea; in return, Sparta had to sign away the freedom of the Greek city-states on the west coast of Asia Minor. With Athens defeated, Spartans were divided about whether to continue honoring the deal or whether to invade Asia Minor on behalf of their countrymen.

The Greek scene was equally unsettled. Athens was disarmed and forced to accept a pro-Spartan junta, but a powerful guerrilla movement threatened a return to democracy. Some of Sparta's staunchest allies were also restive. The traditional basis of Spartan power was the Peloponnesian League, a loose organization of some fifty Greek city-states under Spartan leadership. Now, Thebes and Corinth, the two most powerful allies after Sparta, were at odds with Sparta over the disposition of the spoils of victory and the nature of the postwar world.

Finally, there was the home front. Victory brought wealth to Sparta, and wealth brought dislocation. Wealth undermined the traditional Spartan ethos of austerity and egalitarianism. The uneven distribution of wealth forced some Spartans to drop out of the ruling elite, which led in turn to a drastic shortage of elite military manpower. The wealthy, however, had political power, and they balked at the necessary reforms.

All in all, Sparta's victory in 404 was less an exclamation point than a question mark. Sparta faced problems at home and abroad, in its own elite and in its alliance, with Athens and with Persia. Sparta had won the Peloponnesian War, but the key to a stable and healthy future was a good strategy for the postwar world.

THE GLOW OF VICTORY

On an April day in the year 404 B.C., to the festive music of flute girls, and before a crowd of smiling dignitaries garlanded with flowers, work crews began tearing down chunks of Athens' defense walls. At the same time, the Athenian fleet was being burned in its own home port. The day was hailed as the beginning of freedom for Greece. Exaggeration, perhaps, but for Sparta, it was undeniably a day of triumph. After seventy-five years of conflict between Spartan and Athenian power blocs, of which the last twenty-seven had been spent in the grueling Peloponnesian War, Sparta had emerged victorious. Two men were to guide Sparta's destiny in the coming years, the admiral Lysander and the soon-to-be king Agesilaus. We do not know if Agesilaus was present on that glorious spring day, but Lysander certainly was, and he had reason for satisfaction. In the previous autumn at the battle of Aegospotami, Lysander had personally delivered the coup de grâce to Athenian power. Now the fearsome Athenian fleet was destroyed, and many cities of Athens' former empire had already welcomed Spartan liberators.

The signs of triumph were many. At Delphi, the religious center of the Greek world, the Spartan conquerors dedicated a group of about forty bronze statues, a tableau in which the gods themselves crowned the victors with wreaths. Surely, the hour of Spartan ascendancy, of the *pax Laconica*, was at hand.

Or was it? In 404, no one could have seen that victorious Sparta was heading toward the greatest failure in its history—indeed, toward the destruction of its military and economic power—only thirty-five years later. Nevertheless, to the farsighted, some storm clouds were visible on the horizon even in 404. Abroad, there were many dangers, among them rivalries within the Peloponnesian League, an uneasy Persian alliance, the status of the Asia Minor Greeks, and the instability of Athens' former empire. At home, manpower problems loomed. For thoughtful Spartans, it was a moment to reflect upon the price of overseas entanglement. For most of its history, Sparta had been extremely reluctant to engage in major military expeditions far from home, and with good reason. Sparta was a serf society. The majority of its laborers were so-called helots, most of them Messenian Greeks conquered centuries before and forced ever since to work the land for their Spartan masters. Given the opportunity, the helots would and, not infrequently, did revolt. Whatever else the Spartan military did or did not do, it had to keep the helots in line.

We are running up against one of the central paradoxes of postwar Sparta. For Sparta to be Sparta, the Spartans had to stay home and enforce a security regime. But for Sparta to protect itself from foreign threats, it had to play some role in Greece and the Aegean. Could the Spartans afford to do both? Could they afford not to?

Lysander and Agesilaus never doubted the necessity of interventionism, and in the long run they got their way. At first, however, there was a great debate. In 404, the Spartans faced three questions of grand strategy. First, Sparta had to decide what to do about the former Athenian empire. Should it be reorganized as a Spartan empire or left to its own devices? Should Greek Asia Minor be conceded to Persia or wrested back by force? Second, Sparta had to decide how to treat the prickly Peloponnesian allies. Thebes, in particular, was champing at the bit, having emerged as one of the big winners of the Peloponnesian War. Thebes had consolidated control over the central Greek region of Boeotia, which it organized as a Theban-led confederacy. Should Sparta compromise and share power with its allies or beat them into submission?

Third, Sparta had to put its own house in order. In 404, that house suffered from two severe problems: a breakdown of the old standards of austerity and civic virtue and, even more serious, a drastic military manpower shortage. These problems began before the Peloponnesian War and were greatly exacerbated by it. Indeed, Sparta's victory in 404 mustn't be treated like some physical examination that gives the system a clean bill of health. "Sparta won the war, so its regime must have been sound": so the argument goes. On the contrary, Sparta could not have lasted long against even the limping, post-Sicilian-disaster Athenian fleet without the massive and continuous injection of Persian aid. After 404, however, the future of Spartan-Persian relations was in doubt.

Once the glow of victory had faded, therefore, the strategic tasks before the Spartan leadership were tremendous. Abroad, they had to choose between compromise or conflict. At home, they had not only to avoid factionalism but, tougher still, they needed to open up the doors of the Spartan military fraternity, admit thousands of new members, and pay for the expense out of their own pockets.

Bitter pills: as it turned out, Sparta was unwilling to swallow the medicine. The country's leadership proved incapable of facing hard decisions. Instead of making a realistic assessment of their limitations and acting accordingly, they tried to do everything. A respectable middleweight, Sparta after 404 tried to act like the heavyweight champion of the world. The result was one fall after the other, but Sparta learned nothing from them. Finally, it was easy for Thebes to land the knockout punch, at the battle of Leuctra in 371. Within a decade, Sparta had lost two thirds of its territory and the foundation of its social system. In international affairs, Sparta was reduced to the roles of Peloponnesian traffic cop and occasional hired gun for dictators overseas. Truly, the mighty were fallen, the victory of 404 notwithstanding.

The ironic story can be told in terms of two men who shaped Sparta's future against a powerful image of the past. The first, Lysander, was the all-too-human architect of victory in the Peloponnesian War, who ended his days bitterly planning a coup d'état against the Spartan government whose servant he was supposed to be. The second, King Agesilaus, came to the throne in or just before 400 and presided over Sparta both in its glory days and its utter collapse after Leuctra. The past is summed up by the phrase "the laws of Lycurgus," Sparta's proud and austere way of life. The story of Sparta after the Peloponnesian War is a cautionary tale of vision turned to blindness, civic virtue turned to greed, justice turned to cronyism, and steadfastness turned brittle.

THE LAWS OF LYCURGUS

Sparta had a unique social and political system, the wonder or curiosity of all Greece. Spartans believed that the system had been put in place by the great Lycurgus, who lived (according to the most common version) in the eighth century B.C., about 350 years before the Peloponnesian War. Nowadays, most scholars argue for gradual innovations in Sparta rather than a dramatic, single change; few date the beginning of the process before the mid–seventh century; and many are skeptical as to whether there ever was a Lycurgus. To make matters worse, classical Sparta was short on literacy and long on mythologizing and secrecy. We will probably never know the truth about Lycurgus, nor ever be quite sure where reality begins and myth ends when it comes to Spartan society. This much is, however, clear: Sparta was unique.

Let us describe Sparta according to what currently seems to be the likeliest reconstruction. Society was divided into three classes: the serfs, or helots, who had the lowest status; the *perioikoi* ("those who live round about"), a middle group, not fully Spartan, and who had no political power at the state level, but who were free and locally autonomous; and finally, the full citizens, the Spartiates— or Equals, as they were known. In a sense, the helots and Equals were mirror images. The helots existed to support the Equals, the Equals existed to suppress the helots. The system was a closed circle, created by military means, and propagated to serve military necessity.

What made the Equals equal was, above all, their common status as Spartan soldiers. As soldiers, the Equals were expected to live an austere life, abjuring luxury or even money. Each Equal was given a minimum land allotment worked by helots—in effect, his salary as a soldier. Of course, many Equals owned additional, private land, and a wealthy few owned large estates. In the beginning, however, even the poorest Equal had enough land to live on. Equality Spartan-style did not mean economic equality, and the wealthy had a leg up in politics, but sumptuary laws and the Spartan educational system went a long way toward establishing an egalitarian ideology.

As one would expect in a communal society organized along military lines, Sparta's government was neither a democracy nor a dictatorship, but rather an oligarchy: a headquarters run by a committee of generals, if you will. Sparta had an unusual arrangement of two kings, each of whom led military expeditions. A small council of elders and a board of overseers were among the top policymakers. The Equals composed the assembly, which was more than a rubber stamp but less than an independent legislative body. In theory, no one man could dominate the regime, but quite often in Spartan history, an outstanding individual became rather powerful.

Sparta's ideology was transmitted by a system of public education, male initiation, and indoctrination to which the Equals alone were admitted. Known as the *agoge* ("bringing up" or "raising"), the system was intended to produce superb soldiers and, until Leuctra, it was a stunning success.

Sparta's crack soldiers were the product of a rigid system of state control, a thoroughgoing attempt to subordinate private life to the public good. Plutarch comments in his *Life of Lycurgus:*

> Altogether [Lycurgus] accustomed citizens neither to want nor know how to have a private life, but rather to be like bees, always attached to the community, swarming together around their leader, and practically ecstatic with enthusiasm and ambition to belong entirely to their country.

Unattractive as this image may be to the modern democrat, many Greeks admired Sparta's civic virtue. Political philosophers down to modern times, including such strange bedfellows as Plato and Karl Marx, have been inspired by the Spartan communal vision.

Both Lysander and Agesilaus were raised in the agoge, so to understand them, we need to examine it and its role in the Spartiate's life cycle. To begin at the beginning, the Spartan newborn was examined by the tribal elders, who condemned deformed or unhealthy specimens to be left in a chasm near the city. Having passed this test, a boy lived with his mother until the age of seven, when he was taken from home and billeted with a group (literally, a "herd") of his agemates, under the leadership of the toughest boy. Girls remained with their mothers, but they too (unlike Greek girls elsewhere) had a public education—though much more limited than the boys'—with an emphasis on preparation for motherhood. Boys were taught to be soldiers: the agoge emphasized obedience, discipline, toughness, physical fitness, and violence. Only the rudiments of reading and writing were taught. While other Greeks learned to deliver grand and complex orations, Spartans were taught to speak in a blunt and pungent "laconic" fashion.

Rewards and punishments were an important part of Spartan education. In order to be taught to fend for themselves, boys are supposed to have been underfed and forced to go out and steal food. Fights between boys were not only permitted but encouraged and punishments were omnipresent. Life from ages seven to eighteen was one long combination of boot camp, fraternity, and gym class. Homosexual liaisons between older and younger boys were encouraged, in order to reinforce the authority of older males.

Between eighteen and twenty, many boys served in the *krypteia* ("secret service"), in which they spent their time spying on, and often killing, helots. At twenty, having completed his formal education, a boy became eligible to serve in the army. Before achieving full adult status, however, he would be elected to a common mess, a small, fraternitylike group of about fifteen men, to which a Spartiate belonged for life. Every Spartiate took his main meals in the mess, and each messmate contributed to the meals from his own land. The messes reinforced Sparta's civic-minded ideology and were meant to promote equality, but in practice, some messes were exclusive and aristocratic.

By thirty, a Spartiate had married, and was admitted to the assembly. Having completed the transition from initiate to initiator, he would take his part in the system of coaching, coaxing, and punishing the next generation of boys. The adult male also served in the Spartan army and, if he was wealthy and well born, in the government. Otherwise, the Equal need do absolutely nothing. Supported by the helots, prohibited from learning a trade or making money, the Spartiate devoted all his time to fighting, thinking about fighting, talking about fighting, and training others to fight.

Thanks to the agoge, the adult Spartan, at his best, was patriotic, warlike, austere, egalitarian, obedient, and uncorrupted by foreign ways or by money. But he might also be unsophisticated, close-minded, and undiplomatic. When it came to the complex world of international relations, the laconic mind-set might prove not only simple but simplistic.

Worse still, by the end of the Peloponnesian War, the very socioeconomic underpinnings of the Spartan system were eroding badly. The main problem was the inherent and ever-growing economic inequality among the Equals. There had always been wealthy Equals, large landowners who vigilantly refrained from marrying their children to their poorer brethren, and who thereby concentrated wealth within a few families. The forbidden fruit of money found its way into the hands of these wealthy houses, especially after Sparta's victory in 404.

Meanwhile, the poorer Equals found it increasingly difficult to make do on their state land allotments. The precise details of what happened are unknown, but it is a good guess that as Spartan tastes grew ever more luxurious, the struggle to keep up with the Joneses depleted many an Equal's purse. Since individual financial initiative was forbidden, the only legitimate way to get new wealth was to marry it, but since the rich only married each other, that avenue was closed to most Equals. When they found themselves unable to meet the payments for the common messes, as increasing numbers did, they were demoted from the status of Equal to that of Inferior, (an ill-defined but clearly undesirable status). Thus, over time, the number of Equals plummeted. Other factors, such as battle casualties, the great earthquake of the 460s, and what family planning was available in ancient Greece (as the Equals got poorer perhaps they tried to have fewer children) may have contributed to the decline. The numerical estimates are striking. In the seventh century B.C. there had been about 9,000 Equals; according to current scholarly estimates, in 480 there were about 8,000; in 431 about 4,000 to 5,000; by the early fourth century a maximum of 3,000; at the time of the battle of Leuctra, only about 1,500; by the late fourth century, fewer than 1,000 (according to Aristotle); by the mid–third century, only 700 (according to Plutarch). No wonder the loss of 400 Spartiates at Leuctra was so disastrous.

The fewer Equals there were, the fewer men to go through the full Spartiate education system, the fewer superbly trained elite soldiers to serve the country. In short, what began as an imbalance in the distribution of wealth ended up as a crisis in military manpower. The authorities were not blind to the problem, but while they should have responded with a restructuring from the ground up, they tried to make do with a tinker's dam. First, in the mid–fifth century, they began to include *perioikoi* troops (infantrymen from the neighboring towns) in the same regiments as Spartiates. Second, beginning in the 420s, they took the even more drastic step of emancipating many helots (eventually thousands) to serve in the military, preferably in campaigns far from the Peloponnesos (though deployment closer to home was sometimes necessary).

But what of a third step, recommended by no less an authority than Aristotle: a redistribution of wealth to restore the downwardly mobile Inferiors to the status of Equals, hence replenishing Sparta's elite military manpower? This was too much for the powers that be, who were unwilling to part with any of the huge estates they had built up over the generations. Their resistance was paid back with the threat of revolution. Just a few years after the defeat of Athens, the Spartan authorities uncovered a group of plotters who, we are told, would have practically eaten the Spartiates raw! The authorities squelched the plot by executing the ringleaders, but the underlying problems were not so easily solved.

Hence, at the very time when Sparta, as self-proclaimed leader of the Greek world, needed a stronger army than ever, the strength of its elite force was declining precipitously. A reformer was desperately needed, but the Spartan premium on conformity and obedience all but guaranteed that none would arise. And so it turned out. Sparta's two main leaders after the Peloponnesian War made a bad situation even worse. Lysander, who had only a brief taste of power, treated the other Greeks like a bunch of Spartan schoolboys, and was deposed only when it looked as if he had the same fate in mind for adult Spartans. King Agesilaus, who dominated postwar Sparta, turned a blind eye to his country's weaknesses and refused to make the necessary compromises with its allies. The carnage at Leuctra was not far off.

LYSANDER

It hardly seems likely that the first man in Greek history to be worshiped as a god could turn out to have been a Spartan. Yet not only is it so, but the man in question is also famous as an extraordinarily ambitious schemer, as a man who wanted to be king of Sparta but apparently only as a stepping-stone to the dictatorship of all Greece; a man who, though personally frugal, was obsessed with money; who broke oaths with swashbuckling gusto, and whose bootlicking was shameless and relentless. It was a long way from the laws of Lycurgus, but in the person of Lysander, it was all too true.

Lysander was not lucky in his dying. Had he passed from the scene at the end of 405, flushed with his victory over Athens, he would probably have gone down in history as the brilliant and tricky general who had won the Peloponnesian War, the "new Spartan" who could match Athenian intelligence tit for tat. By lasting another ten years—he died in 395 at the battle of Haliartus, which he clumsily lost—Lysander showed posterity both his insouciance about kicking over the Lycurgan applecart in order to get ahead and his utter career failure. Not that the stymieing of Lysander signals the strength of the Spartan system; rather, even in defeat, Lysander hurt his country both at home and abroad.

At home, Lysander symbolized a new low in factional bitterness and disunity. Himself of questionable background (possibly an Inferior who had been championed by a wealthy Equal), Lysander may have felt more than the usual sting of ambition. Perhaps he compensated for his own obscure and impoverished beginnings by emphasizing the making of connections, which became a leitmotif of his career. He became famous both for fawning on great men, and for demanding that others fawn on him in turn. In his late teens, he scored the coup of a love affair with the royal prince (later king) Agesilaus; as an admiral, he wrapped Prince Cyrus of Persia around his finger and extracted from him the money necessary to hire top-notch rowers for the Spartan fleet. As a diplomat, he specialized in making personal connections with oligarchs in the various cities of the Athenian empire; after Sparta's victory, he promoted them to power, establishing narrow juntas wherever he could.

Before the home government knew it, Sparta's promise at the start of the Peloponnesian War to free the Greeks was dissolving into an empire of Lysander's creation. The new regimes set up by Lysander came with Spartan governors, garrisons, and tax collectors. All that was missing was an emperor, and there were signs that he would not be missing long. In addition to the statues (including the tableau at Delphi with which this chapter opened), there were songs of triumph and festival games—called (what else?) the Lysandria—as well as the novel fact of deification. The colorful anecdotes about Lysander's bribes to various oracles in order to have them open up the Spartan kingship to none other than himself may even be true. But if not, Lysander was still doing enough to raise considerable uneasiness, both abroad and in Sparta itself.

As exemplified by Lysander, the new Spartan was a break with the old in several ways. He thrived on imperialist entanglements rather than restricting himself to the Peloponnesos. Never one to follow the leader, the new Spartan put his own ambition first, much as Alcibiades the Athenian had done—indeed there is much of the Alcibiades syndrome in Lysander. Far from ignoring money, the new Spartan brought home a small fortune, from Persia and from the new empire. Although Lysander may have been personally indifferent to lucre his countrymen were not.

If Lysander's imperialism was novel, his treatment of other Greeks was not. The "ugly Spartan," who behaved in an aggressive and overbearing manner abroad, was an old story. The ancients traced the root of this problem to the Lycurgan system itself, arguing that it made the Spartans as domineering abroad as they were obedient at home. Aristotle quips that Lycurgus produced crack soldiers, not governors of an empire. Nor, we might add, strategists. Take Lysander: he was brighter, more talented, more ambitious, and more ruthless than the average Spartan, but did he have a coherent grand strategy?

Lysander's ambitions so frightened Sparta's allies that in 403, Corinth and Thebes gave aid and comfort to a democratic rebellion by enemy Athens against its Lysander-installed oligarchy. Lysander's ambitions frightened Spartans, too. A Spartan king himself gave the final boost to the democratic revolt by marching out an army to support the restoration of Athenian democracy. "Better free than Lysander-led" might have been the motto of most Spartans and their allies when it came to Athens, and not only to Athens. It was probably at around this time that the Spartan government did an about-face and abolished the narrow oligarchies that Lysander had established, and recalled Lysander himself home to Sparta.

The upshot was that, while defeating Athens, Lysander had destabilized both the Spartan regime and the Peloponnesian League. By attempting to bend the postwar settlement to his own personal ambition, he had thrown away goodwill and support throughout the Aegean. Worse still, having botched the job of replacing Athenian democracy with a friendlier regime, he ended up with a reinvigorated democracy. Imagine if the Allies had been forced to tolerate a neo-Nazi uprising in Germany in 1946 and then had accepted it as the legitimate government: such was Sparta's position vis-à-vis Athens by the end of 403.

Lysander was down but not out. When his former patron, the Persian prince Cyrus, tried to grab the Persian throne in 401, Lysander was perhaps one of the movers behind Sparta's decision to support him. When Cyrus failed, Lysander probably had much to do with Sparta's expedition shortly afterward to free the Asia Minor Greeks from Persia. Far more impressive, in 400 he steered his former lover Agesilaus through the shark-infested waters of domestic politics and had him proclaimed king in place of his older brother (who was tarred with the brush of possibly being the illegitimate son of Alcibiades!). Yet, although King Agesilaus owed his throne to Lysander, he was no man's patsy. In 396 Agesilaus entered Sparta's military crusade in Asia Minor with great fanfare. When Lysander, present on Agesilaus's staff, attempted to rekindle his old patronage network there, Agesilaus dumped him, and Lysander had to return home humiliated.

There was no shortage of opportunities for action at home. The great growth of Spartan power—in the Aegean, in the campaign against Persia in Asia Minor, and in a series of intrigues in central Greece—convinced Sparta's former allies Boeotia and Corinth to join with Athens in a revolt. Sparta had unwisely refused to share the glory or booty of victory with allies. Moreover, Sparta had underestimated the diplomatic sagacity of the king of Persia, who responded to Sparta's invasion of Asia Minor by bankrolling the anti-Spartan revolt in Greece. This so-called Corinthian War, which began in 395, eventually forced Agesilaus and his army back from Asia Minor. At first, however, the Spartans tried to quell the revolt with their forces in Greece. The command went to Lysander, who led an army into Boeotia in summer 395.

Was Lysander troubled by the prospect of a two-front war (Greece as well as Asia Minor)? On the contrary, some ancient sources argue that he welcomed it, and that he had actually stage-managed the policy that pushed Boeotia into fighting. If so, Lysander had made one scheme too many. Boeotia was no pushover—a miscalculation Lysander would pay for with his life. Lysander declined to wait for the full complement of Spartan troops to arrive before attacking a fortified enemy city; the Boeotians, not frightened by an inferior Spartan force, rushed out and butchered Lysander and a thousand of his men. It seems that no one had been more dazzled by his ambition than Lysander himself; and no one paid more dearly for the illusion.

In 395 Lysander was dead, but his legacy lived on. Instead of establishing a generation of peace after the Peloponnesian War, Lysander's policies had committed Sparta to a state of war against every one of its former major allies as well as a resurgent Athens. Although the Spartan government had disavowed Lysander's narrow and repressive oligarchies, people throughout the Greek world blamed Sparta for them nonetheless. By dropping the principle of liberation when it suited their interests, the Spartans had lost the ideological high ground. In domestic politics, instead of uniting the Spartan leadership, Lysander had been the source of bitter divisions. He had failed to deal with the problem of the ongoing decline in elite military manpower; in fact, the huge amounts of money Lysander brought home from the Aegean tended to let the rich become richer, and so contributed to the financial pressure driving Equals down to the status of Inferiors. In sum, both abroad and at home, although he beat Athens in the Peloponnesian War, Lysander's policies brought Sparta less rather than more security. Nevertheless, had a man of vision replaced him at the helm, a man tough enough to force through the necessary internal reforms and realistic enough not to take on the whole world as an enemy, Sparta might have regrouped and come out stronger than ever. But the leader Sparta got was not that man: Sparta got Agesilaus.

AGESILAUS

After Lysander's Athenian-like energy, cunning, and fondness for novelty, it is fitting that Sparta got a leader who prided himself on his old-fashioned, all-Spartan character. Although he would travel widely and meet foreign potentates, Agesilaus remained a man of simplicity, austerity, and plain speech. Although a king, he shared hardships and camaraderie with his troops. In fact, Agesilaus was the only Spartan king to have gone through the full agoge: a second son, he had never been groomed for the throne, and hence had been allowed to be just one of the boys. In short, Agesilaus was the ideal Spartan.

Few Spartans were as successful as he in living up to the dictates of Lycurgus. Agesilaus excelled in self-discipline and bravery in battle, he subordinated everything to the interests of Sparta (as he conceived them), he was decisive and ambitious, he stood second to none in taking care of his friends, and he went the old Greek maxim ("Help your friends, hurt your enemies") one better by trying to win over even his enemies with favors and flattery. He served at various times as commander of his country's troops in the Peloponnesos, in central and northern Greece, and in Asia Minor. Measures of his political success: Agesilaus was unusually powerful for a Greek constitutional monarch, and a near contemporary called him, with little exaggeration, the most powerful and most famous man of his day.

Psychologists might seek explanations for Agesilaus's drive for success in his physical makeup. He was short, and was often reminded of it. Worse still, in so physique-conscious a society, he was born lame. In theory this should have qualified Agesilaus for exposure as an infant, but perhaps the son of a king was exempt, or perhaps manpower-short Sparta did not throw away a perfectly good boy child because of a limp. Whatever the case, if anyone had a motive for overcompensation, it was Agesilaus.

In spite of all his achievements, Agesilaus is in the end a tragic figure, because he lived to preside over the dismantling of Spartan hegemony; in fact, he helped to bring that disaster on. Of course, a tragic figure is supposed to be conscious of his or her fate, and Agesilaus was prevented by his Spartan upbringing from acknowledging, much less lamenting, his failure. For that matter, he was ignorant of classical tragedy—and proud of the fact. Hence, some may doubt whether he deserves tragic status. Yet, Agesilaus was a man of undeniable greatness, as tragic heroes ought to be, and he was a man whose character carried its own seeds of destruction within. So perhaps Agesilaus's story can be called a tragedy after all, the tragedy of a man who succeeded too well.

As an ideal Spartan, Agesilaus possessed a vision that was as narrow as it was pure, never able to see beyond the confines set by Lycurgus. Experience had taught him that devotion to the old Spartan ways would bring success in the state; after all, he himself had unexpectedly ascended the throne at the age of about forty-five. He saw no reason to doubt that the same skills that had made him king would allow him to maintain and even increase Sparta's dominance of Greece. Unfortunately, Agesilaus had not learned that international diplomacy required a broader theme than cronyism. He had not learned to respect or adopt the new military tactics that would ultimately defeat Sparta on the battlefield. Like so many Spartans, he had not learned that other Greeks expected to be treated as equals rather than as buck privates. Above all, Agesilaus was unwilling to recognize the seriousness of Sparta's military manpower problem.

Perhaps one of the keys to Agesilaus's problematic standing at home and abroad is his use and misuse of symbolic gestures. In a society proud of its illiteracy, vivid and visual communication is essential. Agesilaus often used such symbols deftly; perhaps the need to overcome his own visible handicap had given him special skill in manipulating symbols. For instance, Agesilaus never lost an occasion to demonstrate his Lycurgan austerity, be it by wearing his coarse Spartan cloak everywhere, or by sleeping on a hard bed while on campaign, or by refusing to replace the old wooden doors of his house. To take another example of his adept use of symbols, when on campaign in Asia Minor (396–394) he wanted to demote Lysander, Agesilaus made his point by naming Lysander as his meat carver.

On other occasions, however, Agesilaus mishandled symbolic communication disastrously, which suggests that he had a large blind spot. For instance, back in Greece in 394, after winning the battle of Coronea, he chose not to let a still-intact crack Theban infantry unit retreat from the field, but insisted on attacking the enemy head-on, to demonstrate Spartan strength. Heavy casualties ensued on both sides, including severe wounds to Agesilaus himself, and the Thebans succeeded in pushing through anyhow. Agesilaus's vain gesture shows both how little he understood the limits to Sparta's power and, a related point, how naively he believed in the ability of Spartans to sweep all before them. It is interesting to compare this failed gesture with a more successful ploy before the battle when, for the sake of morale, Agesilaus covered up the news of a major Spartan defeat at sea. Instead, he announced a victory, put on festive flower garlands, and sacrificed in thanksgiving. What the two incidents have in common is that both were theatrical gestures—as if by staging scenes of Spartan invincibility, Agesilaus could render Sparta invincible. Yet, one by one, the unpleasant realities of power, like the Thebans at Coronea, would force their way into sight.

Perhaps the most interesting of Agesilaus's symbolic failures was his sacrifice at Aulis. In 396, Agesilaus took personal command of Sparta's faltering expedition in Asia Minor. Agesilaus mustered the reinforcement troops, both

Spartans and those he had managed to get from the recalcitrant allies, at Aulis, a town on the Boeotian coast.
Aulis had been specifically chosen for its mythological significance as the jumping-off point for the Trojan War. It
was a dubious parallel, however, since the Trojan War
had dragged on for ten years, and the leader of the
Greeks at Troy had been Agamemnon, proverbial as an
overbearing and arrogant ruler, who came to a bad end as
a cuckold murdered by his own wife—hardly a good role
model for Agesilaus. We can, however, learn something
from Agesilaus's inappropriate choice. In invoking
Agamemnon, he shows his belief that he could rule the
other Greeks by carrying a big stick. Diplomacy in this
view was unnecessary, and might even appear as weakness to men who, although fellow Hellenes, were palpa-
bly inferior to Spartans. So Agesilaus had learned from
the agoge, but he was wrong. The allies would not play
subhumans to his master race.

Indeed, Boeotia, Corinth, and Athens had all refused to
contribute troops to Agesilaus's campaign. Now the Boeotian government showed further what it thought of
Agesilaus's expedition by dispatching horsemen to throw
his sacrifice at Aulis off the altar. It was a vivid and sting-
ing insult, one that Agesilaus would never forget.

Meanwhile, misled by the illusion of Spartan superiority, Agesilaus had made a key strategic error. Sparta
could not go off and make successful war on Persia without securing its rear in Greece. When his turn to fight
Persia came, for example, Alexander left a large army at
home to guard his potentially restive Greek allies. Moreover, he and his father, Philip of Macedon, also knew
how to use the carrot of kind words and lots of bribe
money with the Greeks. Agesilaus neither secured his
rear, nor did he mollify his allies: indeed, he practically
sought out occasions to insult them. As an ideal Spartan,
Agesilaus was used to the military chain of command, not
to diplomacy.

Agesilaus may not have had the spectacular success of
an Alexander, but he did well against the Persians in

western Asia Minor from 396 to 394. The larger strategic realities, however, robbed him of his success. First, in 394, the anti-Spartan alliance dragged Agesilaus back to the Greek mainland, forcing him to abandon the gains he had made in Asia Minor. Second, also in 394, the Persian fleet, commanded and to a large extent manned by Athenians, smashed the Spartan fleet at sea. Agesilaus had unwisely put the Spartan navy in the hands of an inexperienced crony, his wife's brother. Sparta's sea empire was gone, almost at a stroke. Third, during the Corinthian War, Agesilaus had to face the unpleasant reality that while he could win a big battle or two, he lacked the power to bring the rest of the Greek world to its knees.

In order to defeat his enemies in Greece, Agesilaus had to give up the war with Persia. Thus, Sparta had to accept a return to the sellout of 412, when it had handed over the Asia Minor Greeks in return for Persian support in the Peloponnesian War. In 387, the king of Persia agreed to a similar bargain in exchange for supporting Sparta's current war effort, which enabled Sparta to defeat an Athenian fleet. Peace followed in 386. The most important provision of the treaty, known as the King's Peace, was an autonomy clause, which forbade the formation or continuation of federal leagues. The primary target of the clause was Sparta's archenemy Thebes, now required to give up its confederacy in Boeotia.

By winning this victory over Thebes, Agesilaus had shown what he was made of. Neither the rebellion of his Greek allies, nor the destruction of Sparta's fleet, nor the shocking massacre of a Spartan unit by light-armed skirmishers had shaken his resolve. If Agesilaus had been as perceptive as he was steadfast, he could have taken Sparta far. We get a clear insight into his limitations through a comment he made shortly after the peace was negotiated.

When asked how Sparta, ostensible champion of the Greeks, could collaborate with Persia, Agesilaus replied cheerfully that Sparta wasn't collaborating with Persia—rather Persia was collaborating with Sparta. It was a quintessentially laconic comment, terse and pungent. Laconic discourse, however, was just about the least appropriate way to approach the immensely complicated reality of fourth-century B.C. Greece. Nor would Agesilaus be able to dismiss an unpleasant fact simply by denying it. His laconic witticism about the King's Peace boded ill for his future.

In 386 Sparta had regained hegemony in Greece but still faced complex problems. Sparta could not maintain control of Greece without Persian support. Moreover, Athens had made great advances during the Corinthian War, even temporarily reestablishing part of its Aegean empire. Hence, Athens was an anti-Spartan rallying point again. Finally, Sparta had just about exhausted any of its remaining reservoirs of goodwill in the Hellenic world. Spartan hegemony could only be maintained by force. Yet it was almost mathematically certain that such an enterprise would prove impossible.

It was impossible first because Persia had no interest in seeing strong leadership in Greece—quite the contrary. One could predict in 386 that as soon as Sparta grew strong again, Persia would withdraw its support. Second, the reality principle, in the form of Spartan demography, would intervene in fairly short order. There simply were not enough Spartiates to keep fighting all of Greece. Eventually, Sparta would run out of men, and Lysander's disaster in Boeotia had proved that given the right odds, Spartan infantry were far from invincible.

So in 386, just as in 396 and 404, common sense dictated that the Spartans seek a compromise. But they made no more use of the breathing space offered by the King's Peace than they had of previous opportunities. Much, though certainly not all, of the blame goes to Agesilaus, by far the most powerful political player in Sparta. It is worth remembering how he attained and maintained that power. One reason for Agesilaus's near lock on Spartan policy was the network of friends which he carefully built up by favors, threats, and flattery. In addition, however, there was his successful manipulation of the national mythology—his image as the ideal Spartan. The more Lycurgan his behavior, the more Agesilaus was rewarded with power. Yet the same policies that made Agesilaus into Sparta's darling—toughness, inflexibility, simplicity, cronyism, the bullying of non-Spartans, faith that the Spartan army could plow through all opposition, including the demographic problem—precisely these same policies led to Sparta's failure abroad.

Agesilaus's actions after 386 are not without merit. After all, he was in his sixties and seventies, yet he continued tirelessly to lead Sparta's armies throughout Greece, incurring serious wounds in the process. Even more than in previous years, however, his ideological blinders impeded his vision, and Sparta paid an ever greater price. Three areas stand out for special comment: Agesilaus's relationship with his Greek allies, his lack of response to novel military tactics, and his inattention to the ever growing Spartan manpower problem.

A first point concerning the allies is Agesilaus's cronyism. Agesilaus had been brought up on the twin notions that justice was rarely as important as friendship and never as important as the short-term good of Sparta. Although most Greeks held similar ideas about their own countries, few would have taken them to the point the Spartans did. As king of a self-proclaimed world-class power, however, Agesilaus saw no reason to temper his principles when abroad. After all, the way Sparta did things was clearly the best way to do them. Time and again, therefore, he made enemies for Sparta by intervening on behalf of his personal friends.

Moreover, in the years following the King's Peace of 386, Agesilaus constantly followed a policy of armed intervention in other Greek cities, in violation of the autonomy clause of the peace. Spartan armies intervened in the Peloponnesos, Boeotia, Attica, and even Macedon. An unpleasant policy, but one that might have given Sparta security and assured military superiority if properly implemented. Agesilaus had miscalculated the force he could bring to bear, however, and his policy was dominated by an obsessive hatred of Thebes.

Whether it was born of the insult at Aulis, as some would have it, or simply from a natural rivalry with the second greatest infantry power in Greece, Agesilaus's pursuit of anti-Theban policies was relentless and ultimately suicidal. Like all of Sparta's attempts to impose its will uncompromisingly against a powerful enemy, it failed. After Thebes' liberation in 378 from the pro-Spartan puppet-regime installed by one of his cronies in 382, Agesilaus personally led two invasions of Boeotia in successive summers, but he achieved nothing beyond giving the Thebans practice in infantry skirmishes. In fact, fired with revolutionary zeal, the Thebans went from strength to strength, and had reestablished their confederacy in most of Boeotia by 374. They also made an uneasy alliance with the Athenians, who were busy in the Aegean, trying to reestablish their naval confederacy.

Agesilaus had much to answer for. The Peloponnesian allies were tired of risking their lives in Boeotia, and accused him of indulging a private grudge. A leading member of Sparta's ruling faction warned Agesilaus that he was achieving nothing but giving the Thebans a free lesson in how to fight. The critic was right.

Thebes' ever improving army was an ominous addition to the international power equation. The foundation of Sparta's power had been its unsurpassed elite infantry corps. Now, in addition to endemic manpower problems, the corps also faced competition in the area of battle skills. Already, in the Corinthian War, the Thebans had smashed through the Spartan line at Coronea, and on another occasion, a group of mercenaries, lightly armed mobile skirmishers, had massacred a unit of 250 heavily armed Spartans (including some Equals) near Corinth.

The Theban revolutionaries of the 370s, led by Epaminondas and Pelopidas, applied the latest advances in tactics to the always formidable Theban infantry. First, they created the elite strike force called the Sacred Band, 300 picked soldiers trained to a high degree of skill and united by homoerotic bonds. Next they drilled the rest of the army in novel and effective tactics, including an emphasis on the left rather than the right wing of the phalanx, where men would now be massed fifty ranks deep rather than the usual twelve, and the efficient use of cavalry to disrupt the enemy's advance. With a deeply massed left wing, the Sacred Band at its head as a striking force, the Theban army of the 370s presented an increasingly serious threat to Sparta. In 375, at Tegyra in Boeotia, the Thebans routed an enemy force twice their size, and killed two Spartan generals. The stage was set for Leuctra.

The Leuctra campaign of 371 began when a Spartan army invaded southwestern Boeotia to try, once again, to defeat Thebes. The other Spartan king, Cleombrotus, was in command, but Agesilaus was the guiding spirit of the campaign, his anti-Theban obsession the motive: had he not been suffering from a leg injury, he would have been present himself. As the great battle approached, Cleombrotus had some 10–11,000 men, but many were allies, and only about 700 were Spartiates. The Boeotians, with Epaminondas and Pelopidas in command, had 6–7,000 men. It was a battle fought according to Epaminondas's new precepts. In the first phase, the Boeotian cavalry prevented the enemy from advancing. Then, Epaminondas moved forward with his left wing, composed of about 4,000 Thebans massed 50 shields deep, the Sacred Band in front. They smashed through the enemy's right wing, which was occupied by the Lacedaemonian contingent (Spartiates, *perioikoi*, possibly some Inferiors), and won a decisive victory. In fact, Leuctra turned into a rout, with some Spartans running from the field after most had fought bravely. Their casualties were enormous: 1,000 Lacedaemonians were dead, including 400 Spartiates and King Cleombrotus himself.

Thebes' victory at Leuctra was a great shock to most Greeks, but it is only part of the story. What is equally or more important is the aftermath. Had Sparta been a world-class power, as it had proclaimed since 404, it would have been able to roll with the punch and reassert hegemony. Instead, Spartan power collapsed. In the following years, Epaminondas and a large army marched into the Peloponnesos and into Laconia itself, which he ravaged at will. The city of Sparta probably owed its survival less to Agesilaus's defense than to Epaminondas's intention to keep it alive as a counterweight to the newly liberated Peloponnesians. For liberate he did indeed: after some three hundred years, Messenia was restored as an independent state. The cities just north of Sparta, once tightly controlled clients, were freed and organized in a new federal league of Arcadia. Sparta had lost most of its helots and their land as well as its cordon sanitaire of allies. Sparta had been the dominant land power in Greece for some two hundred years and then, suddenly, it was all over.

Sparta would still fight battles here and there, still go its own gruff way in diplomacy. It was, however, no longer a major player on the Greek international scene. As for Agesilaus, having organized the defense of Sparta in his seventies, in his eighties he served two years as a mercenary captain in Egypt, in order to earn "hard currency" for the national treasury. What can have gone through the mind of the man who once commanded a Panhellenic army in a new Trojan War? Did he lament his fate? It seems doubtful, because before all else, Agesilaus was Sparta personified. He was tough, he was fighting, he was serving the interests of his country: nothing else mattered. He earned a respectable commission and died on the trip home, aged eighty-two.

THE LESSON

Sparta went from riches to rags in the thirty-five years from 404 to 371, about a generation. Sparta's downfall was even worse than Athens' had been, but in both cases, the defeat was largely of the loser's own making. Not that Sparta had ever been strong enough to carry out the full imperial program of Lysander or Agesilaus. The Spartans could have maintained and consolidated their position in Greece, however, and perhaps slowly built up to the point of mounting a challenge to Persia's control of the Asia Minor Greeks. Instead, Sparta fought a war on two fronts and lost on both.

Sparta's victory in 404 spelled trouble. Perverse as it seems, winning the Peloponnesian War was probably the worst thing that could have happened to Sparta. If the war had ended in a stalemate, as it almost did (in the last phase, Sparta twice offered Athens a compromise peace, and was twice turned down), the world would have looked very different to the Spartans. The Spartans would not have been the Victors. There would have been no forty-statue tableau at Delphi, no flute girls at Athens' walls. Lysander would not have been deified. Instead of being encouraged to indulge its arrogance and sense of power, Sparta would have been forced to contemplate its limits. And well it should have, because even after winning the Peloponnesian War, Sparta's power was severely limited by, among external constraints, its dependence on Greek allies, its need for Persian subsidies, and Athens' potential for recovery.

Had the Spartans been confronted with a negotiated peace, therefore, they might have treated their allies more gingerly. The Spartans might not have bit the Persian hand that fed them. They might not have overlooked Athens' recuperative powers.

Maybe and maybe not, because beneath the matter of postwar psychology, there is an underlying structural problem: the mentality of the Spartan elite. In a society that was not merely military but militaristic—organized from top to bottom on military lines—diplomacy went against the grain. Aristotle was right: after all those years of Lycurgan schooling, Spartans were soldiers, not ambassadors. So Sparta might have treated its allies better after a compromise peace, but probably would still not have treated them very well. Besides, the allies were not the heart of the problem; the heart of the problem was

Sparta's social crisis, which led to the collapse of elite military manpower. Had there been 9,000 Equals in 371 and not 1,500, Sparta might have won at Leuctra—or, if it had lost, it would have survived to win another day.

Once again we run up against the problem of the elite's mentality. Sparta's rulers had been brought up to believe in their own propaganda. Sparta was Sparta; it was the greatest place on earth and had no need to change. Were thousands of Equals slipping to Inferior status over the years? Well, as long as people in one's own communal mess were still well off, then the phenomenon was invisible. Was wealth spilling over the Lycurgan walls? As long as men still wore rough cloaks, slept on hard beds, and spent their lives fighting, so what? The Spartan elite was virtually unable to absorb unpleasant realities; to use the current jargon, they could not process cognitive dissonance. Spartans were famous for acting expediently and calling it justice; worse, they sincerely believed their own warped logic; worse still, their expedients were expedient only in the very short run.

The truth is, Sparta was miscast as an imperial power. Sparta's elite was not merely untrained in diplomacy: it was untrained in making the compromises with reality which any kind of long-term success demands. Spartans lived by the comfortable illusion of their military omnipotence, and they died by it. Agesilaus and Lysander lost because they would not face up to rapidly changing internal and external realities. Unfortunately, theirs was far from the last such case in history.

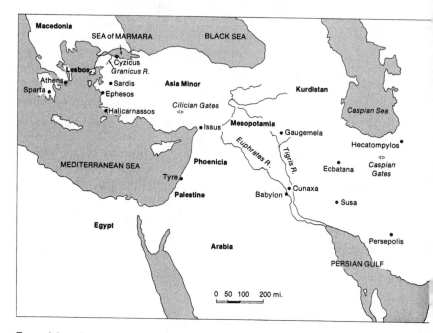

From Macedonia to Persia, 334–330 B.C.

Darius III of Persia: Why He Lost and Made Alexander Great

Bactria

Iran

to India
→
to Indus R.

INDIAN OCEAN

THE FIFTH CENTURY B.C. showed that Athens and Sparta were unable to share the hegemony of Greece. The fourth century showed that no Greek city-state was able to go it alone as hegemon either. After winning the Peloponnesian War in 404, Sparta tried, but the attempt was shaky, and it came to an end on the battlefield of Leuctra in 371. The victorious Boeotians then tried to dominate the Greek world, but it was too big a job. Boeotia freed the helots and set up an independent Messenia to the west of Sparta and an Arcadian confederacy to the north, but these new states were no Boeotian puppets. Athens, whose power was reviving, proved to be a thorn in Boeotia's side. By 360, with plenty of opposition, with its leadership decimated and its people exhausted, Boeotia was in retreat.

It looked as if the real winner of the Greek wars of hegemony was Persia, whose diplomats had helped keep the Greeks fighting each other. That judgment turned out to be premature, however. In 359, on the fringes of the Greek world in Macedon, a new king came to the throne who would set in motion a revolution in Greece and the

Middle East. Philip II displayed Athenian energy, Spartan discipline, the Boeotian flair for military innovation and for instilling esprit de corps in his troops, and a combination of skills at conquest and administration that recalled the Persian kings Cyrus the Great and Darius I. The kingdom of Macedon won the hegemony that had eluded the city-states.

The main instrument of Philip's success was the new Macedonian army. Year-round training, new weapons, an original combination of infantry and cavalry tactics, a streamlined baggage train, and a steady source of pay for the troops all led to victory. Philip was an excellent strategist and diplomat too. Under his leadership, Macedon expanded in Greece throughout the 350s and 340s, and won a final showdown with Athens and Thebes at the battle of Chaeronea in 338. The Greek city-states accepted Philip as hegemon.

He now turned to what he considered the main event: Persia. For years, Greek propagandists had been floating the idea of exploiting Persian weakness. Given its weakness in infantry, Persia depended on Greek mercenaries. Recent decades had seen a series of provincial revolts and palace coups. Their appetite whetted by these signs of Persian fallibility, enlightened Greek opinion-makers called for a frank war of expansion against Persia, whose western lands could then be colonized by Greeks. Racist slogans of Persia's "natural" inferiority were not lacking.

Philip was preparing for the big day when in 336 he was assassinated by a disgruntled courtier. Gossip said that his wife, Olympias, and son, Alexander, were in on the plot, but as the new king, Alexander ruthlessly put down opposition in Macedon and Greece. In 336, by coincidence, a new king, Darius III, came to the throne of Persia, too. The stage was set for war.

THE MYTH OF INEVITABILITY

Sometime in the autumn of 334 or the winter of 334–333, a group of bearded, splendidly robed men probably held a meeting where they decided to entrust the future of their country to a foreigner. They were proud men, of a great country, and their decision was not made lightly. They may have considered the matter twice—once sober and once drunk—as was the custom of the land, but there is no doubt that theirs was a rational and careful decision. The men were Persian nobles, something on the order of the "seven Princes of Persia and Media which saw the King's face, and which sat the first in the kingdom," mentioned in the Book of Esther. Their leader—dressed in purple, bedecked with gold jewelry, anointed with unguents and cosmetics, seated on a high throne, attended by a corps of slaves—was the Great King himself, the chosen of God, Darius III. The foreigner in whom he and his advisers put their trust was a Greek, Memnon of Rhodes. A Greek: for Persians, this was frustrating, inauspicious, humiliating. Yet Memnon had served Persia faithfully for fifteen years; he had even married a Persian woman, and left her and his children as hostages at court. Besides, after the decisive defeat of a Persian army on land the previous summer, it was time to turn to a maritime strategy, and Memnon was far and away Persia's best naval commander. So a Greek it would have to be. Never mind: if the fleet won victories, if Darius continued to trust the new strategy, if Memnon kept his command, then Alexander of Macedon's invasion of the Persian empire might be stopped. As it turned out, the fleet was victorious but Memnon died. Darius impatiently opted for another land battle, and Alexander went on to greatness.

He also went on to dominate the history books. With little or no record of the Persian side of the story, many historians have written as if Alexander's victory was inevitable. Again and again they point to once great Persia's decadence in the late fourth century, Alexander's unique genius as a general, and the extraordinary excellence of the Macedonian army. How could Alexander the Great have been anything less than . . . the Greatest?

Great he was, but his victory was not inevitable at the outset. Alexander was the young king of a small country that had been a great power for less than thirty years. He had inherited an empty treasury and a throne surrounded by would-be traitors: the stormy factions of both the Macedonian aristocracy and the Greek city-states who hated him, looked down on Macedonians as barbarians, and manned the untrustworthy "allied" fleet. Darius, on the other hand, wore the ruler's diadem of a two-hundred-year-old empire that was vast in size, that was rich in money and manpower, and that had survived many previous military challenges. Alexander had a first-rate army and he promised brilliance as a general, but that does not automatically spell victory over an empire. If it did, history would be rote, like arithmetic, but there are many counterexamples. Stalin's Russia, for example, however weak in 1941, managed to crush the vigorous Nazi invader. Or the Roman Empire in the third century A.D., which, after tottering for years, triumphed over a host of enemies. Or France, who lost battles on a heroic scale during the Hundred Years' War (1337–1453) but produced Joan of Arc, outlasted the English invader, and went on to thrive. Or finally, to return to Alexander's part of the world, the "sick man of Europe," the dismembered Ottoman Empire, which should have been an easy target for Greek irredentism after World War I. Instead, under Ataturk's generalship, the Turks crushed the invading Greek army in 1922 and drove over a million Greek refugees out of Asia Minor. Persia was not a dead duck on the day that Alexander began his campaign. It took talent on Alexander's part to win; it also took errors on Persia's part to lose.

The Persian emperor who faced Alexander, Darius III (called Codomannus before ascending to the throne) is a little-known figure. His strategic choices, however, stand out in clear relief. There were several turning points, moments when Darius or his commanders made decisions with fatal consequences for Persia. A series of different decisions might have changed history. The subject of Persia's strategy—or rather strategies, because several were tried—against Alexander needs more attention than it usually gets, and for a simple reason: had Darius chosen the right strategy and followed it consistently, he could have beaten Alexander. Persia was not doomed to fail.

Persia's defeat therefore can and should be explained in terms more sophisticated than Alexander's genius or Persia's decadence: it has to be explained in terms of strategy. We can understand Persia's loss by paying particular attention to the interplay of war, diplomacy, and finances; and to Clausewitz's dictum that the victor will be the one who is willing to sustain defeat(s) on secondary fronts as long as he wins the main event.

Second, we must explain why Persia failed to choose the correct strategy. The answer seems to lie in ideology and domestic politics. As a man who owed his personal success to the fortunes of war, Darius was drawn back, step by step, to the time-honored Persian dream of victory in battle. As a late ascendant to the purple, Darius was seduced by the illusion of the omnipotence of the Persian monarchy. Finally, as an uneasy and recent pretender to the throne, Darius could not take the strategically sound but politically unpopular actions that might expose him to a coup d'état.

Before proceeding, let us briefly survey Alexander's road to victory. To put it simply, Alexander conquered Persia because he won battles. His three big victories were at the Granicus River (334) in northwestern Asia Minor, at Issus (331) on the Mediterranean near the modern Turko-Syrian border, and at Gaugamela (330) near the modern-day city of Mosul in northern Iraq. Alexander crushed the enemy army in all three battles, and in each one the superiority of the Macedonian army shines through. Still, the Persians fought bravely, and at Gaugamela, it appears they may have even come close to winning. The more fundamental question is why the Persians did Alexander the favor of facing him in battle at all! The Persian High Command had received a steady stream of advice not to risk conclusions with the crack Macedonian army. Indeed, an alternative strategy was readily at hand: a scorched-earth policy in Asia Minor while raising the standard of rebellion in Greece and the Aegean. But Darius wanted to fight; Alexander and his veterans took care of the rest. When it was over, the Macedonian sat on Darius's throne; Darius lay dead in an oxcart by the roadside, stabbed by his own disgruntled nobles.

PERSIA AND ITS EMPEROR ON THE EVE OF WAR

In 336, the Persian Empire was still the greatest empire the world of the Near East and eastern Mediterranean had ever seen—and it had seen many. True, the great days of Cyrus the Great, Darius I, and Xerxes were gone. True, the loyalty of the western satrapies was in question. True, palace intrigue had put a new and untested king on the throne. Nevertheless, the strengths of the empire were formidable.

It was, first of all, huge. Conquered territories in the west and east, roughly equivalent to today's Bulgaria and Pakistan, had been lost. What was left was nonetheless enormous: nearly two million square miles, extending from modern-day Afghanistan in the east to modern-day Turkey in the northwest and Egypt in the southwest. The empire included an enormous variety of peoples and terrains, difficult enough to visualize, let alone to conquer or administer. As many have noted, the huge and daunting expanse of Persian territory was in itself a defensive weapon.

The Great King (as the Greeks called Persia's ruler) could summon an enormous army, many times larger than anything his enemies could put together. In 330, for example, when Darius had already lost two big battles as well as control of his subjects in the west, his army at the battle of Gaugamela was several times larger than Alexander's 50,000 troops. We don't know exactly *how* large, but large enough for Alexander to offer a special sacrifice to the gods on the eve of battle. The Persian navy was similarly impressive: 400 warships from Cyprus and Phoenicia, compared to only 160 for Macedon.

The Persians were famous as tough fighters, particularly as cavalrymen and archers. For instance, in an inscription of about 513 at Persepolis, the capital, Darius I speaks of "this land Persis, . . . which is beautiful; possessing good horses and good men, . . . it has no fear of an enemy." In infantry, on the other hand, Persia could not compete with the Greek or Macedonian hoplite. Still, what the Great King couldn't command, he could buy. It is estimated that nearly 50,000 armed Greek infantrymen fought as mercenaries for Darius against Alexander. Although mercenaries are notoriously unreliable, these Greeks did fight well for Persia—motivated both by traditional Greek-Macedonian animosity and by Alexander's massacre of mercenaries at the Granicus.

Given the state of ancient technology, an empire this large could not be tightly governed, but its administration is impressive, even so. The empire was divided into some twenty provinces, each governed by a satrap. The satraps held civil and military authority; they were responsible for collecting taxes, administering justice, and raising troops when needed. Several key strong points held imperial garrisons, and Iranian military colonists were settled in many locations. Bureaucrats and scribes maintained contact between local authorities and the royal court. King's agents (men known as "the Eyes of the King") traveled the empire. The capital city of Susa (in Iran) was connected to Sardis (in western Turkey) by the Royal Road; the trip took three months under normal conditions, but teams of royal couriers using Pony Express–style changes of mount could do it in a week.

By the late fourth century, some western satraps were virtually independent of the Great King, but except in times of open rebellion, they continued to send him the annual tribute. The Great King was rich, dizzyingly rich by Greek standards. In the golden fifth-century days of empire, Athens took in an annual tribute of 600 talents. His Persian expedition had put Alexander in debt to the tune of 800 talents. The Great King, on the other hand, took in over 10,000 talents as annual tribute, while his precious metal reserves amounted to 235,000 talents, some in coin, most in ingots (compare Periclean Athens' 6,000-talent reserve). Darius could buy a lot of military might with this kind of money.

One of the assets that Persia bought regularly throughout the fourth century was Greeks: not merely mercenaries, but politicians. From the late Peloponnesian War, when Persian money financed Spartan fleets for use against Athens, to the Corinthian War, when Persian gold greased the palms of the leaders of the anti-Spartan alliance, to the various Common Peaces and King's Peaces of the 380s to 360s, the Great King had been quite successful at winding up the Greek city-states and aiming them against each other—thereby keeping them off his territory. The King's Peace of 386, which settled the affairs of mainland Greece, was, for example, negotiated far away from Greece in Susa, and its terms were read aloud by a royal official to the assembled Greek representatives at Sardis. That Peace restored Cyprus and the Greek cities of Asia Minor to Persian rule after a century of independence. Above all, it marked the official failure of Sparta's invasions of Asia Minor in the 390s. Although some Greeks, like the Athenian Isocrates, urged their countrymen to take up the anti-Persian burden, there were no takers until Philip and Alexander, and they were Macedonians.

The Great King did not always project his power so successfully, however. At the beginning of his reign Artaxerxes II (405–358) was faced with the rebellion of his brother Cyrus, who hired 10,000 Greek mercenaries and came within an ace of beating Artaxerxes. Even after the King's Peace, the independent-minded king of Cyprus remained a thorn in Artaxerxes' side. Shortly afterward, the Great King risked his prestige by personally commanding an expedition against rebels southwest of the Caspian Sea; the expedition failed, but Artaxerxes scored points by sharing his men's suffering on the freezing retreat home. In the west, the Greeks made trouble by supporting a series of Satraps' Revolts. By the late 360s, it looked as if the whole west might go, but a strategically placed traitor saved the day. What had happened was that the satrap Orontes, a veteran commander and the king's son-in-law, managed to get named as leader of the rebellion, and then promptly betrayed his colleagues. The 350s saw a new Great King, Artaxerxes III (358–338), and more rebellious western satraps. These were suppressed in turn, some by armies led by the king himself. Egypt represented another, long-standing crack in the dike, but it was not beyond repair. In a state of semipermanent revolt from the mid–fifth century on, Egypt was finally reconquered by Persia in the 340s.

The Persian Empire had been shaken severely in the 360s and 350s, but by the 340s the structure had been firmed up nicely. The Great King had triumphed in person over rebels in Phoenicia and Egypt; the satraps in Asia Minor were loyal again. The rest of the empire, as far as the sources tell us, held firm. Even the Caspian rebels were finally defeated. Artaxerxes III had able advisers like the eunuch Bagoas, and excellent generals like Mentor of Rhodes, hero of the Egyptian campaign, and Mentor's brother Memnon, who became commander in the west when Mentor died in 336. Persia's resources in money, manpower, and armies were still great. There were still men willing to fight for the empire, men like Darius III (then called Codomanus), cousin of Artaxerxes III: the man who defeated a Caspian champion in single combat and was named satrap of Armenia as reward.

What Persia needed to survive and prosper was a little luck and a lot of strong leadership. It got neither. It was bad luck that between 338 and 336, the Great King and his son were both poisoned. Thus the government's grip on the periphery of the empire was very loose by 336 when the new, inexperienced monarch, Darius III, came to his throne. But with a little luck, the Greeks would continue doing what they did best: killing each other off before they could kill Persians. Again and again, fourth-century Greeks obliged by destroying their leaders. Even Philip of Macedon, who dominated Greece more decisively than Lysander or Agesilaus during the height of Sparta's power, was knifed by an assassin before he could lead his planned invasion of Asia Minor. Philip himself had barely resisted the temptation of killing his obstreperous son Alexander, and after Philip's death there were other Macedonian nobles ready to finish the job. It was bad luck that Alexander turned out to be more than a match for them.

The leadership Persia needed was a king on the model of Tissaphernes, satrap of Sardis, a dominant figure in imperial politics around the year 400. Like Alcibiades, whom he took on as adviser after the latter fled from Sparta in 412, Tissaphernes was both a fox and a lion. His policy during the Peloponnesian War was to play a double game: to help both Sparta and Athens until they wore each other out and Persia could call the shots. Other leaders prevailed, however, and, against Tissaphernes' judgment, Persia tipped toward Sparta. Tissaphernes might have felt grimly vindicated when, in 401, the chickens came home to roost in the form of Spartan soldiers fighting for the Persian rebel Cyrus. But Tissaphernes was tough and loyal. Not only did he lead a successful cavalry charge during the battle of Cunaxa, where Cyrus and his rebel cause perished, but Tissaphernes arranged afterward for the murder of the Greek generals during a parley.

There was no Tissaphernes in the 330s. Instead, there was the vizier, Bagoas the eunuch, the schemer who poisoned first Artaxerxes III in 338 and his son, Artaxerxes IV, shortly thereafter. Bagoas then offered the throne to Codomannus, who became Darius III in 336 and beat Bagoas to the punch by forcing the eunuch to drink his own poison. Darius had moved decisively, but he was no fox. Neither he nor his servants ever took full advantage of the possibility of using diplomacy to raise a Greek rebellion against Alexander and Macedon. Indeed, considering the emphasis in Persian elite culture on telling the truth—imagine what a master of strategic duplicity like Sun Tzu would have thought of that!—foxes are likely to have been in short supply among Persian commanders.

Darius's background did not promise foxiness. He was

a man of action, blunt and direct action, who had built his reputation on beating an enemy in single combat. How easy to go from that heroic feat to the dream of taking on Alexander in battle. How much easier when, as the new Great King, Darius suddenly found himself in the midst of a Versailles of flattering court ritual. In the hothouse of the palace Darius was allowed to nurture his ambitions without having to face unpleasant facts. The Great King was exalted to his pleasure and isolated to his peril. Consider, for instance, the Greek writer Heracleides' description of meals in the palace:

> Of the king's dinner guests, some dine outside, and anyone who wishes can see them, while others dine inside with the king. But even these do not really dine with him: rather there are two rooms opposite each other, in one of these the king takes his meal and in the other the guests take theirs. The king can see them through the curtain at the door, but they do not see him. Sometimes, however, on a festival day, they all dine in one room with the king, in the great hall. When the king has a drinking party, as he often does, he has up to a dozen drinking companions. When they have finished dinner, the king by himself and the guests in the other room, one of the eunuchs calls in the drinking companions. When they go in they drink with him, though not the same wine, and while they sit on the floor, he is on a golden-footed couch. After having drunk too much they leave. Most of the time the king has breakfast and dinner alone, but sometimes his wife and some of his sons dine with him. During dinner the king's concubines sing and play the lyre; one of them is the soloist and the others sing in chorus.

His rough-hewn path to the throne shows that Darius had once been a man with open eyes, but it was too easy to succumb to myopia in the palace. Except when he met Alexander in battle, he knew only as much as his advisers told him. It is not even clear whether Darius could check what they said against written reports, for there is some evidence that Persian nobles could neither read nor write.

At the moment when Persia needed a fox, it got a lion—that is, a convinced believer in the myth of triumphant Persian courage and strength. At the moment when Persia needed an unassailable monarch, secure enough to take on domestic opposition to unpopular but necessary maneuvers (such as a scorched-earth policy), Persia got a new leader whose legitimacy was open to question, and who faced a legacy of assassination and disorder. Darius did not have the luxury of taking his domestic power base for granted. If he avoided battle, if he was seen relying too heavily on Greek advisers, if he allowed Persian land to be burned, then he opened himself up to charges of cowardice and treason. Neither Darius's life experience nor his domestic political position was what Persia needed against Macedon.

To judge from the pictures on his coins and on the tomb he prepared for himself at the beginning of his reign (as was the Persian custom), Darius was a mature, bearded man when he came to the throne. One source tells us that he had contempt for Alexander's youth: the temptation for the seasoned champion to teach the kid a lesson on the battlefield might have been great. By meeting Alexander's army head-on, Darius demonstrated his old-fashioned courage, but he threw away his best card.

THE GREEK CARD

In the era between Napoleon and the Kaiser, British policy in Europe was to maintain a balance of power by preventing any one power from becoming dominant. Similarly, Persian policy toward Greece since the Peloponnesian War had generally been to prevent any one power from dominating Greece, intervening when necessary with ships and money. There had been two Persian slip-ups, though: the blind support of Lysander in 407 and the failure to stop Philip in the 340s. Within twenty years of taking the throne in 359, Philip had turned Macedon into the leading power of Greece. His victory over the armies of Athens and Thebes at the battle of Chaeronea at 338 in Boeotia sealed Macedon's dominance. While Persia had been distracted with rebellious satraps and court intrigue, its longtime nightmare had come true: a strongman had emerged in Greece who was capable of taking up where Agesilaus had left off in his "second Trojan War" of the 390s.

At first, Artaxerxes III made do with a nonaggression pact with Philip. Perhaps he was too busy in Egypt to pay sufficient attention to the Macedonian threat; perhaps he was unconvinced of its danger. In 346, Persia asked Athens to supply mercenaries for the Egyptian campaign, but Athens turned down the request. By the end of the decade, however, when Philip was threatening Athens' grain supply at the Dardanelles, the Athenians were singing a different tune. They sent an embassy to Artaxerxes urging him to make war against Macedon. Philip responded with a letter to the Athenians complaining about their trafficking with the national enemy, but Artaxerxes was willing to do business: in 340 he sent a mercenary force under an Athenian general to the strategic region between the Black Sea and the Aegean. Philip was stymied.

It was a good start, but only a start, and there was little follow-through. If the Great King had financed mercenaries to help the Greeks at Chaeronea, he might have saved Persia a lot of future trouble. Faced by only the national levies of Athens and Thebes, however, Philip swept the field. By the end of 338, he had organized the Greek city-states into a malleable league. Using Persia's intervention of 340 as an excuse, Philip secured a declaration of war from the Greek league and prepared to launch the expedition which Alexander eventually led.

Persia's Greek friends had suffered a major setback, but they were not out of the picture yet. When Philip was assassinated in 336, the Greeks rose in revolt. The great orator Demosthenes, the Winston Churchill of fourth-century

Athens, the indomitable enemy of Macedon, fanned the flames of Greek pride. Gossip said the Persians had arranged for Philip's assassination, but as we have seen gossip blamed various people including Alexander and his mother, Olympias. Whoever killed Philip, it was the perfect time for Persian intervention. Yet, when Athens requested Persian money for a revolt, it was apparently denied. The latest victory in Egypt and the youth of Alexander may have made Darius overconfident. Perhaps Demosthenes deserves some of the blame for overstating Alexander's weakness in the letters he wrote to Persia's generals. At any rate, Darius soon had second thoughts. He sent 300 talents to Greece, but the moment had passed. Only Sparta had the courage to accept money; Athens publicly refused although Demosthenes reportedly took 70 talents privately. Too little, too late. Alexander crushed the Greek rebels and destroyed the powerful city of Thebes in 335. Having secured the home front, and with 12,000 Macedonian infantry and 1,800 cavalry left behind in case Demosthenes got any new ideas, Alexander was ready to turn to Asia Minor.

Still, a revolt in Greece remained one of Persia's best hopes. Officially, the entire Greek league was committed to war with Persia under Alexander's leadership. Yet the league only provided 7,000 infantrymen and a few cavalry, and Alexander seems to have treated these men more as hostages than fighting resources. Although the Athenians had 300 ships available, they gave Alexander only 20: a sign both of their enthusiasm for Alexander and of *his* confidence in Athenian loyalty. Greek discontent with Macedon awaited only a signal from Persia to be aroused, as Athenian exiles at the Great King's court no doubt informed him. One of his chief military advisers proposed building a grand strategy around Greek discontent. Memnon of Rhodes had been a Persian general for over a decade. He was a hardened professional and a good commander. Before Alexander ever crossed the Dardanelles, Memnon proved himself against the Macedonian advance force, which he defeated in battle near the important city of Ephesos, thereby driving the Macedonians back to the northwestern corner of Asia Minor.

Memnon's greatest contribution, however, was as a master strategist. He had no illusions about the difficulty of the task ahead. Ephesos (and a failed attempt to recapture another Macedonian-held city, Cyzicus) was atypical, for Memnon's plan avoided direct confrontation. To quote the Greek historian Diodorus of Sicily:

> [Memnon] advised a policy of not risking a battle face-to-face, but of ravaging the countryside and through the shortage of supplies preventing the Macedonians from advancing further, while at the same time [the Persians] sent naval and land forces across to Macedonia and transferred the whole war to Europe.

In other words, Memnon proposed to build on the traditional Persian policy of pitting Greek against Greek. This policy had worked beautifully in 394, when Agesilaus had been forced back from his successful campaign in Asia Minor to face Sparta's enemies at home; it might work again now. In a sense, Memnon was a proto-Clausewitz, willing to accept defeat on a secondary front (Ionia) in order to concentrate his forces at the decisive point (Macedon). Memnon's improvement on traditional Persian strategy was the scorched-earth policy. This is never an easy strategy to sell a government, and would hurt both Persia's pocketbook (many Persian landowners were settled in western Asia Minor) and its pride. On the other hand, Memnon had been an exile in Macedonia about ten years before, and he knew just how formidable Alexander's army was.

ALEXANDER AND MACEDON

If Alexander had lost and Darius had won, a list of Macedon's woes similar to those now said to have afflicted Persia in 336 would probably be trotted out by conventional historical wisdom today. For instance, in 336, the Macedonian treasury was empty. King Philip, who had almost single-handedly built Macedon into a great power, was dead by assassination. The nobility had been divided by the struggle over his successor. Philip's son and heir was an inexperienced and narcissistic twenty-year-old whose name did not strike terror in the minds of the country's numerous enemies. The Greeks were lining up to revolt; Macedon's non-Greek neighbors to the north and west were ahead of them. Because of hindsight, though, these troubles are easy to pass over, the "growing pains of a vigorous conqueror" rather than the "death rattle of a nine day's wonder."

As Memnon correctly reckoned, Macedon was far from invulnerable. First, with no reliable navy and little money to pay rowers, Alexander was even more dependent than most ancient commanders on local food supplies. When he left Macedon in the early spring of 334, he only had thirty days' worth of food supplies with him; by the time he got to Asia Minor, that had dwindled to ten. He would soon be dependent on foraging for winter grain, now ripening in the fields, and on requisition from the locals. Hence, Memnon's scorched-earth policy would have cost Alexander dearly.

Second, Greek disaffection with Macedon, coupled with Macedonian naval weakness, opened a golden opportunity. Sparta was ready for revolt, Athens could be cajoled and bullied. A general Greek uprising against Macedon might well force a food-scarce expeditionary force to head home. The next step would be negotiations with Alexander's rivals in the Macedonian nobility; in return for a nonaggression treaty, Persia could support a coup d'état—and, with Alexander gone, Darius would be sitting pretty.

Much prettier, at any rate, than if he had to face the Macedonian army. What made Memnon so adamant about Persia's need to avoid that army at all costs? The army which Philip had built and which Alexander had successfully commanded in 335 against a variety of rebels (not to mention Alexander's leadership of the cavalry at Chaeronea in 338, when he was only eighteen years old) was a uniquely strong and supple instrument. It combined the virtues of a professional force that drilled year-round with those of a national army fighting for its own country. Furthermore, unlike the citizen militiamen of the Greek city-states, who made prudence a virtue and had a healthy respect (and then some) for their own persons, the Macedonian soldiers were hard drinkers who thought nothing of risking their safety with a smaller shield if it freed a hand to hold a longer spear.

Philip had studied the tactical innovations of Epaminondas of Thebes and improved upon them. Traditionally, the infantry had been the deciding force in Greek warfare; the cavalry merely protected the flank and harassed stragglers. Macedon had a superb cavalry tradition, however, and Philip built on it. In his army, the infantry served mainly to hold down the enemy; the cavalry became the key shock weapon, the one that won battles. Philip's infantry was so well drilled that, at Chaeronea, for example, they were able to execute a feigned retreat up a hillside backward! The enemy took the bait, rushed after in pursuit, opened up a gap in their ranks and—like lightning, the Macedonian heavy cavalry charged in and polished them off.

To make matters worse than Memnon could have known, Alexander was to prove himself a superb leader of men. He knew when to go for the common touch and when to be a king. He was a natural at prebattle oratory. He risked his own body in combat without hesitation in order to spur his soldiers on. Moreover, like Hitler, he had an uncanny ability to take the psychological measure of his opponents—for example, correctly reading Persia's lack of self-confidence in its choice of the high ground at the Granicus and Issus.

Was there, then, no hope for the Persian army? Would numerical superiority, Greek mercenaries, the bravery of Darius, the pride of the Persian nobility—would this all count for nothing against the well-oiled Macedonian ma-

chine? Of course, these strengths would count for something. At the Granicus, for instance, a little more muscle
in a Persian's arm would have split Alexander's skull and
sent the Macedonians home; as it was, the Persian cut
open Alexander's helmet and inflicted a flesh wound to
his head. At Issus, Persia's Greek mercenaries ground up
a large part of the Macedonian phalanx. At Gaugamela,
the Persian cavalry broke through the Macedonian line.
Hopeful signs, but still, at best, battle would be a tremendous risk for Persia. As it turned out, three battles were
fought, and Alexander won each decisively. In retrospect,
Memnon's plan looks better and better.

DEFEAT ON LAND, VICTORY AT SEA

No one tried to prevent Alexander from crossing the Dardanelles, probably because the Persian fleet was busy
putting down yet another Egyptian revolt. The Persian
satraps and generals of Asia Minor gathered their armies
not far from Alexander's crossing point and took counsel.
They rejected Memnon's advice and decided to meet the
enemy in battle. The sources suggest various motives for
their decision: pride, jealousy of Memnon's influence with
Darius, disinclination to see their rich possessions destroyed. One local governor supposedly told Memnon
that he would refuse to set fire to a single one of his subjects' houses.

The Persians took up a strong defensive position on the
steep eastern banks of the river Granicus, which flows
into the Sea of Marmara. Alexander advanced and faced
them from the opposite bank. The numbers are uncertain,
but it is clear that Alexander outnumbered the Persians,
perhaps 50,000 to 35,000. The sources differ widely about
the details of the battle, but in the end it came down to a
fight between the two cavalries. The tactical skill and
tougher lances of the Macedonians shone through, but
perhaps the crucial factor was the presence of Alexander
himself, fighting in the thick of things. Alexander was

wounded but not seriously; the Persian elite, on the other hand, was decimated, the death toll including several satraps and generals. Memnon and his sons had fought fiercely and proved their loyalty to Persia before escaping. As for the captured Greek mercenaries, Alexander ordered that most of them be massacred, to send a message to other would-be Greek "traitors."

For Persia, it was time to give Memnon's strategy a chance. The fleet returned to the Aegean from Egypt, 400 ships strong. Memnon was promoted to the leadership of western Asia Minor and the fleet. In turn, he sent his wife and children to Susa, a sign both of his seriousness of purpose and the suspicion under which he suffered as a Greek. He made his base at the coastal city of Halicarnassos, capital of the southern province of Karia, and fortified the city in preparation for a seige.

Since the Granicus, Alexander had been advancing in triumph down the coast. He seems to have had no illusions, however, about the danger which Memnon's fleet posed. Realizing that he had neither the money nor the ships to beat Memnon, Alexander simply dissolved most of his fleet. He kept only 20 Athenian ships, which would carry his siege equipment and whose 4,000 Athenian rowers would serve as hostages. Alexander had not given up on fighting the enemy fleet, but he had changed his strategy: he would render the Persian fleet useless by denying it access to the land bases and manpower of Asia Minor and Phoenicia. One by one, Alexander would attack the cities of the coast down to Egypt, besieging them if necessary.

The real object in all of this was Greece. Alexander could not afford to head east so long as the Persian fleet could raise a rebellion in his rear. He was a fine strategist to appreciate this point, and as long as the Persians appreciated it, too, they were a match for him. Unfortunately, Persian resolve wavered.

For a year Memnon gave Alexander a run for his money. The Macedonians eventually took Halicarnassos by siege, but for two months the defenders put up stiff resistance, bloodying the Macedonians considerably. Even after surrendering most of the town, the Persians managed to hold the city's fortified promontories, which served them as a naval base for another year. Memnon himself escaped to the nearby island of Cos, where Darius named him supreme commander of Persian forces in the entire western empire.

In the spring of the next year, 333, Memnon launched his naval offensive with money from Darius and 300 ships, a huge fleet. Heading toward the Dardanelles, he took the important island of Chios and most of the island of Lesbos: only Mytilene held out for Alexander, and Memnon blockaded it thoroughly by land and sea. According to one ancient source, as news of Memnon's successes spread like wildfire, most of the Cycladic islands sent embassies to him. The rumor that he was planning to sail next to Euboea, an island off the coast of Athens' territory, raised a frisson of hope (or horror) throughout Greece. Memnon's liberal distributions of Persian money also won him many Greek allies.

Alexander was sufficiently impressed to send 500 talents to the troops back in Macedon. He also sent 600 talents to his agents to raise a new Greek fleet, an amount that would finance no more than 150 triremes for the rest of the sailing season—a force only half the size of Memnon's fleet. On the other hand, Memnon himself might have faced some financial restrictions, now that he had lost Asia Minor, the only Persian region that paid its tribute in coin. Still, there was piracy, to which Memnon indeed resorted, and Darius could probably send more coinage from his Persepolis treasury.

At least other Persian commanders were now in step with Memnon. We hear, for example, that the governor of Cilicia, the rich province on the southern coast of Asia Minor, was laying waste his territory "with fire and the sword in order to make a desert for the enemy" (Curtius). He did not even attempt to hold the easily defensible pass into his province, the so-called Cilician Gates, preferring to follow Memnon's strategy and lure the Macedonian army to starvation.

Fate now stepped in. In June, Memnon fell sick and died outside of Mytilene, "the most serious setback which Persia received during this period of the war" (Arrian). On his deathbed Memnon turned the command over to two Persian generals, one of them his nephew. It is an indication of their promise that, although a small Persian naval contingent would be defeated in the Cyclades, their main fleet not only took Mytilene, but went on to take the island of Tenedos—one step closer to the Dardanelles. This last success came even after the fleet had been stripped by the Great King of half of its ships and most of its Greek mercenaries: the news of Memnon's death, it seems, had made Darius do an about-face.

"Darius had expected Memnon to transfer the whole war from Asia to Europe," Diodorus of Sicily says; "if he had lived," Plutarch comments, Memnon "was likely to have offered the most stubborn resistance to Alexander's advance and caused him the most trouble." With the commander's death, Darius gave up on Memnon's strategy and returned to the idea of a go-for-broke battle. Perhaps this was the path of least resistance for the former champion of single combat; perhaps his position as a relatively new king from outside the main line of descent demanded this "manly" alternative; perhaps he simply considered a naval strategy unfeasible without Memnon to command it. Was he right? The victories of Memnon's successors lead us to doubt it—and if Memnon himself had lived his name might be better known today than Alexander's.

A final footnote to Memnon's strategy: two years later, in the late summer of 330, Sparta finally roused itself to fight Macedon in the Peloponnesos. But once again it was too little and too late, and besides, memories of Lysander and Agesilaus were still too bitter to allow many Greeks to rally to Sparta's banner. Sparta had little help, therefore: outnumbered two to one by Macedon and its allies—*Greek* allies—Sparta went down fighting, no help to Darius as he prepared to face Alexander in battle again.

DARIUS'S BLUNDERS

Darius gathered his advisers at Susa in midsummer, 333. There the choice was between an army commanded by generals or one led by the king personally. Charidemus, an Athenian general whom Alexander had sent into exile in 335, advocated the former course, arguing that Darius should stay behind with most of his men and maintain control of the kingdom. Charidemus claimed that a force of 100,000 men would suffice against Alexander, as long as a third of them were Greek mercenaries and as long as the right general—hint, hint—was in charge.

According to the sources, the parley degenerated into verbal mudslinging, with the Persians calling Charidemus a treacherous Greek, while he called the Persians cowards. At this point Darius, who did not take kindly to anti-Persian remarks, is supposed to have "seized Charidemus by the belt according to the custom of the Persians, turned him over to the attendants, and ordered him put to death" (Diodorus of Sicily). It is, alas, too good a story to command confidence, but other evidence seems to confirm that Charidemus was executed after his policy was rejected. Proxy-generalship was out. Darius would command a large army, and he would command it personally.

Whether he had made the right choice is another matter. Darius's force mustered at Babylon in the heat of summer and moved with impressive speed to the coast, where the big battle—Issus—was fought about November 1. Nor was Darius's army small: as usual we don't know quite how big it was, but it certainly much outnumbered Alexander's 50,000 or so troops. Apparently, Darius was returning to the strategic idea that one would have thought discredited forever by Xerxes' fate—that a big army would scare the enemy. In order to have a big army, Darius had to call up every able-bodied man, including the royal Persian youth corps. There is also some indirect evidence that the Persian military colonists around Babylon were having difficulty in meeting their quota. Darius's big army, therefore, had big holes in it; he might indeed have been better off with the smaller but more solid force that Charidemus had advocated.

In any case, Darius did not use his army's size to his advantage. A Macedonian deserter on his staff, one Amyntas, urged the Great King to wait for Alexander in the Syrian desert, whose flat plains would be the perfect setting for outnumbering an opponent. We have seen, though, the spirit in which Persians were accepting advice from Greek-speakers in 333. Darius preferred to cross the mountains to the coast where, as luck would have it, he actually cut off Alexander from his supplies in the rear. "Now I've got him," Darius might have thought. The battle, however, would have to be fought on a narrow strip of land between mountains and sea: once again, as at Thermopylae and Salamis in 480, Persia's numerical superiority could not be brought to bear. And against the superb Macedonian army, Darius was in no position to throw away advantages.

In the battle the Greek mercenaries inflicted serious injury on the Macedonian infantry, but the Macedonian and allied cavalry devastated the Persians. Darius, in the center of the Persian line, was already in danger on both sides when suddenly and only briefly, he found Alexander practically facing him. It should have been the moment that Darius had pitched himself for, the chance to slay the enemy with his own hands and so to avenge his country. But with the wheels of fate turning all around him, Darius could no longer ignore reality. The Great King swallowed his pride and fled from the field. He was alive, and could fight another day, but would he or his subjects ever forget his failure?

Issus was a serious defeat for Persia: heavy casualties; an army destroyed; the king's wife, mother, and children captured; treasure lost; honor lost. Unfortunately, it was also a defeat from which Darius drew the wrong lessons. He might now have withdrawn into a "Fortress Asia," keeping the formidable Tigris river crossings closely guarded. If Alexander advanced, Darius could have made him fight for every city; he could have burned the food supplies. Instead, after flirting with a diplomatic solution, Darius decided to call up another, grander army from his eastern dominions and fight another battle with Alexander. The failed diplomatic initiative had offered Alexander the kingship of all of Asia west of Mesopotamia. Alexander refused, as might have been foreseen, since most of this land was his for the taking anyhow after Issus. Darius gained nothing by this offer; in fact he suffered a loss of face.

Perhaps the offer was merely a political ritual, a last proof needed to rally the Persians for the climactic battle ahead. Because Persian religion placed great emphasis on the struggle between good and evil, by refusing to negotiate, Alexander helped Darius's propagandists to cast him in the appropriate role. In any case, if Alexander *had* negotiated, Darius might well have been assassinated as a weakling and replaced in short order. Persian honor would now accept nothing less than a struggle against the evil enemy. If he had lobbied hard enough for it, Darius might have been able to sell his nobles on a "Fortress Asia" strategy. There can be little doubt, however, that the most "natural" policy, the one most in keeping with Persia's martial traditions, the one most appealing to a king under domestic political pressure, was to go *mano a mano* against the enemy in a big battle. Persia demanded a Hollywood epic, and after Issus Darius was in no position to argue for art over box-office appeal.

Alexander, for his part, now finished the Persian fleet off once and for all by capturing Tyre, its last remaining Phoenician port, after a great, seven-month siege. Tyre is a tribute to Alexander's tenacity, patience, and strategic insight. After Issus, a lesser strategist might have given in to the temptation to go after Darius. Alexander understood that he could not leave the coast until he had captured the bases from which the Persian fleet might launch a second front in Greece. Again, it was Persia's bad luck to face such an intelligent commander. After Tyre, Palestine and Egypt all but fell into his lap. By spring 331, Alexander was ready to turn east.

What did and what did *not* happen during Alexander's march into Iraq throws a fascinating light on what Darius might have thought he was doing. In the two years since Issus, Darius had raised an enormous army from Persia proper and the eastern satrapies, perhaps 250,000 men against Alexander's 50,000. Alexander did not know exactly where Darius planned to meet him in battle, but a location somewhere north of the key city of Babylon was a good guess. To meet Darius, therefore, Alexander would have to march into little-known territory where, as usual, he would depend on local food supplies. The desert left only two routes southward into Mesopotamia: one along the east bank of the river Euphrates, the other along the east bank of the river Tigris. The second route was longer and more difficult, because the Tigris was deep, fast, and its banks easily defensible, which made the river difficult to cross (see the experiences of Julian's army in retreat, Chapter 8). Darius ordered the crops burned along the first route, which forced Alexander to take the second.

When Alexander got to the Tigris, however, he found no Persian cavalry to disrupt his crossing, and the plentiful food supplies on the opposite shore had not been burned. He was no doubt delighted, as Curtius has him tell an adviser on the eve of the great battle that ensued: "When Darius was burning the land, destroying villages and our food supplies, I was beside myself with despair. But now that he is preparing to decide the issue in battle, what do I have to fear? Good heavens, he has answered my prayers!"

Had Darius completely lost control? Was he an incompetent? Perhaps, but another explanation has been suggested: that is, Darius *wanted* to lure Alexander ahead approximately 75 miles from the Tigris crossing to Gaugamela, Darius's chosen battle site. There, the emperor's righteous soldiers would surely avenge the enemy's prior insults. The last thing Darius wanted now was to discourage Alexander from advancing to his doom.

Alexander may have had his moment of hesitation when he saw the enormous army awaiting him, so much larger than the one at Issus, but after a day's reconnaissance, he resumed his customary poise. The battle of Gaugamela on about October 1, 331, is especially difficult to reconstruct. It is clear that Alexander won by drawing the Persians to their left, which opened a gap in the center of their line, a gap to be exploited with a Macedonian cavalry charge. His center threatened, Darius once again fled, this time into the Kurdish mountains toward his Iranian homeland. The battle was lost, but the unanswered questions are tantalizing. For example, Alexander's charge left a gap in his own infantry ranks; the Persians poured in, but instead of turning on the Macedonian flank, which could have been devastating, why did they make for the baggage camp, where the Macedonian reserves fell on them? With proper tactical leadership, the Persians might have done much better at Gaugamela.

Technically, it was not yet all over. Alexander had wealthy Mesopotamia, but Darius might still rally resistance in the Iranian homeland. He fled to Ecbatana (modern Hamadan) with loyal troops, and wintered there while Alexander conquered Susa and Persepolis to the south. But if Darius tried to organize new resistance, he did not succeed. He neither prepared Ecbatana for a siege, nor raised new troops, nor prepared a redoubt farther east in Bactria (Afghanistan), where many Persian nobles were based. In early spring, Alexander hurried north after Darius, who in turn retreated with his forces eastward toward the mountain pass of the Caspian Gates (about 40 miles beyond modern Teheran). Darius proposed to hold the Gates. It was all over now, however. There is some reason to think that Darius was finally ready to surrender to Alexander and perhaps even to acknowledge Alexander's sovereignty—a disaster to those Iranians bent on further struggle. The King was Great no longer, but he could still give Alexander the seal of approval. Determined to keep that prize from Alexander, or perhaps just tired of their failed king, the Bactrian nobles arrested Darius; with Alexander in hot pursuit, they assassinated him on the road, about 250 miles east of Teheran. When Alexander finally caught up with his rival in July 330, he found only a corpse.

Alexander paid for his failure to take Darius alive; the price was several years of tough fighting in eastern Iran against the Persian nobility. Perhaps Darius wavered at the end, but his death at least bought his people a little more time. As for his corpse, it may only have been a political gesture, aimed at the hearts and minds of Alexander's new subjects, but Darius's body was given a proper royal burial at Persepolis. It was a fitting ceremony, and doubly so: first, because however much he had been deluded by his own mystique, Darius had fought the good fight; and second, because like the dynasty whose last member Darius had been, Persepolis itself was now only a shadow; Alexander had torched the royal palace in January 330.

THE LESSON

Call it a weakness for history's orphans: it is hard not to sympathize with Darius. His enemy, Alexander, turned out to be one of the most celebrated military geniuses in the history of the world. Darius himself is usually denigrated as a fool, an incompetent, a coward, or all three. Persia is usually presented as a decadent empire, incapable of resisting the vigorous Macedonian advance.

The standard version makes splendid melodrama, but it is poor strategic analysis. "Young Alexander rode in from the west," as the story goes, and it has gone on to inspire more than two millennia of myth and romance. The truth is that he would have ridden straight out again if Persia had adopted the right strategy. Persia could have beaten Macedon, but its leader made the wrong choices. Darius is a textbook case of someone prevented by ideology from taking the road to victory. Domestic politics played an important part in keeping Darius from choosing the correct strategy, but the main impediment was ideological.

Had Darius followed Memnon's strategy from the start, he stood a good chance of stopping Alexander cold. There were, however, overwhelming problems. First, Memnon was a Greek, and while there was plenty of precedent for a Greek leading Persian forces, it probably still stung the amour propre of the Persian nobility. Second, Memnon's strategy would deny Persia the emotional release of a pitched battle. Third, both for Darius himself and for his nobles, self-esteem was tied to battle performance. The days of Cyrus the Great and Darius I were long gone, but the empire's military fortunes had revived in the 340s, which may have encouraged nostalgia. Fourth, the court ritual surrounding the Great King made it increasingly difficult for a man like Darius, who had not been raised to discount court ritual, to see beyond the illusion of omnipotence that thousands of his servants worked night and day to create. Fifth, as a fairly new king and one of questionable legitimacy, Darius could push his nobles only so far. If he absolutely refused their demands for battle, if he instead burned their fields and entrusted their soldiers to Greek commanders, then, at a certain point, he too, like his predecessors, could be assassinated and replaced.

Darius should have known better, and it is clear that at least from time to time, he did. The policy of exporting war to Greece from Asia Minor was a hallowed Persian tradition, and Darius surely knew its efficacy. He did entrust Memnon with a great command after the Granicus and he did turn to a scorched-earth policy. But only temporarily. Darius gave up too easily. If no worthy successor to Memnon was immediately at hand, then Darius should have sought one out. In the meantime, he should have burned Alexander's supplies, defended his own cities, rallied the population, and refused battle. Instead, he gave in to the temptations of Issus and Gaugamela. Behind the twin myths of Alexander's omnipotence and Darius's incompetence, there is an invaluable lesson. To adopt the right strategy and win, a leader needs to make long-term effectiveness a main criterion. Although no one can escape ideology completely, a strategist must examine his own ideology and attempt to keep his preconceptions from impeding an effective plan. He must also attempt to rally domestic political opinion behind his strategy. Darius attempted neither. It was courageous to fight Alexander in battle, but it was not the way to save Persia.

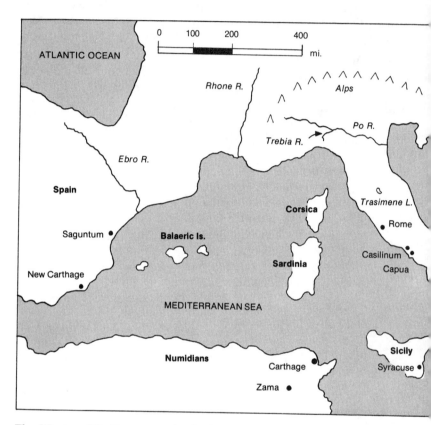

The Western Mediterranean in the late third century B.C.

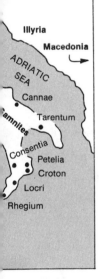

Illyria

Macedonia

ADRIATIC SEA

Cannae

Tarentum

Samnites

Consentia

Petelia

Croton

Locri

Rhegium

Chapter **5**

Hannibal Versus Rome: How to Win Battles and Lose a War

IN THE CENTURY AFTER the death of Alexander, his greatest generals and their sons proclaimed themselves kings and carved up much of the eastern Mediterranean world and the western end of the old Persian Empire into Macedonian-ruled kingdoms. The most important of these were the kingdoms of the Antigonids in Macedonia, the Seleucids in Mesopotamia, parts of Anatolia and the Near East, and the Ptolemies in Egypt. The eastern regions conquered by Alexander quickly reverted to the control of native dynasts. In south and central Greece and in the Aegean Islands, some city-states maintained a precarious independence; others formed themselves into federal leagues.

This "Hellenistic" era was an exciting one in terms of diplomacy, culture, and trade, but it was highly stratified socially: the Greeks in Asia and Africa remained a narrow and exclusive administrative, military, urban elite. As a result, the native populations were seldom brought into the armed forces. Furthermore, Alexander's dream of world empire was quickly extinguished. By the later third century B.C. the Hellenistic powers had fought one another to a standstill. The Greeks paid relatively little attention to the affairs of the western Mediterranean, where Rome was rapidly rising to the status of a genuine world-class power.

In the fifth century B.C., when Athens was at the height of its imperial might, Rome was still a second-tier city-state in central Italy. But in the early fourth century, Rome became the leader of a "Latin League" that quickly established itself as the dominant power in central Italy. By the early third century, the Romans were the strongest force in Italy; by 264 all of Italy south of the Po River Valley had been integrated into a Roman alliance. This expansion was not easy; the Romans fought continuously and had gotten very good at the business of war. Moreover, the Romans achieved long-term strength from their battlefield victories. The Italian peoples defeated by the Romans were not crushed under the victor's heel, but rather were allowed to maintain home rule and were brought into a tightly structured alliance system. A new "ally" might grumble at this arrangement at first, but the Italian tribes and towns soon learned that Rome was a dependable overlord. Stern in retribution if crossed, the Romans were equally reliable as defenders and they maintained a stable status quo in Italy.

Rome's Italian alliance system was tested in the long, hard First Punic War with Carthage (264–241 B.C.). Tens of thousands of Romans and Italians died in the war, especially in naval disasters. But the allies proved loyal, and the defeat of Carthage gave Rome its first overseas province: Sicily. Sardinia and Corsica were soon added (much to Carthage's dismay). By 220 B.C. the Romans had defeated the Gauls of the Po Valley in north Italy, and had begun to colonize the area. Rome was clearly the dominant power of the west.

The Roman success was in part due to a cohesive sociopolitical system. The social system, based on intertwined loyalties to family, clan, and state, was cemented by bonds of patronage and clientage. Every Roman knew who his patron was and who his clients were; patrons watched out for the financial and legal interests of their clients, while clients did "favors" for their powerful patrons and supported them in their political ambitions. The political system was a republican oligarchy: two annually elected consuls served as generals and as executive officials. Legislation and elections were held in republican assemblies that theoretically represented all Roman citizens. A senate, a body of about three hundred heads of great families, advised consuls and assemblies alike, and provided general oversight for the regime. The whole system still worked quite well in the third century B.C. It would have to work very well indeed if Rome were to survive the challenge of the Second Punic War.

THE BATTLE OF CANNAE

As dawn broke over the plains of southeastern Italy on the morning after the battle of Cannae (216 B.C.), revealing the dead bodies of tens of thousands of Roman soldiers, Hannibal, chief general of Carthage, surely believed that the war against Rome was nearly over. His mercenary army, a polyglot mélange of Africans, Gauls, and Spaniards, had just annihilated a force of trained Roman legionaries twice its size. The invasion of Italy was proceeding according to Hannibal's audacious game plan. Despite their huge advantage in manpower, Rome's best generals were helpless in the face of Hannibal's supreme tactical skills. Indeed, Cannae was the third overwhelming battlefield defeat Hannibal had handed his opponents in as many years. Total victory—and in its wake the reduction of Rome to a third-rate Italian power—seemed just around the corner.

HANNIBAL, CARTHAGE, AND ROME

Hannibal had come very far, very fast. Still only thirty years old at Cannae, he was the eldest son of the Carthaginian commander Hamilcar Barca. Hamilcar had fought with distinction against the Romans in the First Punic War. Rome won that war. The peace treaty of 241 stripped Carthage of the strategic island of Sicily, crippled her sea power, and ended her lucrative trade monopoly in the western Mediterranean. But Hamilcar was an optimist. He saw that Carthage could bounce back by exploiting new sources of revenue and new markets.

In 237 B.C. Hamilcar led a Carthaginian army into southern Spain. The Spanish tribes were tough fighters, but Hamilcar's military skills enabled him to carve out an empire that brought great mineral resources under the control of the North African city. Carthage once again grew immensely wealthy. With money came strength—Carthage was back in the ranks of the major Mediterranean powers within a decade of the devastating loss in the first war against Rome.

Hannibal had been raised by his father for a military career. According to Polybius and Livy, the Greek and Roman historians who are our main sources for this period, Hamilcar Barca received special permission from the Carthaginian government to bring his ten-year-old son with him to Spain and to train him as a military commander. According to a legend, just before embarking for Spain young Hannibal was ordered by his father to swear an oath of eternal enmity to Rome. The Romans later claimed that this oath sowed the seeds of a bitter hatred that led to the outbreak of the second great war between Carthage and Rome.

Young Hannibal proved an apt student of the military arts. While still a teenager he became his father's most trusted battlefield lieutenant. When Hamilcar died in 229 Hannibal was still just seventeen, and so the supreme command in Spain passed to Hannibal's uncle Hasdrubal. An adroit diplomat, but a dull general, Hasdrubal consolidated Hamilcar's gains by establishing a network of Spanish alliances. Spanish loyalty was guaranteed by the sons of leading Spanish families, whom Hasdrubal held as hostages. Hasdrubal's most important legacy was the foundation of the port city of New Carthage (modern Cartagena).

Built on a cape, the fortified city was thought to be unassailable by land and possessed one of the finest natural harbors in the western Mediterranean. Hasdrubal's new city became the secure linchpin of Carthaginian military and economic operations in the Spanish peninsula.

When Hasdrubal was murdered by a slave in 221 the Carthaginian army in Spain demanded that twenty-five-year-old Hannibal be named their supreme commander; the home government acquiesced. It was a day for which Hannibal had long been groomed. The young commander amply fulfilled his early promise with dramatic victories over recalcitrant Spanish tribes. He was his father's son, a dashing commander with a penchant for the unexpected bold stroke and an uncanny tactical ability. Hannibal's military genius gave rise to hopes for revenge on the Romans—surely if anyone could beat Rome it was Hannibal. But doubts remained; at the outbreak of the second war with Rome in 219, sober-minded Carthaginians may have regretted the series of events that had led their government to take on the Roman juggernaut.

There were so many uncertainties: How would the young commander fare against trained legionaries? Was he mature enough to go the distance against a genuinely resolute enemy? Could even the greatest general find a way to neutralize the overwhelming Roman advantage in manpower? But Hannibal had quickly silenced the doubters. The first three years of the war went extraordinarily well for Carthage. By late 216, the great victory at Cannae made all those former trepidations appear foolish; Rome was evidently teetering on the edge of total collapse.

Perhaps on the morning after the battle of Cannae Hannibal allowed himself the luxury of reviewing the daring strategy that had brought within his grasp the seemingly impossible goal of overthrowing Rome. In the absence of autobiographical sources we can only guess at Hannibal's actual thoughts. But the origin and development of the Carthaginian strategy for fighting the Second Punic War can be reconstructed with confidence, thanks to the detailed historical accounts by Polybius and Livy, and the biographies of Roman commanders by Plutarch.

A primary strategic determinant for the Carthaginians was their experience in fighting Romans in the First Punic War. At the outbreak of that conflict the two states had been quite similar in terms of their internal government: both were republics, ruled by an elite of established families. In economic terms they were quite different: Rome was almost entirely devoted to agriculture, while Carthage had a mixed economy based on farming and trade. But perhaps the starkest contrast was in the nature of their military forces.

Carthage had started the First Punic War with an apparently invincible navy. The Carthaginians had regarded the western Mediterranean as their private lake for centuries; even the fifth-century Athenians had been unwilling to challenge the African city at sea. By contrast Rome had very little in the way of a fleet at the outbreak of the First Punic War; Rome had always been a continental land power and Roman armed might was concentrated in the legionary infantry, a force made up of Roman citizens and citizens of Italian states allied to Rome. Carthage's land army was largely a mercenary force, composed of men recruited from across her wide imperial holdings.

The First Punic War might have bogged down into an elephant-versus-whale conflict along the lines of the early Peloponnesian War. It did not, because early in the war the Romans realized that they could never beat the Carthaginians without a fleet. Rome recruited rowers and built a navy from scratch. Roman engineers devised a combination grappling hook and landing bridge (called the Crow) that made up for the Roman lack of experience at sea maneuvers. The landlubber Romans were soon a sea power to be contended with.

Roman admirals startled the Mediterranean world by soundly defeating their Carthaginian counterparts in naval engagements early in the war. But if the Romans had proved they could fight at sea, that hardly meant they were decent sailors. Rome lost hundreds of ships to storms, and as a result the war seesawed for two decades. The casualties were staggering on both sides. But the tougher the going, the grimmer was Roman resolve. Because of determination and demographic realities Rome could absorb more casualties at sea and man more ships than Carthage. Rome's manpower advantage eventually made possible an invasion of the Carthaginian North African homeland. With their capital city threatened by land and sea the Carthaginians surrendered. In the end, then, Roman victory in the First Punic War had been a product of superior manpower: the Romans outlasted the Carthaginians in a naval war of attrition because of the immense population base provided by the Italian peninsula.

Shortly after the First Punic War, Carthage was in the midst of another war for survival. Thousands of mercenaries hired for the war against Rome remained in North Africa, but the Carthaginians were unable (or unwilling) to give their hired soldiers the back pay they demanded. The mercenaries rose in revolt and attempted to seize control of the city of Carthage. Thus began the savage Truceless War. Hamilcar Barca (along with other generals) organized a Carthaginian citizen land army that fought and ultimately defeated the mercenaries.

The victory against the rebels gave the Carthaginians renewed faith in their ability to fight land engagements. With the loss of her control of the sea after the First Punic War and with the Truceless War victory, Carthage turned away from a dependence on naval power, and concentrated on building up land forces. But neither conflict persuaded the Carthaginians to give up their reliance on mercenaries. The citizens of Carthage now knew they could fight if they had to, but old habits were evidently too strong to break; Carthaginians were willing to command, but would only serve as foot soldiers in the direst emergencies.

Though they refused to rethink the issue of citizen-soldier versus mercenary, the First Punic War and its aftermath taught the Carthaginians a few lessons that they took very much to heart: that Rome was invincible at sea;

that Rome's strength lay in her access to Italian manpower; and that Carthage could win wars on land. Application of these lessons determined Carthage's strategy in
the Second Punic War. But were the lessons Carthage had
learned in the first round with Rome the right ones?
It is puzzling that the new Carthaginian strategy largely
ignored the possibility of launching major offensive naval
operations. How to explain this rapid turnabout, from a
sea power–based strategy to a strategy in which sea power
was virtually absent? In the interwar period (241–219),
Carthaginian strategists saw that Rome's fleet commanded the western Mediterranean and they were well
aware of the fact that Rome controlled the islands between Africa and Italy and so dominated all potential
naval bases. Rome's monopoly of naval bases made the
possibility of a combined Carthaginian land-sea strategy
appear too risky. If the Carthaginian navy were rebuilt it
would have to operate without the logistical support of
nearby bases. This would make resupply terribly difficult
and would leave Carthage's fleets vulnerable to storms.
As a result of these factors, there was evidently no
thought in the Carthaginian high command of a major
strategic role for the Carthaginian navy in a new war with
Rome. At the outbreak of the Second Punic War Carthage
did have a small fleet, but it played no significant role in
Carthaginian planning.
On the other hand, a land invasion of Italy seemed to
offer splendid strategic opportunities. The Carthaginians
now knew that the Romans had won the First Punic War
because superior manpower reserves had given them an
insuperable advantage in the long war of attrition. But
they also realized that Roman manpower was based only
in part on Roman citizens. At least half of the men who
fought for Rome were not Romans, but rather citizens of
once independent Italian states—states that had been for-
cibly incorporated into a Roman confederacy in the course
of the fifth, fourth, and early third centuries B.C. Hence,
Hannibal and other Carthaginian strategic planners could
reasonably hope that if they could bring the war to

Rome—fight in Italy instead of on the seas or within Carthaginian territory—they might turn Rome's allies against her. A revolt by the Italian allies would deprive Rome of tens of thousands of potential soldiers. And if those non-Roman Italian soldiers could be persuaded to fight on Carthage's side, the manpower advantage would be reversed.

A Rome bracketed by a hostile, pro-Carthaginian Italian League would be permanently crippled. And it was not only the central and southern Italians who might be turned against Rome: the numerous and warlike Gauls of the Po River Valley in northeastern Italy had recently come under the Roman sway; the Po Valley Gauls hated the Romans and were an obvious source of allies for an invader who offered them a chance to break Rome's grip. The Carthaginian conviction that an army of liberation would be welcome in Italy was reinforced by their own imperial experience. Carthage was a harsh mistress. The Carthaginians knew that many of their own "allies" in North Africa and Spain would leap at the chance to stab Carthage in the back if an army of liberation showed up. Why suppose that the members of Rome's Italian confederacy would behave any differently?

By 219 the question of war with Rome was no longer just a strategic "what-if?" speculation. Many Carthaginians had become convinced by recent events that a military reckoning was inevitable, and that the only real choice was whether to attack Italy or to wait for Rome to take the offensive and then attempt to defend Spain and Africa. A series of incidents in the interwar period appeared to signal Roman belligerence. In 238, during the crisis of the Truceless War, the Romans had opportunistically grabbed control of Sardinia, a rich and strategically important island that had been left to Carthage in the treaty ending the First Punic War. The Carthaginians protested this unilateral action; the Romans responded by declaring war. Still reeling from the carnage of the Truceless War, Carthage was completely unprepared to fight. The Carthaginians had been forced to knuckle under and to offer a humiliating pro forma "surrender." The Romans agreed to this, but only after upping the already high war reparations demanded of their defeated opponents.

After the Sardinia incident, the Roman imperial appetite appeared to be satiated for a time, and relations between the two powers ostensibly improved. In 226, while Hasdrubal the diplomat commanded in Spain, Carthage and Rome had negotiated an agreement that implicitly recognized a Carthaginian sphere of influence south of the Ebro (Iber) River in Spain. Unfortunately, we know about the terms of the agreement (like everything else about the Punic Wars) only from Roman (or Roman-influenced) sources. The Roman sources state that the accord forbade the Carthaginians to march in arms north of the Ebro. The ancient sources do not mention a quid pro quo, but modern scholars generally assume that there was one. Certainly Hasdrubal and the Carthaginians supposed that the agreement left them free to pacify the towns and tribes south of the river.

But in 221 the Romans broke the spirit of the Ebro accord by agreeing to serve as arbitrators in a civil war that broke out in Spanish Saguntum, a coastal town located 100 miles south of the Ebro and thus well within the Carthaginian sphere of influence. (One pro-Roman source tries to fudge the issue by claiming that Saguntum was north of the Ebro—a patent falsehood.) Not surprisingly, the Roman arbitrators found in favor of an anti-Carthaginian element in Saguntum; and after the negotiation the Romans felt that a special relationship existed between Rome and the Saguntines.

Given the deliberate vagueness of the Roman sources and the total disappearance of all Carthaginian sources, we have no way of knowing what the Romans were really up to in Saguntum. Maybe they had no long-term policy aims in mind. But they were certainly stirring up trouble in the short term. The Carthaginians refused to accept any Roman meddling in southern Spain and rejected the legality of the Roman arbitration. Hannibal received his government's permission to besiege Saguntum in 219; the town fell seven months later. The Romans were outraged at what they regarded as unilateral aggression against a town friendly to Rome. A commission of Roman senators was sent to Carthage to demand that the siege be raised and Hannibal turned over to Rome for punishment. When Carthage refused to accede to Rome's demands, war was declared.

What part Hannibal's own attitude toward Romans played in the Carthaginian decision to call Rome's bluff we really don't know. Once again we have no ancient sources that tell Hannibal's own side of the story. The Romans believed that he lusted for war because he hated them and in the Roman sources Hannibal's "irrational" hatred was the prime cause of the war. Maybe there really would not have been a war in 218 without Hannibal to lead Carthage's armies, but it is unnecessary to assume that Hannibal was driven by insane hatred to begin a war. Perhaps Hannibal felt for his enemies nothing more than the impersonal distaste of the exterminator for pests that must be wiped out, or the cool perspective of the chess master ready to challenge his opponent with a bold new opening. But whatever his personal feelings about Romans, Hannibal must have been sanguine about the turn of events. He was personally ready for war with Rome: sure of himself, sure of his troops, and sure of the strategic plan that would allow him to strike quickly and fatally at central and southern Italy, the vital center of gravity of the Roman state.

HANNIBAL'S INVASION OF ITALY

The campaign of invasion went pretty much according to plan. Hannibal had set out from his base in Spain in the early spring of 218 with an army of at least 35,000 men, including a large cavalry contingent and a good number of trained war elephants. He crossed the Rhone River just ahead of a Roman land army that had been sent to intercept him; his way now lay across the Alps and into northern Italy. The Alpine crossing is justly famous. The climb up the mountains was difficult. The terrain was steep, the paths narrow, the climate harsh, and the Alpine tribes bellicose and treacherous by turns. Hannibal's cavalry was no use to him in the mountains and the local tribes inflicted terrible damage on his baggage train. Luckily, the Gauls were terrified by the elephants, and refused to attack any part of the line in which the great beasts were posted. The descent was equally tough. Landslides had closed the path and early snows sent men and beasts alike slithering to their deaths into the ravines below. But Hannibal persevered. He rallied his troops, rebuilt the road, and fought his way across the high passes (the exact route is a matter of endless debate) before the autumn blizzards closed the route. He had lost many men and animals—his forces now numbered about 20,000 infantry and 6,000 cavalry. But the main thing was that he was across.

Hannibal's daring march across the mountains and sudden arrival in the Po Valley bollixed Roman plans for a pincers attack on Spain and Africa: the Roman force sent to Spain was allowed to proceed, but an expeditionary force in Sicily under the consul Tiberius Sempronius—intended for a seaborne thrust at North Africa—was withdrawn to defend northern Italy. This was all according to Hannibal's plan. The pressure was now off Africa and the defense forces Hannibal had left in Spain should be able to contain the Romans north of the Ebro. The Po Valley Gauls proved to be gratifyingly receptive and offered Hannibal their immediate military support.

But Hannibal had learned in the Alps the quicksilver nature of Gallic loyalties. In order to secure the long-term allegiance of the Po Valley Gauls, Hannibal needed a rapid and dramatic victory over the Romans. He did not have long to wait. The more cautious of the two Roman consuls sent against him, Cornelius Scipio (father of Scipio Africanus), was badly wounded in a cavalry skirmish. Tiberius Sempronius, the other Roman consul, was thus left as sole Roman commander, and Sempronius was hungry for glory. He hoped to engage the invaders before his command lapsed and Hannibal was happy to oblige him. The Carthaginian took up a position on the Trebia River and set an ambush in what appeared to be an open field. He then used his crack Numidian cavalry to execute a harassing maneuver that provoked Sempronius into launching a precipitous attack across the freezing-cold river. The ambush was sprung successfully and Hannibal's defeat of Sempronius's legions was decisive. Trebia assured Hannibal winter quarters and a secure Italian base. The victory was marred only by the death by pneumonia of all but one of his elephants.

By capturing some non-Roman Italian troops at Trebia, Hannibal got the chance to kick off a propaganda campaign that he hoped would win him the support of Rome's Italian allies. Unlike his Roman captives, who were forced to fight as gladiators for the amusement and elucidation of Hannibal's men, the Italians were released without ransom. They were sent back to their various homes to spread the word that Hannibal was the deadly enemy of all Romans but the friend of all other Italians. This gesture broadcast the message that Hannibal's quarrel was with Rome alone. To the rest of the Italians he advertised himself as Liberator, not Conqueror; he proclaimed that Carthage planned to free the Italians, not enslave them.

The Romans were shocked by the loss at Trebia. Against the wishes of the normally authoritative Senate, the Roman citizens elected as consul for 217 the popular and experienced general Gaius Flaminius. His mandate: find and destroy Hannibal, and do it quickly and surgically before the invader causes any serious damage. When the campaigning season of 217 opened, Hannibal skillfully played upon Flaminius's sense of his own mandate. The Carthaginian commander managed to slip past his Roman opponent by risking a dangerous march through the swamps near Faesulae (modern Fiesole). The maneuver worked and the way to central Italy was now open to Hannibal. Flaminius, horrified by the prospect of Hannibal at large in central Italy (and the political ramifications this would have for his own political career), set out in hot pursuit. He caught up with the Carthaginian at Lake Trasimene, where at first conditions looked good for Rome. Hannibal seemed foolishly to have allowed his forces to be trapped in a misty dead-end valley. Flaminius sent his men in for the kill. Only when the fog began to lift did the Roman general see the trap: the men at the end of the valley were only the bait; most of Hannibal's troops were on the hillsides above and they were now charging down from both sides! Flaminius and his men were outflanked and massacred. After the battle, captured allied Italian troops were once again sent home with Hannibal's message of friendship and freedom.

Following his victory at Trasimene there had been a disquieting (from Hannibal's perspective) lull in the action. Rome's Italian allies proved stubbornly loyal even after Hannibal's reiterated demonstration of battlefield superiority. Furthermore, the Romans seemed determined to deny Hannibal the chance for another dramatic follow-up victory. Under the cautious military leadership of Fabius Maximus, who had been appointed Dictator with emergency powers, the Romans refused to meet Hannibal in battle for the remainder of 217 and for most of the campaigning season of 216. Hannibal marched more or less unimpeded through central Italian territory held by Rome's allies, but with little obvious effect. Fabius and his army dogged Hannibal's tracks, while avoiding major battles. The presence of Fabius's army made it tactically unwise for Hannibal to disperse his troops to plunder. When he did send his men out on foraging expeditions they were vulnerable to attack in force by Fabius's men. These conditions limited the amount of plunder Hannibal was able to accumulate. They also limited the amount of damage he was able to inflict on the economies of the Italian towns that still pigheadedly refused to be liberated from the Roman yoke.

Hannibal's big break came in late summer of 216 in the region of Apulia in southeastern Italy, where he surprised and captured the town of Cannae, a key Roman supply depot. The prospect of Carthaginian occupation of a permanent base in southeastern Italy was ugly enough to convince the Romans to risk an open battle. The odds were overwhelmingly favorable to the Romans: according to Polybius, over 80,000 legionaries against Hannibal's approximately 35,000 mercenaries (his African-Spanish forces were now augmented by Gallic contingents) on open terrain. Yet Hannibal's generalship stood the test: he deployed his troops in a crescent with its apex toward the Romans. The shock of the Roman charge caused the crescent to bend inward, but its center held, and soon the Romans found themselves enveloped as the arms of the crescent converged. Only the legionaries in the outer ring of the compressed Roman mass could reach the enemy with their weapons, and thus Roman numerical superiority was nullified. As the Carthaginians slaughtered their confused and almost helpless opponents the battlefield turned into a killing-ground.

The defeat at Cannae was perhaps the greatest military disaster ever suffered by the Roman Republic: some 25,000 soldiers were dead and another 10,000 captured. The Romans had now lost three great battles to the invader in three years, and each loss had been attended by catastrophic losses of men. There was no Roman general alive who dared to meet Hannibal in the open field, and no reserve of trained legionaries. Hannibal's tactical and strategic domination of his opponents was complete. Hence, on the morning after Cannae, a conviction on Hannibal's part that the end of the war was imminent would have been quite rational. Rome's allies must now surely revolt en masse and the Romans would have no choice other than to try (and of course fail) to defeat Hannibal in the field. With these considerations in mind, Hannibal sent word to Rome that he would allow them to ransom the Roman legionaries taken at Cannae.

AFTER CANNAE

Perhaps Hannibal's ransom offer was meant to initiate treaty talks (on his terms, of course); perhaps he simply planned to raise some quick cash with which to reward his mercenaries. In any case, he was disappointed. The Romans seemed not to realize when they were whipped and they refused even to discuss the possibility of ransom. Rome grimly chose to consider Hannibal's prisoners of war as dead men. Within a few weeks after the battle it had become clear to the Carthaginian general that the war was not yet won. The Romans showed no signs of giving up the struggle. They shook off the initial trauma of the defeat and set about recruiting new legionaries. Rome was clearly prepared to fight a long war of attrition even though the enemy was on their own territory. Within a few years of the disaster at Cannae, Rome was able to field 25 legions, some 150,000 men.

Many of these new recruits were Roman citizens, but many others were from allied cities: in the aftermath of Cannae, a number of towns in southern Italy had in fact gone over to Hannibal, but the central Italian core of the confederacy held firm. The Romans returned to Fabius Maximus's approach of dogging Hannibal's footsteps and refusing battle. As we saw in the previous chapter this strategy is a difficult one for an invaded state to maintain, because it results in no great morale-building victories, and may give the appearance of indecisiveness on the part of the high command. But when applied consistently, as it was in the years after Cannae, Fabius's strategy of exhaustion had a powerful double effect. First, because Hannibal's men were prevented from plundering efficiently, Hannibal stayed strapped for cash. Without a significant cash surplus the Carthaginian commander could not continue to enlarge his mercenary army. And with a relatively small army Hannibal's strategic options were strictly limited. Second, the "Fabian strategy" (as defensive strategies of exhaustion have been called ever since) diminished the economic effect of Hannibal's ravaging. Since his men could not disperse, the damage they could inflict on the agricultural base of Italy remained localized and limited. Thus Hannibal was prevented from exerting effective economic pressure upon Rome's allies.

Hannibal's cavalry was the key to his tactical strength

and his strategy was based on rapidity of movement. He lacked a powerful siege train and so was unable to capture big towns by assault. The weakness of his assault technique was graphically demonstrated soon after the battle of Cannae, at the Campanian fort of Casilinum. The place was located in the open plain, and was defended by fewer than a thousand Roman and allied troops. Hannibal brought up his entire army, and yet failed to take the little fort by assault (it eventually surrendered after a long siege). Since he could not hope to storm major towns, Hannibal had to depend on a carrot-and-stick approach to subverting the loyalties of Rome's Italian allies. He had offered a "carrot" of liberation from Rome, but this had not been regarded as palatable by many of the Italian allies. The Fabian strategy much reduced the weight of Hannibal's "stick" of economic coercion. As a result, the Romans were able to limit the number of defections, and Hannibal had to struggle for each city he brought over to his side.

Because the Romans maintained the core of their confederacy intact, they retained their primary manpower base. And this meant that they were able to operate in several military theaters simultaneously. Most important, Rome maintained its army in northern Spain, an army ultimately commanded by the great Scipio Africanus. The Roman army in Spain prevented the Carthaginians from establishing an overland supply line across the Alps to northern Italy and kept pressure on Carthage's economically vital imperial holdings. No Carthaginian relief army managed to follow Hannibal's route across the Alps into northern Italy until 209 b.c.

Meanwhile, in Italy, the Romans' manpower advantage meant that they could simultaneously engage in siege operations against towns which had joined Hannibal and attack the siege lines the Carthaginian might attempt to deploy against loyal towns. Since he had neither the machines nor the trained men who could successfully assault fortified positions, the only way Hannibal could take a city by force was by an extended siege. It had, for example, taken Hannibal seven months to take Spanish Saguntum by siege. In Italy, however, he could not often risk tying down a major part of his limited forces in such lengthy siege operations. He knew that if he lost the advantage of mobility, he would lose the war. When Hannibal did attempt a siege, his army was vulnerable to a countersiege by the more numerous Roman forces, and this risked tying him up in a static contest that would be fatal to his chances of final victory. Hannibal's inability either to assault or to engage in protracted sieges of major towns, therefore, further limited the size of the stick Hannibal could use against the allies.

Meanwhile, the Romans went on the offensive against Hannibal's allies. Many Samnite hill towns had jumped to Hannibal after Cannae, but by 215 destructive Roman raids on their territories led the Samnites to doubt the wisdom of their action and they sent a delegation to Hannibal complaining about his failure to protect them. Citizens of wavering allied towns weighed the Carthaginian's limited capacity to protect his friends against the prospect of brutally harsh Roman reprisals. In many cases the Romans could depend on relatives of men who were serving in Rome's armies (and who were thus effectively hostages to Rome) to fight against the spread of pro-Hannibal sentiments in their towns. Popular leaders who advocated cooperation with Hannibal were hunted down and ruthlessly executed by Roman military commanders. Those who were considering jumping to Hannibal's side might well consider the fate of Tarentum, a major city in southern Italy that went over to Hannibal after Cannae. When Tarentum was retaken by Fabius in 209 the Roman commander ordered many of the Tarentines killed outright; 30,000 of the survivors were sold into slavery. The town was systematically plundered and then sacked. The reward/punishment equation clearly did not favor defecting to Hannibal; indeed, the Roman destruction of Tarentum is said to have convinced Hannibal that the conquest of Italy was impossible.

Furthermore, Hannibal got remarkably little military

advantage from the towns he did succeed in taking and holding. Hannibal had to persuade the Italians that Carthage would be a more acceptable overlord than Rome, so he could not levy heavy taxes on his new allies, nor could he demand oppressive military service of them. Consequently, the piecemeal defections he was able to spark brought him but few assets and considerable liabilities, in particular the need to expend part of his limited forces and to compromise his mobility in defensive operations.

For much of the war, Hannibal's Italian allies were limited to the Gauls in the north, Capua in Campania, and a patchwork of towns in the south. In other words, Rome retained firm control of the bulk of central Italy. Their centralized geographical position gave the Romans the benefit of short and internal lines of communication, based on the famous system of Roman roads. These roads were originally built as military highways for the conquest of Italy; now they defended central Italy against the Carthaginian invader. Even in the south, where many towns had a weaker and more recent connection to Rome's confederacy, there were many places that rejected Hannibal: Petelia, Consentia, Croton, Locri, and Rhegium all stayed loyal despite Rome's limited ability to defend them after Cannae. Thus, Hannibal never gained secure control of a major part of Italy. Because the Romans retained bases of operation in every part of Italy, they were able to resupply their multiple armies.

While the Roman land armies were thwarting Hannibal's hopes for expansion in Italy, the Roman navy—200 ships strong (another 50,000 men!)—stymied new Carthaginian strategic enterprises. Hannibal could not expect much seaborne resupply from Carthage, since every convoy that departed Africa risked capture and sinking by the Roman battle fleet. Rome's control of the waves also blunted Carthaginian diplomatic initiatives. The disaster at Cannae had sent shock waves around the Mediterranean, but Carthage was unable to capitalize diplomatically as long as the Romans were able to deploy their fleet in a show of strength. A Carthaginian alliance with the Macedonian King Philip V (a descendant of one of Alexander the Great's generals) offered the exciting promise of opening a second front against Rome in Illyria. The plan collapsed when Philip panicked at the sight of a Roman fleet off the Macedonian coast.

The Romans followed up their humiliation of Philip with a diplomatic initiative of their own. They persuaded many of the independent city-states and tribal leagues of Greece to form an anti-Macedonian coalition that then fought a proxy war in Rome's interest against Philip. Often scorned as a dull lot in comparison with the clever Greeks, the Romans in fact played a masterful diplomatic game. The Greeks themselves kept Philip busy and out of Rome's way; Rome's contribution to the war amounted to little more than inexpensive naval displays off the Macedonian coasts. The failure of the Carthaginian-Macedonian alliance kept the war centered in the western Mediterranean and so prevented Rome's resources from being stretched thin. After the Macedonian debacle the Carthaginians tried to open a front in Sicily. The Carthaginians did succeed in making a landing on Sicily and the strategically vital city of Syracuse revolted from Rome. But the Carthaginian army on Sicily was rapidly contained by the Romans and Punic admirals never dared challenge the Roman battle fleet. When Syracuse was recaptured by the Roman general Marcellus in 211 the Sicilian front collapsed.

Rome's strategic response after Cannae prevented the massive collapse of the confederacy—a collapse that Hannibal had counted on. As a result, although the Romans could not field an army capable of meeting, much less beating him in open battle, the Carthaginian soon went on the defensive in Italy. Meanwhile the Romans took the offensive in Spain, and finally found a military genius of their own: the young Cornelius Scipio—the man who would ultimately be surnamed "Africanus" for his victories in Carthaginian Africa. Like Hannibal, Scipio had been raised by a general-father to be a warrior and showed a precocious genius for innovative tactics. And Scipio, young though he was (only twenty-five years old when, in 210 B.C. he was made Roman commander in Spain), was an astute student of military history—and most particularly a student of Hannibal's campaigns. He may have been the first Roman really to understand Hannibal's strengths and weaknesses as a general, and through understanding him, he found a way to beat him.

In 209 Scipio captured the vital Carthaginian base of New Carthage by an audacious surprise attack. The victory set the stage for his eventual defeat of the Carthaginian army in Spain, but in 209 the Carthaginians were far from ready to admit defeat. Scipio's coup at New Carthage was matched by Hannibal's brother Hasdrubal, who, late in 209, succeeded in bringing a second major Carthaginian army over the Alps into the Po Valley.

The arrival of the new Carthaginian army in northern Italy might have spelled real trouble for Rome. But Hannibal was already losing support and was suffering from decreased mobility. His forces remained tied down in southern Italy and so Hasdrubal had to go it alone against Roman commanders in northern Italy. Hasdrubal did not have his brother's genius, while Roman commanders were getting better. Hasdrubal's army was wiped out in the battle of Metaurus before the two Carthaginian commanders could link their forces. Claudius Nero, Roman victor of Metaurus, informed Hannibal of the outcome of the battle by having Hasdrubal's severed head thrown into his brother's camp.

After 209 Hannibal was trapped in southern Italy, although the Romans still did not dare to meet him in open battle. In 206 Carthage made another attempt to save the situation: Mago, Hannibal's son, sailing from the Balaeric Islands, managed to avoid the main Roman battle fleet and landed at Genoa in northwest Italy. But once again, he was unable to link up with his father. Mago had a difficult time recruiting soldiers: the Gauls were no longer enthusiastic about the Carthaginian cause. After Mago had

engaged in a few years of indecisive action and had suffered a major defeat the Carthaginian high command ordered him out of Italy. Yet another Carthaginian relief
force ran into a storm and was captured by the Romans
on the island of Sardinia in 205.

Meanwhile, Rome was on the move. By 206 Scipio had
completed the conquest of Carthaginian Spain, and was
forging alliances with anti-Carthaginian tribes in North
Africa. Two years later he sailed for Africa. Linking
up with his Numidian tribal allies, Scipio whipped the
Carthaginian home-defense forces and soon threatened
the great city itself. The Carthaginian government now realized the war was lost. In 203 Carthage initiated surrender negotiations and Hannibal was recalled to Africa.
The dream of beating the Romans on their own turf was
over.

STRATEGIC ASSESSMENT

The Second Punic War had dragged on for fourteen long
years after Cannae. But within a few months after his
greatest victory Hannibal had begun to learn that (as Polybius later pointed out) "the Roman people are most formidable, collectively and individually, when they have
real reason for alarm." The string of disastrous defeats—
Trebia, Trasimene, Cannae—failed to break the spirit of
the Roman people or to precipitate a collapse of the core
confederacy. Because the ideological effects of his battlefield victories remained limited, Hannibal lost his
chance at a quick victory in the war. After Cannae he was
reduced to fighting a war of attrition. And that was the
sort of war Rome always won.

Despite his apparently strong position, Hannibal's strategic options in the years after Cannae were really quite
limited. Some of his lieutenants suggested that he march
on the city of Rome itself. But Hannibal knew how
chimerical this was likely to prove. Rome was a huge,
densely populated, walled city. Hannibal's army had

failed in assaults of even small forts; he had neither the manpower, nor the artillery, nor the financial resources for a protracted siege of a city the size of Rome. Even if Hannibal did somehow succeed in breaking into the city, victory was far from assured. His men would be vastly outnumbered in the street fight that would ensue, and their mobility would be cramped in the narrow, twisting lanes of the residential quarters. The Romans would fight like cornered rats in a maze they knew intimately, and every Roman man, woman, and child would be a combatant. Perhaps Hannibal remembered the fate of the last foreign invader of Italy, the brilliant Hellenistic Greek general Pyrrhus, who had died in a street fight in the Greek town of Argos, done in by a roof tile thrown by an Argive woman. This was not an end the heroic Carthaginian general or the troops under his command would relish.

After Cannae failed to knock out Rome or her allies, Hannibal's only real hope for victory was massive resupply from Carthage. Only great infusions of money, men, and material could give him the manpower resources necessary to divide his armies, generalize the conflict in Italy, and so force the Italian towns to break with Rome. Immediately after Cannae, Hannibal dispatched his son Mago back to Africa to report the victory and to ask for grain, money, and reinforcement troops. But Mago failed in his mission. In order to open a reliable line of supply to Hannibal's base in southern Italy, the Carthaginians must challenge the Romans at sea, and this they were unwilling to do. But why?

Carthage probably had the resources to construct a fleet big enough to attempt a naval confrontation with Rome, but Carthage never built enough ships to make this a viable option. If Carthage *had* built the ships, could Carthaginian naval commanders have used them to good effect? On several occasions Carthaginian admirals displayed a distinct reluctance to engage Roman warships—even when they enjoyed a momentary numerical advantage.

Apparently the Carthaginians had lost the will to fight at sea after their failure in the First Punic War.

The naval challenge strategy would have been a big, expensive, dangerous venture and in the years immediately after Cannae, the Carthaginians were not gambling men. Why should they take the risk? From a North African perspective the war seemed to be going fine. When Mago arrived, begging for a massive new commitment of men and funds, the Carthaginians must have asked themselves: Is this really necessary? After all, the Romans were on the defensive in Italy and had made no real inroads into Carthaginian Spain. Why, wondered the complacent Carthaginians in the years following 216 B.C., should they exert themselves when Hannibal was doing so well? It was not until 209 B.C., when Scipio seized New Carthage, that the Carthaginians seriously faced the possibility of a Roman victory in the war. They suddenly realized the need to get more men to Hannibal in Italy, and attempted on several occasions to do so. But by 209 it was too late for the resupply effort to do any good because Hannibal was pinned down in southern Italy and the Romans had recovered from the loss at Cannae.

So, in the end, Hannibal was stuck with the strategy he had come to Italy with: attempting to overthrow the power of Rome by subverting her confederacy, using for this purpose his existing forces and any allies he could recruit locally. The Fabian strategy of exhaustion robbed Hannibal of his operational momentum after Cannae and prevented the tidal wave of defections he had counted on. In the war of attrition that followed, Rome held all the winning cards, and Hannibal had no way to change the game. His tactical brilliance and leadership skills were undiminished. His army remained loyal for the sixteen years (218–203) that they occupied Italian territory: no small feat when one considers that plunder was thin after the first few years, and that even the dullest of the mercenaries must eventually have realized that the war was not going very well. But tactical brilliance and leadership skills were not enough to beat Rome.

When he was recalled to Africa in 203 Hannibal and his army were still undefeated in major battle. A peace treaty was signed, but there was bad feeling on both sides. In a confused incident the Carthaginians seized supplies from a Roman convoy driven off course onto the North African shoreline. The Romans sent envoys to investigate the incident; they were murdered on their return journey. As a result the peace broke down, setting up the final battle of the war. Hannibal was put in command. He would fight on African soil for the first time in his life, and he would try his skills against Rome's greatest general. At the Carthaginian town of Zama, Hannibal and his veterans faced Scipio. The Carthaginian launched a preliminary elephant charge but this failed to disrupt the Roman lines. On the Roman side, Numidian tribal cavalrymen provided the tactical mobility Roman armies typically lacked. The battle was bitterly contested, but in the end Roman legionary discipline and superior cavalry overwhelmed the Carthaginian forces and handed Hannibal the first major battlefield defeat of his career. He returned to Carthage and urged his countrymen to accept peace with Rome. Surrender meant survival, but it also meant that once-proud Carthage was reduced to the status of a second-rate city-state.

After the war, Hannibal went into politics, and initiated a number of constitutional reforms in Carthage. But his political career was cut short when his enemies whispered to the Romans that Hannibal was plotting a new war. He fled east, to the court of Antiochus III, the Macedonian king of Mesopotamia (a descendant of another of Alexander's generals). There he was given a minor naval command, and fought against Rome a final time when the Romans invaded Antiochus's kingdom in 190 B.C. Both Hannibal and Antiochus were defeated. Again Hannibal fled, ultimately to the Black Sea kingdom of Bithynia. He was not to find peace. The Romans accused him of stirring up Bithynia against their allies in Asia Minor and demanded his extradition. In 183 B.C., now in his mid-sixties and unwilling to run any more, the Carthaginian took his own life. Forty years later the Romans initiated an un-provoked war of aggression; in this Third Punic War the city of Carthage was burned, its inhabitants enslaved or scattered. Despite all his brilliance and his many victories Hannibal ultimately lost and his failure destroyed his nation's standing as an independent power. Where and why did he go wrong?

THE LESSON

First, Hannibal made the fatal error of mirror-imaging his enemy—of viewing the Roman alliance system as an ana-log of the Carthaginian empire. Because Hannibal under-stood the depth of the resentment of the peoples under Carthaginian control, he assumed similar resentment on the part of Rome's allies. Thus, he assumed that once he raised the standard of liberty and proved himself able to whip Roman armies in the field, the allies would flock to him. He did not properly assess the ties that bound the allies to Rome: notably Rome's demonstrated sincerity and prowess in the role of protector and guarantor of peace in Italy. Most allied states had prospered (at least relatively) under Roman rule. The ruling elites of those states had been supported by Rome and their members were treated as near equals by the Romans. In the late second century Roman demands on their allies were not especially onerous (at least not by ancient standards), and the Romans did not ask their allies to do anything in terms of military service that they did not ask of them-selves. Hannibal's banner of liberty found few to salute it, because most of the Italian allies did not see themselves as oppressed slaves but rather as Rome's willing partners in the governance of the Italian peninsula.

Nor did Hannibal adequately assess the public relations difficulties of presenting himself to the Italians as an at-tractive suitor. The Carthaginians had a bad reputation as overlords; anyone who heard about how they treated their subjects hesitated to put himself under their thumb.

Carthaginians looked strange (they dressed oddly and wore earrings), spoke an odd language, even smelled bizarre to Italian noses because they favored strong perfumes. Carthaginian culture was desperately foreign in the eyes of the Italians and some aspects of that culture were regarded as revolting and barbarous—for example, the practice of sacrificing their own infant children to the god Baal. The Italians were perfectly happy to trade with foreign oddities, but they were unwilling to put themselves under foreign rule. Moreover, the Carthaginians were allied with the Gauls. Roman mothers scared their children with stories of the nightmarish Gauls—the monsters who had sacked the cities of Italy (including Rome) in the fourth century B.C. There had been wars between the Gauls and the Italians since time immemorial and most Italians tended to regard Gauls as among the most dangerous and hateful of their external enemies. He who allied himself with Gauls would find it difficult to present himself as a friend of the Italians.

If mirror-imaging was the problem, it is fair to ask why Hannibal, an intelligent man by any standard, was so ready to mirror-image Rome. Perhaps, as the Romans supposed, he was blinded by his own irrational hatred of all things Roman, but there is little in the historical record that supports the idea that Hannibal was a slave of wild emotion. It seems more likely that the great tactician was dazzled by his own tremendous abilities. The invasion plan Hannibal adopted was perfectly designed to highlight his own magnificent skills in deploying mobile troops and using surprise against superior numbers of slow-moving and indifferently led infantrymen. Because Hannibal knew (and he was right) that he could beat any Roman general living at almost any odds, he also knew (but he was wrong) that he could win the war.

Finally, Hannibal's strategy was perfectly tailored to cushion the impact of the war on Carthage. This might have been an advantage if the Carthaginians were fully committed to a total war from the beginning, but apparently they were not. Insulated from the realities of the conflict because the main theater was in distant Italy, the Carthaginian people were slow to develop a sense of the conflict as a total war for national survival. Reports from the front carried cheering tales of tens of thousands of Romans slaughtered. If the Italians were proving a bit more stubborn than originally predicted, surely that was little cause for immediate alarm. Hannibal's army was an army of mercenaries; there were no grim funerals for dead citizen-soldiers to drive home the reality of the conflict. Some Carthaginian politicians were quite content to have the ambitious Hannibal, scion of the powerful House of Barca, out of the way fighting a lengthy war in distant Italy: as long as Hannibal was in Italy he could not be in Carthage, dominating the political scene there, or in Spain setting up a personal fiefdom. Other Carthaginians simply carried on their lives of farming and trading in a business-as-usual atmosphere that was unconducive to making the sort of financial sacrifices Hannibal's dispatches asked for. Thus, Carthage did not commit itself as a society to the war until it was too late for the war to be won.

Hannibal and the Carthaginians undoubtedly regarded the Roman decision to abort the invasion of North Africa in the first year of the war as vindication of their strategic plan. That decision to abort was made (or at least agreed to) by Tiberius Sempronius, the Roman general who became Hannibal's first major victim when he botched the battle of Trebia. Tiberius Sempronius's name does not loom large in the annals of military history. He was a stolid politician and general; unlike Hannibal, he has never been accused of being any kind of genius. But ironically, dull Sempronius's decision to return to Italy, by encouraging Carthaginian complacency, helped to seal genius Hannibal's fate.

In the end, Hannibal failed because he could not see beyond the battlefield. His self-confident conviction of his own ability and of his men's discipline led him to overlook the ideological factors that would undermine his stra-

tegic plan and render his battlefield successes meaningless. Because he misjudged the nature and resiliency of
the Roman confederacy and the depressing effect early
successes would have on the Carthaginian war effort,
Hannibal devised a strategy that made the most of his
own genius and led his state to ruin.

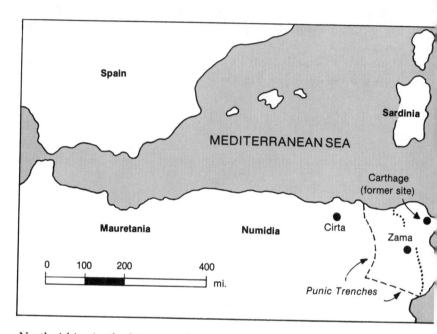

North Africa in the late second century B.C.

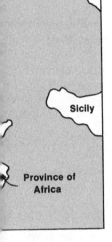

Rome

Sicily

Province of
Africa

Chapter 6

Jugurtha Versus Rome:
How Both Sides Can Lose

THE NINETY-YEAR PERIOD from the end of the Second Punic War to the outbreak of the Jugurthine War (202–111 B.C.) saw a tremendous growth in the amount of territory controlled by Rome. Immediately after the Second Punic War, the Romans had declared war on Philip V, the Antigonid king of Macedon, a conflict called the Second Macedonian War in the Roman tradition. Rome's exact motives are unclear, but it is hardly coincidental that Philip had allied briefly with Hannibal after the battle of Cannae (precipitating the First Macedonian War, 215–205 B.C., which was fought largely by Rome's Greek proxies). The Roman legion proved to be more than a match for the Macedonian phalanx. Philip surrendered in 196 B.C. and was allowed to keep control of a reduced kingdom. Much to many Greeks' surprise, Rome quickly pulled her armies out of Greece. But to no one's surprise, the legions were soon back. Various Greek states had become clients of Rome in the course of the first two Macedonian wars. This meant that when the Seleucid king Antiochus III brought his armies over to Greece in 192, the Romans felt obliged to get involved. The Romans chased Antiochus back to

Asia Minor, and handed him a catastrophic defeat at the battle of Magnesia in 190 B.C. Seleucid power in Asia Minor was crippled, and Rome filled the vacuum by allowing the loyal client state of Pergamum to grow quickly in size and influence.

Trouble soon cropped up again in Macedon; Perseus, son of Philip V, was acting altogether too independently for Roman tastes. Thus Rome launched, and won, the Third Macedonian War (171–167 B.C.). The historian Polybius fought on the wrong side, and was taken prisoner in this war. The Macedonian Kingdom was eliminated, and Macedon was divided into four independent republics. Even this did not do the trick. The Romans felt obliged to launch one more Macedonian War (149–148 B.C.), and in the aftermath decided to annex Macedon as a province. Greece was attached to the province as an administrative district. The age of Greek independence had come to an end. Meanwhile, Rome was acting more and more aggressively and more overtly as an imperialist. Both Corinth and Carthage were sacked in 146 B.C. The kingdom of Pergamum was added as the Province of Asia (western Asia Minor) in 133 B.C. In northern Italy, all the territory south of the Alps was regained and colonized. In the west Roman armies had begun the long process of turning Spain into a province. In the second century B.C., Rome was well on the way to becoming not only the dominant power, but the only power, in the Mediterranean world. It remained to be seen what impact that shockingly rapid growth would have on the Italian Confederacy, on Roman society, and on international politics.

MARIUS'S TRIUMPH

In January 104 B.C. the city of Rome was treated to a favorite spectacle: the triumphal parade of a successful Roman general. A Triumph was truly something to see: the victorious general, splendidly dressed in a purple toga and riding in a magnificent four-horse chariot, led the parade through the Arch of Triumph, along the streets of the city, and up to the Capitol Hill. The general was followed by his troops—the only time Roman soldiers ever (legally) marched in arms within the precincts of the walled city. Behind the Roman legionaries came wagons filled to overflowing with booty: gold, silver, spices, statues, slaves. The goods varied depending on the defeated enemy, but there was always plenty of loot on display. Although the bulk of the booty would eventually be deposited in the state treasury, the general kept a good chunk for himself and generous triumphal generals were in the habit of tossing gold coins and other souvenirs to the spectators. Not surprisingly, triumphal parades always had a fine turnout. Behind the booty came the prisoners of war: in the eyes of the crowd these dejected men represented despicable revolutionaries who had dared offend against the majesty of SPQR—the Senate and People of Rome. At the conclusion of the parade some of these prisoners (often including their leader) were executed by stoning or strangulation. This showed the world what happened to the rabble who raised weapons against the masters of the Mediterranean.

At the head of this particular Triumph in 104 was the general Gaius Marius. Beloved of the Roman lower classes, Marius was hated by many in the senatorial elite. Friend and foe alike respected him as a tough soldier, a good battlefield commander, and a no-holds-barred politician. At the rear of the parade, marching to his death, was the opponent Marius had defeated: Jugurtha, one-time king of the North African state of Numidia. The Roman people were thirsty for Jugurtha's blood. They had been forced to wait a long time for the spectacle of this particular African king in chains. Hostilities with Jugurtha had broken out over seven years ago (in 112 B.C.) and no less than five Roman commanding generals had been dispatched to fight him. The first four had failed to crush the African's arrogance. Only the fifth general, Marius, had won the great honor of a Triumph.

The seven long years of what the Romans called the

Jugurthine War had been tough ones in Roman internal politics, too. The other four commanders were old-family senators who had played politics the old way: through manipulating a network of friends, relatives, and "clients"—that is, people who owed them favors. A big-name old-style senator was typically the "patron" of hundreds, maybe thousands, of clients ranging in status from slum-dwelling citizens who depended on an occasional handout, to fellow-senators, to foreign kings. But Marius represented a new style in politics and was elected consul by a newly politicized constituency: the disenchanted and dispossessed lower classes of Roman citizens. This meant that the political system could no longer be easily manipulated through strings pulled by a few master puppeteers in the Senate. By 104 the old social and political order was in deep trouble, well on its way to the chaotic Civil War that would kill off the republican form of government.

Despite its length, the ultimate outcome of the war fought by Rome against Jugurtha was really never in doubt. Jugurtha won only one significant engagement in the course of the entire seven years! Thus, it initially seems odd that this war is the subject of a detailed narrative written by Sallust, an important Roman historian. Why did Sallust choose to describe the Jugurthine War, when there were so many other wars (for example Marius's later campaigns against the Germanic tribes of the Cimbri and Teutons) which offered more glorious battles, and whose outcome was less certain? The answer is that the war against Jugurtha exposed key weaknesses of the Roman political system. Sallust wrote about the Jugurthine War, not because Jugurtha could have won it, but because a crisis in Roman politics turned what should have been a quick victory into a long, drawn-out struggle that had devastating effects on "the folks back home." Sallust's *History of the Jugurthine War* was a morality tale, rather than a straight history. This makes the book both interesting and potentially misleading. Sallust told only the parts of the story that fit his view of moral decay.

Viewed from a modern perspective, North Africa in the

age of Jugurtha was, in many ways, Rome's Vietnam. Although in 104 the Roman Marius rode a chariot at the front of the parade, and the Numidian Jugurtha slogged along at its back in heavy shackles, when we judge by the long-term effect of the war on their respective nations, both men were big losers. The Jugurthine War is the story of two failures: on the one hand, the failure of the Romans to find a strategy that would determine the appropriate level of force needed to maintain sound and stable foreign policy; on the other hand the failure of a client king to control his troops or to find a way to persuade his masters that his small nation was not a fierce lion merely disguising itself as a mouse. The Romans thought they heard the mouse roar, and that perception led to a comic war with tragic consequences.

ROME AND NORTH AFRICA IN THE SECOND CENTURY B.C.

In order to understand why the Jugurthine War represented almost as great a loss for Rome as it did for Numidia, we must first jump back a century, to the years immediately following the Second Punic War. Rome had beaten Carthage after a long and desperate struggle. As part of the war booty seized from Carthage, Rome had taken over the Carthaginian domains in southeastern Spain—or rather had taken over the imperial burden of trying to force the recalcitrant Spanish tribes into submission. This proved to be a major undertaking. As long as the Romans were fighting their hated Carthaginian overlords many Spanish tribes had been happy to cooperate with the Romans. But once Carthage was out of the picture, Rome had become the imperialist enemy. No Roman would have imagined in 200 B.C. that it would take two centuries before Spain was fully pacified. But in the generations after 200 B.C. Roman commanders and soldiers learned to their dismay how tough the Spanish tribesmen could be: year after year Roman armies headed out to

Spain, gaining ground only very slowly and at the cost of many Roman lives, and with little loot.

Spain was not the only active theater of war in the years following the defeat of Hannibal. The Romans had a few scores to settle in the Greek East. In the East the fighting proved to be easier than in Spain, and the loot was a lot richer. Beginning in 198 B.C., the Romans launched a series of highly successful campaigns against Macedon and then against other Hellenistic Greek kingdoms of mainland Greece and western Asia. By 130 B.C. Macedon and Asia Minor had been made into provinces; the rulers of Egypt and various minor kingdoms became clients of the Roman people and of individual Roman senators.

The booty from these eastern wars was tremendous. The Greeks had accumulated great wealth over the centuries: massive quantities of precious metals, innumerable statues, paintings, and other works of art were shipped back to Rome by victorious commanders. More backward areas of Greece lacked gold or objets d'art, but the ever resourceful Romans took the people themselves as booty. In a famous incident, some 150,000 prisoners of war were shipped to Italy from the region of Epirus in northwestern Greece. Most of these prisoners were not fated to be executed on the Capitol Hill, but rather were intended for Rome's burgeoning slave market. As the market was flooded with prisoners of war the price of slaves dropped sharply, and for a while the supply of slaves seemed as inexhaustible as Rome's capacity for military success.

Military operations—and thus strategic decision making—were entangled in economic affairs. Clever and wealthy Roman senators commanded the expeditions to the East (while their braver or more foolish relatives served in Spain) and so got their hands on masses of booty. But what should the senators do with their sudden influx of cash? Since the goal of many wealthy Romans was to become even wealthier, the senators looked around for an appropriate investment. Their options were, in fact, limited because it was regarded as improper or even illegal for a Roman senator to derive his income from any source other than agricultural land. Happily for the status-conscious senator with a wad of booty money to invest, in the second century B.C. there was much Italian land available for a good price. Some of this land was actually war booty itself. The allied cities that had supported Hannibal during the Second Punic War were punished by the appropriation of part of their agricultural land: this property was then made available to Roman citizens for long-term lease at generous terms.

Generous, that is, by a senator's standards. Poorer Roman citizen-farmers did not benefit; indeed, many had to sell their own farms. Some Roman farms had been ruined by ravaging during the Hannibalic War. In other cases, the problem was an insufficient labor supply. Through much of the second century B.C. most adult Roman males were drafted to fight in Spain and against the Greeks in the East. These were long campaigns that kept the men overseas for years on end. Meanwhile, their wives and children, who were left behind, often found themselves unable to do all of the manual labor necessary to keep subsistence farms operating. For many families, the only option was to sell the farm, and move to the city.

The failed farms of the Roman poor were quickly bought up by wealthy Romans, who thereby consolidated huge tracts into gigantic estates. Unlike their poor fellow citizens, rich Romans did not have to worry about finding laborers. There was a ready source for the rich to tap: slaves. Because slaves were in such good supply and were (by upper-class standards) so cheap when bought wholesale, they could be worked to death in a few years and then replaced. This system lowered the overhead that would otherwise be expended on providing workers with proper food, shelter, and working conditions, and so increased the profitability of agricultural land. The equation was pretty simple: the more land and the more slaves, the higher the profit for the rich. Thus, it was to the benefit of the wealthy senators to keep wars going that would keep Roman-citizen farms failing and would keep slaves coming into the market. It wasn't that the senators meant to be cruel to their fellow citizens, it was just a matter of good business.

The whole system was shockingly brutal to the slaves (who sometimes rose up in bloody revolt) and destructive to the Roman citizenry, but immensely profitable to the rich landowners. With land consolidated and cheap slaves available, the wealthy Roman tended to grow vastly richer in the years between the Hannibalic and Jugurthine Wars, while the ordinary Roman citizen-farmer fell into utter destitution. The failed farmers were bitterly unhappy but had few occupational options. The only real career open to most of them was more military service. Thus, by the end of the Jugurthine War, the Roman army was largely composed of poverty-stricken, resentful soldiers—men who remembered that their ancestors had fought and died in the war against Hannibal so that their descendants could live decent lives. These angry soldiers were commanded by the very men who had most benefited from the post–Hannibalic War conditions. The Roman army—traditionally an institution in which class interests were submerged in the common goal of the national defense—was, in the age of Jugurtha, a powder keg of social tension and class hatred.

The situation in North Africa in the generations after the Second Punic War was equally complex and troubling. Scipio's final victory over Hannibal at Zama had been made possible in part by the loyal cooperation of Numidian cavalrymen, led by an ambitious and highly competent young king named Masinissa. The Numidians lived in the area of Africa west of Carthage and north of the Sahara (mostly modern Algeria). Some Numidians were settled agriculturalists, others were seminomadic herdsmen—both groups had welcomed the arrival of Scipio in Africa, because he offered them a chance of liberation from the rule of Carthage. Masinissa managed to unite a number of Numidian tribes, but unlike his Spanish counterparts he entertained no notions of independence from Rome after the defeat of Hannibal. Rather, the astute Numidian king quickly recognized that ongoing cooperation with Rome—the status of client king—offered him his best chance to consolidate and then to expand his kingdom.

The peace treaty that ended the Second Punic War between Rome and Carthage called for the Carthaginians to maintain control of the agricultural territory and all towns and villages within the "Punic trenches." But the agreement between Rome and Masinissa said that the Numidian king had the right to rule over all of the towns that had been occupied by his ancestors. Unfortunately for Carthage, the agreement did not define "occupied by his ancestors"—and Masinissa chose to interpret the phrase as meaning any town in which a Numidian band had carried out a booty raid. This definition included places within the area of the Punic trenches, and thus Masinissa found a pretense for launching a series of raids against towns that the Romans had guaranteed would remain under Carthaginian control.

The Carthaginians were upset by Masinissa's raids, but their treaty with Rome forbade them the right to cross the Punic trenches in arms. Thus, they had little recourse against the Numidians within the terms of the treaty, and they knew that breaking the treaty would infuriate the Romans. The Carthaginians complained repeatedly, but unsuccessfully, to the Roman Senate about Numidian provocations. Masinissa took Rome's stance of benign neglect as a license to increase his incursions across the trenches. Eventually the Carthaginians did respond in force, and the Romans took this as an unacceptable display of independence. The eventual result was the Third Punic War (149–146 B.C.), the extermination of the Carthaginian people by Rome, and the establishment of the Roman Province of Africa in what had been the Carthaginian homeland (roughly, modern Tunisia).

Meanwhile King Masinissa had died (in his nineties, in 148 B.C.), leaving as his heir Micipsa, one of many sons. Besides difficulties with jealous brothers, half-brothers, and their progeny, Micipsa had to face the problem of a much more visible Roman presence in Africa. Masinissa had been able to take advantage of Roman distrust of Carthage to expand Numidian holdings eastward, but now there was a Roman province on Numidia's eastern frontier, and no raiders would be tolerated across the line. Micipsa understood the role expected of him by the Romans. According to Sallust he thought of his own kingdom as a Roman possession, and acted as if he were merely the steward for its rightful owners. The Romans liked this sort of obsequious behavior from client kings—indeed it was the only sort of attitude they were willing to tolerate. Any sign of real independence on the part of a client could be treated as a provocation meriting the severest punishment—as demonstrated by the sack of the once great cities of Corinth and Carthage in 146 B.C. The Romans also liked the efficient way that Micipsa kept nomadic raiders from crossing into the province. Under Micipsa's cautious rule, close economic contacts developed between the Roman Province of Africa and the Kingdom of Numidia; the Numidian city of Cirta became a major trading center with a sizable resident population of Italians. Thus, Micipsa was the perfect model of a Roman overseas "ally": useful militarily and economically, and submissive in his public attitudes. And thus Numidia was left in relative peace by its Roman overlords.

As one of his gestures of loyalty to Rome, Micipsa sent his young nephew Jugurtha to Spain, to serve as an auxiliary in the Roman army. The commander of the Roman army in Spain was then Scipio Aemilianus, the grandson (by adoption) of Scipio Africanus, conqueror of Hannibal. It is surely no accident that Micipsa sent his nephew in 134 or 133 B.C. to serve with the descendant of the man who had brought Numidia into alliance with Rome: international diplomacy in this era tended to follow family lines across the generations. Sallust claims (perhaps maliciously) that Micipsa secretly hoped his nephew would be killed in Spain, but Jugurtha distinguished himself in action and earned the regard of his commander and the other Roman officers.

By the end of his tour in Spain, Jugurtha probably

spoke Latin and was personally acquainted with Scipio Aemilianus, one of the most important power brokers in Roman politics. Scipio apparently liked Jugurtha, going so far as to send the following letter to Micipsa:

> Your nephew Jugurtha has distinguished himself in the . . . war above all others. . . . I hold him in affection for his services, and I will do all I can to make him equally highly esteemed by the Senate and People of Rome. As your friend, I congratulate you personally; in him you have a man worthy of yourself and of his grandfather, Masinissa.

Whatever had been Micipsa's opinion of his nephew before, once Jugurtha had returned with this letter, it was obvious to the king that his nephew was going to be a major player in Numidian politics. Jugurtha fulfilled his early promise. A few years before Micipsa's death Jugurtha was formally adopted by his royal uncle, and became equal heir with Micipsa's two younger natural sons, Hiempsal and Adherbal.

ORIGINS OF THE JUGURTHINE WAR

After Micipsa's death in 118 B.C. the three heirs discussed what to do regarding the kingdom. Sallust reports that Jugurtha suggested that since the old king had become senile toward the end, all decrees of his last five years should be declared void. Hiempsal, the younger natural son, quickly supported Jugurtha's motion—and then pointed out that Jugurtha's adoption, and thus his share in the kingdom, was one of the decrees that would be voided. The motion was dropped, but the cards were now on the table: the co-heirs would never rule Numidia as a friendly troika. Given the Roman touchiness about the behavior of clients, an open feud among Numidia's rulers boded ill for the survival of the independent kingdom.

It is worth pausing at this point to ask ourselves how

Rome should have responded to the death of Micipsa. The death of a client king, especially one without a clear and dependable heir, was sometimes a signal for Rome to move in militarily and make the kingdom into a province of the empire. This is what happened in Asia Minor in 133 B.C.: client king Attalus III of Pergamum (in modern western Turkey) smoothed the way by refusing to name a successor and instead leaving his kingdom to the Romans in his will.

But there is no reason to suppose that Rome was ready to turn Numidia into a province in 118 B.C. After all, despite the influence of Roman culture, many Numidians were still seminomads, and nomadic people were very difficult for the Romans to administer under the province system. People who stayed in one place could be taxed, recruited as auxiliaries for the army, watched for signs of restlessness, and (if they proved rebellious) punished by destruction of their towns. Nomads, on the other hand, were hard to tax and hard to control—it was really more economical to rule them through a loyal client king—one whose family had generations of experience in local affairs. Micipsa's reign had proved lucrative for Romans and had provided adequate security. There was no advantage for Rome in breaking the pattern.

There were more pressing problems for the Romans to worry about in the years around 118 B.C.—northern Italy was still vulnerable to transalpine invasion; several newly formed provinces needed to be put on a secure administrative footing, and, as we have seen, there were serious social problems. This was not the time for an imperialistic war in Africa aimed at taking over an area that was already being run in Rome's interest. No evidence suggests that Rome was planning for a Numidian war in the years immediately following the death of Micipsa.

If military takeover of Numidia was not in Rome's interest, what was the ideal outcome for Rome of the squabbles among Micipsa's three heirs? Surely it was for one king to emerge: strongly pro-Roman, competent, and experienced. Jugurtha was the obvious candidate; he had the closest connections to the Roman ruling elite, and had proved his loyalty by fighting for Rome in Spain. This is not to say that the Romans should have assassinated Micipsa's other two sons—if a Roman-sponsored assassination of Numidian princes ever became public knowledge it could destabilize client kings elsewhere in the empire. But on the other hand, there was no rational reason for Rome to interfere with the consolidation of power in Jugurtha's hands—as long as he did nothing to offend the majesty or material interests of Rome in the process.

The Numidian ruling troika was quickly reduced to a dyad: Hiempsal was assassinated by a band of soldiers while staying in the house of a friend of Jugurtha. Sallust tells us straight out that Jugurtha arranged the killing, but Jugurtha is the villain of his morality tale and Sallust was overtly biased against him. Jugurtha may have killed Hiempsal, but Adherbal had just as strong a motive. And it was Adherbal who took the initiative after the assassination: he sent word of the assassination to the Roman Senate (attributing the deed to Jugurtha) and launched a military attack on Jugurtha.

The letter to Rome was a good idea—whoever had killed Hiempsal, the only judges who mattered were the Roman senators, and *they* would decide according to their own perceptions of who among the survivors would make the best client, not on the basis of probable guilt. But Adherbal's military attack was foolhardy: Jugurtha's exploits in Spain had not been mere beginner's luck. Sallust reports that while the majority of the Numidians favored Adherbal, the best soldiers went for Jugurtha, and Adherbal's men were quickly routed.

Adherbal himself fled to the Roman province of Africa, then to the city of Rome. Having lost the trial of arms, Adherbal intended to win a kingdom by engaging Jugurtha in a groveling contest to be decided in the Roman Senate. Adherbal proved to be consummately spineless and delivered a speech to the Senate which, in the version reported by

Sallust, is a masterpiece of bootlicking. "Members of the Senate," he began,

> my father Micipsa advised me on his deathbed to consider that it was merely a stewardship of the Numidian Kingdom that belonged to me, and that the real ownership and sovereignty of it were yours. He also bade me strive to serve the Roman people to the best of my ability . . . and to regard you as my kinsmen and relatives. If I did this, he said, your friendship would protect my kingdom as effectually as an army and a treasury.

The speech goes on and on:

> Such grievous misery was destined to be my lot . . . I am forced to be a burden to you . . . my pitiable circumstances . . . my hapless condition . . . [you are] masters of such a mighty empire . . . where else can I go, to whom else can I appeal . . . you are great and prosperous . . . the worldwide influence and empire you have won make it simple for you to redress the wrongs done to your allies . . . [compared to my dead brother] I am the unlucky one . . . I am an object lesson of the changeability of human fortunes . . . I beg you, as you respect yourself, your children, your parents, and the majesty of the Roman people—aid me in my affliction. . . .

There were no "court stenographers" in the Senate at this time and the speech, as reported by Sallust, cannot be an actual record of Adherbal's (or his interpreter's) words. But it does catch the tone that was expected of a client king when he addressed the Roman Senate in the late second century B.C. and, as we shall see, Adherbal did win some adherents among the senators.

What was Jugurtha to do in response to Adherbal's quick move to grab the sympathy of the Senate? He could hardly afford to leave Numidia, which was on the verge of a civil war. Instead he sent ambassadors to Rome to make his case. Jugurtha relied on the senators' ability to recognize and willingness to act on the plain fact that Roman interest would be served by establishing himself as king. In response to Adherbal's weepy speech Jugurtha's ambassadors stated simply, "Jugurtha asks you [senators] not to let anyone persuade you that he is not still the same loyal ally he showed himself to be [in Spain], and not to attach more weight to an enemy's assertions than to his own actions." The senators then debated, and took the path of least resistance: a senatorial commission was appointed to divide the kingdom. In 116 B.C. the commission completed its work: Adherbal was given the much more prosperous eastern half with its towns and harbors. He had won the groveling match hands down.

The senators' decision to divide Numidia is reminiscent of King Solomon's decision about the baby, and was no more likely to satisfy both disputants. Further conflicts were inevitable and were certainly not in Rome's interests. How then, can we explain the senators' decision? The answer is that the policymaking Senate was a deeply factionalized group of ambitious, greedy, and arrogant politicians. This is not to say that the senators completely failed to take Rome's interests into consideration, but Rome's interests were only one factor among many in their deliberations and decisions. Among the extraneous factors were personal and factional loyalties, the lust for personal aggrandizement and military glory, and the delight they felt in the spectacle of kings and princes begging for aid and succor. In times of genuine national emergency, like the war against Hannibal, these extraneous matters might be temporarily submerged, but there was no real threat from North Africa, and so personal and factional interests dominated the decision-making process.

Beaten by Adherbal's diplomatic strategy, Jugurtha countered with a military one. In 113 B.C. Jugurtha sent an exploratory raid into his cousin's kingdom that met little resistance and provoked no response from Rome. The raid was then followed up by a full invasion. Adherbal, better at whining than fighting, was defeated in a battle outside the town of Cirta; he and the remnants of his army fell back into the town. The Italian residents of Cirta managed to close the gates against Jugurtha's men, but the town was immediately besieged. Once again Adherbal sent off to Rome and once again a Roman senatorial commission was sent to Numidia to deal with the situation. The commissioners met with Jugurtha outside Cirta and were told by the king that he would send ambassadors to Rome to explain the situation; meanwhile the siege continued. Adherbal sent yet another pathetic letter to the Senate; yet another commission was sent to North Africa. This time Jugurtha was ordered to come to the Roman Province of Africa to meet the commissioners, who instructed him to lift the siege of Cirta.

At this point the exact sequence of events becomes rather confused. According to Sallust, when the Italian population of Cirta heard that the senatorial commission had ordered Jugurtha to lift the siege, they advised (read: commanded) Adherbal to surrender the town and himself to Jugurtha. Apparently the Italians assumed that there would be a new division of Numidia and that Jugurtha would be too much afraid of the displeasure of Rome to take advantage of the situation. What happened was that as soon as the town surrendered, Adherbal was killed (tortured to death according to Sallust) and all of the armed men of Cirta—Italians and Numidians alike—were slaughtered.

Several things are unclear about this narrative: Jugurtha apparently did not withdraw his army from Cirta after visiting the Roman commission in the Province of Africa. Did he openly defy the commissioners by continuing the siege? Perhaps, but then why were the Italians of Cirta so sure that he would be lenient? The most likely scenario is that he ceased active assaults on the town (thus hoping to assuage the commissioners) but maintained an embargo (thus pressuring the Italians to turn over the town).

But this leads us to ask a second question: why did

Jugurtha kill the residents of Cirta? The murder of Adherbal has a certain grim logic, but the murder of the Cirtans
was madness: the slaughter of Italian traders, citizens of
the old allied towns of the Roman confederacy, could
never be overlooked by Rome. Rome's relationship with
the Italian allies required that the murder of Italians be
avenged by military force. This meant that open war between Jugurtha and Rome became inevitable as soon as
the Cirtans were killed. Jugurtha may have been a cold-
blooded murderer and a power-hungry opportunist, but
nothing in his earlier career suggests that he was insane.
Because he had served in the Roman army he knew better
than most the awesome power of the Roman military machine, and he must have seen that there was no way he
could win a war with Rome. So why were the Cirtans
killed?

The only reasonable explanation is that Jugurtha simply
lost control of his army of tribal irregulars once they entered the town: the killing was not ordered as a matter of
policy but was done by his men on their own initiative as
they rampaged through the town. If this is right, the
massacre at Cirta was the result of a lapse in military discipline, a tragic mistake all too common in wartime, and
one that Jugurtha knew he would pay for dearly.

ROMAN INVASION OF NUMIDIA

The Roman response was quick and unambiguous. War
was declared and Lucius Calpurnius Bestia, one of the
two consuls for the year 111 B.C., was made commander
of the expeditionary force. Jugurtha desperately sent ambassadors to Rome to explain his mistake. The ambassadors were refused admission to the city, told that the
only message the Romans would listen to was an uncon-
ditional surrender, and then ordered to leave Italy within
ten days. Numidian blood would have to be shed to
avenge the blood of the Italian traders of Cirta.

Bestia's invasion went well; he captured a number of

Numidian towns and met with little resistance. Jugurtha did not lead an army against him and quickly surrendered. Bestia accepted his surrender. As a guarantee of good faith Jugurtha turned over a quantity of cash and military matériel, including 30 war elephants. That should have been that. Jugurtha had taken his punishment (the loss of cities, cash, matériel) and had surrendered. It only remained for the Senate to confirm Bestia's acceptance of the surrender and decide what to do about governing Numidia. The result that both Bestia and Jugurtha presumably expected is that Jugurtha would be given a good scolding and then reestablished as client king. At worst he would be forced into retirement and another relative of Masinissa would be found to rule Numidia. Either course (especially the first, given Jugurtha's demonstrated willingness to acknowledge the superiority of Roman arms) would have served Roman interests well.

But when Jugurtha's surrender was announced in the Senate, the "Numidian problem" quickly became embroiled in politics. The peace agreement made by Bestia was attacked in public speeches by the tribune Gaius Memmius, who portrayed the treaty to the Roman citizenry as a sweetheart deal cut by a dangerous rebel and corrupt senators. Memmius accused the Roman treaty makers of taking huge bribes from Jugurtha. In the atmosphere of resentment that obtained in Rome as a result of the economic squeeze on the poorer citizens, these charges carried weight. Everyone knew that a few Romans were getting very rich at the expense of the rest of society. Since senators as a class were making hay, the Senate was eager to deflect the blame away from structural flaws within the socioeconomic system. So instead, the senators externalized (and distanced themselves from) the problem by blaming the overconcentration of wealth on certain "evil men" who had taken massive bribes from Rome's foreign enemies.

As a result of Memmius's charges, Jugurtha was ordered to Rome in order that he might reveal which Romans he had bribed. Jugurtha had no option but to go.

Had Jugurtha actually bribed Bestia and other senators to support him? Sallust claims he did, but Sallust was far from objective. It is beyond doubt that Jugurtha had given various senators gifts in order to win their goodwill. If giving substantial "interested" gifts is equated with offering a bribe, Memmius's charges must be regarded as true. But Jugurtha *had* to give gifts: presenting gifts to one's patrons was part of the normal and expected behavior of the client. In some vague sense Numidia was collectively the "client state" of the State of Rome, and Jugurtha reigned as client king at the pleasure of SPQR—the Senate and People of Rome. But in Rome, politics was always personalized, and so Jugurtha became a "personal client" of various individual Romans—beginning with Scipio Aemilianus. Failing to give his individual Roman patrons the expected gifts would have been the sort of bad manners that spelled political suicide.

So how should we distinguish between a Roman client king's legitimate gift and a bribe? Presumably by asking, Did the Roman receivers of the gift/bribe act against the best interests of Rome as a result of having received it? As we have seen, keeping Jugurtha on as king of Numidia was indeed in Rome's long-term interests, and so there is no reason to suppose that the gifts offered by Jugurtha and accepted by many influential Romans should be regarded as bribes.

But this sort of rationalistic argument did not cut much ice in the fevered political climate of the late second century B.C. If Jugurtha was forced to list the recipients of his gifts, their political careers would be finished—no defense based on having looked after the national interest was likely to save them. The solution was to ensure that Jugurtha did not testify before the "ethics commission" of the Senate. When Jugurtha was called before the commission, the tribune Baebius interposed his veto. According to the ancient constitution of Rome any one of the ten tribunes elected each year could block all activity of any public agency by declaring a veto. Thus, Jugurtha did not testify. And that should have been that.

But personal ambition once again stirred up the action. One of the two consuls-elect for 110 B.C., Spurius Albinus, was eager for the kind of fame and glory (not to mention the booty) that could be won only by military victory. Bestia's campaign had shown that Numidia had the best features for an easy and lucrative victory: towns full of goods that could be looted and an "enemy" general who respected Roman military might and whose only goal was to surrender before his country was destroyed. But Jugurtha had to be made to play along—his surrender to Bestia had to be invalidated so that he could surrender to Spurius, after the latter had invaded Numidia.

Spurius found the cat's paw he needed in Massiva, one of the seemingly endless supply of Masinissa's grandsons knocking around Rome. Poor Massiva was persuaded by Spurius's minions to declare himself pretender to the Numidian throne and was promptly assassinated by one of Jugurtha's men. This was just the outcome that Spurius hoped for: Jugurtha had come to Rome under a diplomatic guarantee of safe conduct, and so was allowed to leave for Numidia. But the murder of Massiva on Roman soil was sufficient grounds to have the king of Numidia declared an enemy of Rome. Spurius was made commander of a new Roman expeditionary force to Numidia and, after some delay, successfully embarked his army in the summer of 110.

There was some sporadic fighting—the Numidians engaged in guerrilla-type mobile defense—but there were no serious battles. Once again, Jugurtha offered to surrender, but Spurius, perhaps hoping for a slightly more glorious victory, stalled until it was time for him to return to Rome in order to hold the elections (one of the civilian duties of the consuls). Spurius left the Roman army in Numidia under the command of his brother, Aulus Albinus. Spurius presumably hoped that he himself would be allowed by the Senate to continue in command of the campaign in 109, but he failed to reckon with the simultaneous ambitiousness and incompetence of his brother. Aulus attempted a daring winter offensive against

Jugurtha in January 109. Jugurtha continued his offers to surrender, but these came to naught. Eventually, Aulus's bumbling gave Jugurtha an opportunity for a counteroffensive. The Numidian army attacked Aulus's camp at night and captured most of his men.

This was a surprising turnabout, but Jugurtha did not let it go to his head. He neither killed nor tried to ransom his captives, but merely made them walk under a yoke in token of their surrender. He returned them unharmed as soon as the defeated Aulus accepted his offer of a peace treaty. Jugurtha had finally forced a Roman commander to accept the peace he had been offering all along. And that should have been that.

But back in Rome there were political repercussions. Aulus's peace treaty was declared invalid. New accusations of bribery and malfeasance were bruited about. A bill was passed by the enraged poorer citizens that called for criminal penalties against anyone who had taken bribes from Jugurtha. A new commander, Metellus, was sent to North Africa in the summer of 109 to restore discipline in the Roman army and to reopen hostilities against the hapless Jugurtha.

Jugurtha continued to play the only card he had in his hand: his offer of surrender, now on the sole condition that his life and that of his children should be spared. To show his lack of hostile intent Jugurtha kept Numidia on a peacetime footing; no military opposition was offered to Metellus's invasion force. This was not good enough for the Roman commander, who must have known that any quick acceptance of surrender would make Metellus himself the target of bribe-taking charges back in Rome. Thus, instead of opening treaty negotiations, Metellus attempted to bribe Jugurtha's envoys to assassinate their king.

Jugurtha was finally driven to fight back. All of his attempts to accomplish a peace that would be in the mutual interests of Numidia and Rome had failed, so he might as well try hostilities. The bizarre political machinations of Rome had finally transformed the cooperative client king into the rebellious threat to the Roman order that Roman propaganda demanded.

Rebellious, yes, but still not much of a threat. Jugurtha attempted a pitched battle at the river Muthul, but his light cavalry proved no match for the Roman heavy infantry. Metellus responded with a policy of terrorization; burning town after town, killing the inhabitants, destroying crops. The Roman Senate approved of these measures and voted a public thanksgiving for Metellus's successes. Jugurtha responded with a "Fabian" strategy of harassment (see Chapter 5), using his superior cavalry, but he continued to lose important towns, including Zama, site of Hannibal's only battlefield loss. Jugurtha's hit-and-run counterattacks met with very limited success.

In the winter of 109–108 Jugurtha surrendered for the third time, following the advice of his trusted lieutenant, Bomilcar, a man who had actually been "turned" by Metellus's agents. Jugurtha handed over massive quantities of war matériel, including all his elephants, many arms, and horses. But he balked at the Roman's final demand: to surrender his person with no guarantee of safety.

MARIUS

Hostilities recommenced in 108 with Metellus still at the head of the Roman forces. The Romans took more towns, a murder plot against Jugurtha by the treacherous Bomilcar failed, and Jugurtha struck an alliance with King Bocchus of Mauretania (western North Africa; Bocchus previously had been snubbed by the Romans when he offered an alliance to them). But the most significant action of the year was in the field of Roman politics.

Among Metellus's client lieutenants was Gaius Marius, a Roman from an apolitical family who had worked his way up in the ranks and had very high ambitions. Rarely did a Roman without consular ancestors attempt to gain the highest office. Worse yet, Marius failed to get his patron Metellus's support for a bid at the consulship. Ordinarily, a client would regard lack of a patron's support as closing the issue, but Roman society was changing fast. Marius realized the vast political potential of the anger of the Roman poor. Thus, he decided to ignore Metellus and go for it on his own. Marius returned to Rome, and was elected consul for 107 after bitterly attacking the privileges of the senatorial elite, including his former patron.

As consul, Marius quickly raised a large army of destitute Roman citizens, who were eager to follow their political champion into battle. The new army arrived in Numidia in the summer of 107 and Marius immediately commenced active campaigning. Like his various predecessors, Marius discovered that Numidian towns had little hope of holding out against superior Roman siege techniques. Indeed, Marius showed a special genius for siege operations, and he took several apparently unassailable fortresses by clever ruses and surprise attacks during the campaigning seasons of 107 and 106. Jugurtha could not respond effectively; his two major attacks on Marius's army ended in decisive Roman victories.

By the end of the campaigning season of 106 the Roman army was in possession of much of Numidia, but Jugurtha and his mobile forces remained at large. The Roman infantry could not hope to chase down Jugurtha's cavalry. And as long as Jugurtha remained alive, the war could not be declared a Roman victory. Despite (probably because of) ongoing Roman terror tactics, many Numidians remained loyal to the king, who found he could operate guerrilla forces even within the Roman zone of control.

Marius saw that the campaign would end only when the king had been killed or captured and decided that a trap must be set for him. Marius's lieutenant Sulla (later to be self-declared Dictator of Rome) was put in charge of the operation. Sulla's choice of bait was easy: the offer of treaty negotiations, the only goal the Jugurtha had allowed himself to hope for since the massacre at Cirta. Sulla enlisted King Bocchus of Mauretania, who had secretly gone over to the Roman side, to set the trap. Bocchus persuaded Jugurtha to come out of hiding to discuss surrender terms with Sulla. In the summer of 105 Jugurtha rode up to the agreed-upon meeting place with an unarmed entourage. Then, at a signal from Bocchus, ambush parties sprang up and cut down the defenseless Numidians. Jugurtha was captured alive and taken in chains to Rome to grace Marius's triumphal parade. And that really was that.

Or at least that was that as far as Jugurtha and the stability of the Roman client state of Numidia were concerned. The war was over and it was officially a Roman victory. But it had taken and would continue to take a nasty toll. A fair number of Roman soldiers had died in the course of the seven years, but the Romans were used to war casualties. More significant in the long run was the Jugurthine War's exacerbation of social and political tensions in Rome. The war itself had been fueled by social tensions. But it was during the Jugurthine War that open conflict between the upper and lower classes became the main driving force of Roman politics.

After the Jugurthine War, although rich senators would continue to play leading roles in Rome's political arena, they increasingly played before an audience of poor and politically restive citizen-soldiers. Marius and Sulla (who, as Dictator, set himself up as defender of the traditional prerogatives of the Roman upper classes) both got their starts in the Jugurthine War and both went on to careers that were long and liberally stained with the blood of their countrymen. Many, many more Romans died in the Civil Wars sparked by the ambitions of these two men and their supporters than died in North Africa. The Jugurthine War let the cat of overt class conflict out of the bag, and the Roman Republic was never the same again.

THE LESSON

Rome's Numidian policy from 118–105 B.C. was absurdly inconsistent. The Roman Senate meddled needlessly in client-king succession, gave up numerous chances to end the war on favorable terms, wasted the lives of Romans and Numidians alike, ruined the Numidian economy, damaged Rome's international prestige, and shattered their own sociopolitical order. So what lessons are there to be learned from this tragicomic conflict?

There are no obvious lessons for the client state. After Jugurtha made the single error of losing control of his troops at Cirta he and his people were helpless pawns—unable to affect their destiny by fighting or by surrendering. But there are serious lessons for the imperial power. First, the Romans should have learned that it was impossible to set a rational policy for the rest of the Mediterranean world while playing the game of factional politics. The system of provinces and client kingdoms had the potential to be a stable international order operating to Rome's advantage. But this happy situation could pertain only if Rome made clear the duties expected of client kings and the privileges that would be accorded to those who proved loyal. Because Rome failed to present a united front and a consistent policy to submissive and weak client states, the Romans inevitably became involved in the unnecessary foreign wars that first opened and then widened fissures in Roman society at home.

Next, the Romans should have learned to operate according to the simple rules that Clausewitz later laid out in *On War:* that war is always to be regarded as the pursuit of policy by other means and that strategy is the art of using exactly the appropriate amount of force to accomplish the ends of policy. The Romans never *had* a clear policy in Numidia. Thus, they never had a rational strategy for winning the war. As a result they poured a massive amount of military force into the region and accomplished worse than nothing.

Finally, the Romans should have learned that when imperialist wars materially benefit one small segment of society and hurt the great majority of citizens, and moreover when the members of the armed forces who must fight the imperial wars are recruited from the disadvantaged majority, there will be the very devil to pay. The Romans began to pay during the Jugurthine War, but their social debts kept accumulating for another eighty years. The big payment came due in the frightful bloodbath of the Civil Wars.

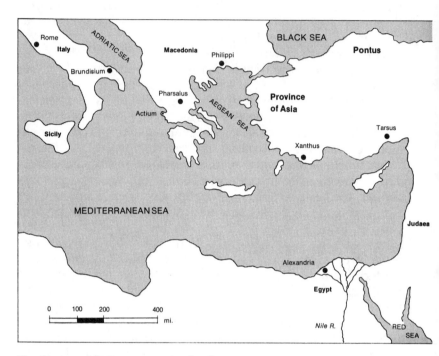

The Eastern Mediterranean in the first century B.C.

Armenia

Tigris R.

Parthians

Syria   Euphrates R.

Arabia

Chapter 7

Mark Antony:
The Man Who
Would Be Caesar

THE PERIOD 105 TO 44 B.C., between the end of the Jugurthine War and the death of Julius Caesar, saw both the continued expansion of Rome's imperial power and the continued decay of her social and political system at home. The greatest imperial growth came in Gaul (modern France). Caesar's spectacularly successful wars in Gaul added vast regions to Rome's provincial holdings. Meanwhile, more and more of Spain was pacified; exploratory raids were sent into Germany and Britain. Several new provinces were added in Anatolia. In the Near East, Syria became a province and elsewhere in the eastern region Rome was universally acknowledged as the patron state. The Province of Africa grew in size to encompass much of Numidia. By the late 40s, the greatest quasi-independent power left in the Mediterranean world was Egypt, which owed its continued existence to Rome's benevolence.

Marius was uncontested leader of Rome for several years after the Jugurthine War, and he spent much of this time fighting against genuinely dangerous incursions by Germanic tribes in the north. Despite his successes in the field, Marius's political career collapsed when he was forced by events to use his veterans to suppress one of his own political allies in 99 B.C. Much of the serious fighting of this era came in what amounted to civil wars: Roman armies fought uprisings of slaves in Sicily and Italy. The Italian allies finally had enough of fighting to gain an empire they benefited little from, and seceded from the confederacy in 90 B.C. Under Sulla's leadership they were defeated (88 B.C.), but in the course of the war Rome offered the allies what they had been demanding for a long time, Roman citizenship. This Italian war was immediately followed by a war in Greece against the client king Mithradates, and this campaign segued into a civil war in Italy between Roman forces loyal to Marius (and his friends) and the forces loyal to Sulla. The latter won out, and established himself as Dictator in 82 B.C. An uneasy interim period of relative peace was followed by renewed civil wars (49–45 B.C.) when Caesar's political enemies in Rome attempted to recall him from Gaul. Caesar won that war, named himself Dictator, and was promptly assassinated. The Civil Wars began anew. By the late 40s B.C. the main question in Roman politics was no longer whether the republic could survive intact, but rather which great warrior/politician would succeed in claiming personal possession of the empire for himself and his family.

THE BATTLE OF PHILIPPI

On an October day in 42 B.C., near the Greek town of Philippi, two armies, both Roman, were preparing for combat. Everyone knew that the fighting would be nasty: for the legionaries this would not be the hot knife through butter of skirmishes with untrained barbarians, but the clash of battle-hardened Roman veteran against veteran. The arms and training of the men on both sides were identical; they all used the same battle cries, knew the same thrusts and parries, had the same weak spots. A lot of Roman blood was about to be shed, and why? To answer the burning question, Who would be master of Rome's world empire?

For the second time in a decade, that question would be answered on the plains of northern Greece. Just six years before, in 48 B.C., Julius Caesar had defeated his rival Gnaeus Pompey at Pharsalus in Thessaly and had gone on to become Rome's Dictator for Life. This proud and controversial assumption of power eventually led to Caesar's assassination on the Ides of March, 44 B.C. Now, outside Philippi, Caesar's assassins—the self-styled Liberators, Gaius Cassius and Marcus Junius Brutus—were confronted by the armies of Caesar's would-be avengers. The avengers were led by Marcus Antonius (Antony), a man who had been the Dictator's most trusted lieutenant, and Gaius Julius Caesar Octavianus (Octavian), Caesar's adopted son and heir.

Brutus and Cassius claimed to be tyrant-slayers who, by killing a would-be king, had acted to uphold the traditional liberties of the Roman Republic. "Death to the king" was a powerful ideological slogan in first century B.C. Rome. The republic had been established half a millennium before (ca. 509 B.C.), when the Roman elite, led by one of Brutus's distant ancestors, revolted against Tarquin the Proud, an Etruscan puppet-king. Brutus and Cassius asserted that by killing Caesar they had been defending the free republic against autocratic monarchy. But, on the other side, Antony and Octavian contended that they were avenging Caesar's bloody murder in the name of friendship and kinship—and these were compelling motives recognized as legitimate by all Romans. Furthermore, the late Dictator had been extremely popular with the Roman poor (that is to say, the overwhelming majority of the citizens) and with the veterans. Caesar's death at the hands of men he had believed were his friends (some even whispered that Brutus was his illegitimate son) had shocked Roman soldier and civilian alike.

So, when the two opposing Roman armies squared off

at Philippi, both sides had a cause to fight for—the generals on either side could rouse their troops with the vision of fighting for a higher ideal. And, on a power-politics level, the stakes were extraordinarily high. The men who emerged as victors from the fields of Philippi would be the rulers of Rome and this meant they would be masters of most of the known world. The Roman Empire, a worthy successor to the Persian Empire of the sixth and fifth centuries B.C., now stretched from Syria to Spain, from France to North Africa.

The stakes were high for the individual foot soldiers, too. Civil war was a dangerous business. Fighting one's fellow legionaries was much more hazardous than chopping down disorganized mobs of barbarians. But the victorious troops who survived expected very generous rewards from their generals. That reward could be fat enough to get a man out of military service for good; the capital he won as battle bonus might allow the civil war soldier to buy a farm and build a real life for his family. Thus, in the conflicts that followed Caesar's death, raw lust for absolute power and personal self-interest were inextricably mixed up with high principles and ideology. The man who could blend power, greed, and values in the right proportions—who could persuade most Romans that their interests and his were identical, and that those interests were within the framework of traditional Roman ideals—that man would come out the final winner in the Civil Wars and would be rightful heir to Caesar's mantle.

There were three highly skilled, experienced generals at Philippi. Brutus, Cassius, and Antony had seen years of service at various levels in Rome's armies. All three had held major military commands in an earlier stage of the Civil Wars (49–45 B.C.)—the period of conflict that had secured control of the empire for Caesar. Brutus and Cassius had served as senior officers in Pompey's forces, but had been pardoned by Caesar after his victory; and he had given both men positions in his own new government. Antony had been Caesar's right hand throughout much of the Civil War; he had been chosen because of his strategic, diplomatic, and administrative skills, and for his proven ability to inspire the troops. Antony had begun his career as a dashing and successful cavalry commander in Rome's eastern provinces. Later he had served for several years under Caesar in Gaul, earning the general's respect. As tribune in 49 B.C. Antony had used the veto to defend Caesar's political interests in Rome; he had rejoined Caesar's forces immediately upon the outbreak of the Civil War. During the period 49–47 he served Caesar well in both administrative and military capacities: he saw action in the early Italian campaign, held Rome for Caesar during the first Spanish campaign, and commanded Caesar's left wing at the decisive battle of Pharsalus.

Octavian was the only one of the four commanders at Philippi who could not boast of much in the way of a military background. He had been an eighteen-year-old schoolboy when, in 44 B.C., he received word that Caesar had been assassinated and that he was the primary heir. The two years between Caesar's death and Octavian's arrival on the plains of Philippi had matured him fast. He had even led soldiers against Antony a year ago, before they had decided to join forces against the "Liberators." But Octavian was too young to have gone through the long years of service as a junior officer that was an ordinary part of the "post-graduate" education of every senatorial-class Roman male. Octavian did not appear to be a natural warrior, either. His health was poor, and he tended to come down with sudden and debilitating bouts of sickliness on the morning before a battle was to be fought.

As it turned out, it took two battles, several weeks apart, on the plains of Philippi to decide the issue. Cassius's camp was captured in the first engagement and Cassius committed suicide before word came that Brutus's forces were still intact. Brutus soon followed his colleague's morbid example, after being beaten in the second battle. With this second victory Antony and Octavian became masters of Rome. Caesar's lieutenant and adopted son could toast each other on their joint success, but many Romans knew that both victories at Philippi were the product of the military leadership skills of a single commander—Antony. Octavian had sat out the battles in his tent; his habitual combat-day ill health prevented him from taking an active role in either engagement.

It did not take a crystal ball for a contemporary observer to foresee that the alliance between Antony and Octavian would not last for long. The two men were radically different in their personalities and tastes: Antony was a hard-drinking womanizer who loved a wild party and the rough male company of the military camp; Octavian appeared to be almost ascetic in his tastes, at least by Roman standards. But, more important, each man hoped to don the mantle of Caesar, and each believed he had a legitimate claim to it: Antony on the basis of his proven ability and years of loyal service at Caesar's side, Octavian on the basis of his adoption and inheritance. Neither man really believed that Rome could have more than one master, and each was determined that he would someday be that one.

In the aftermath of the battles of Philippi, Rome's political pundits were surely giving pretty long odds against Octavian's chances. After all, Antony had what it took to be a successful civil warrior: cunning, administrative ability, connections with powerful men in Rome and throughout the empire, and above all military prowess. Octavian was still just a boy, with none of Antony's proven skills—except, perhaps, cunning. It was to his credit that he had survived the last few years, but all he really had was a name: after his adoption Octavian had taken his new father's name and was officially called Gaius Julius Caesar (he tended to drop the cognomen Octavianus, since it reminded people of his less distinguished natural parent).

The famous name was all Octavian had to go on and our hypothetical tough-minded, realistic political pundits might well ask, "What's in a name?" A lot, as it turned out. Eleven years after the battles of Philippi, Antony lay dead by his own hand, defeated in battle by Octavian and abandoned by most of his troops. Octavian was hailed by civilians and soldiers alike as the savior of the Roman state; he would spend the next half century establishing himself—in fact, though not in name—as the first true emperor of Rome. Caesar's mantle, the Romans found, fit Octavian's shoulders pretty well.

THE LATE REPUBLIC

To understand how Antony, with all his apparent advantages, could have lost to Octavian, with all his apparent disabilities, we must jump back in time, to the late republic: the era of social and political upheaval that followed in the wake of the wars between Jugurtha and Rome. Late republican Rome was ruled by a small elite of well-connected senators who were dependent on the loyalty of the Roman legions, but were increasingly out of touch with the rest of the Roman citizenry. The senators were hugely wealthy. Most Romans were miserably poor. The old class of independent farmers that had long been the backbone of the Roman citizen army was by now largely destroyed. In the late republic the ordinary Roman citizen was likely to be a sharecropper at best, a jobless resident of Rome's urban slums at worst. The urban citizen's main concern was with simple survival: neither food nor shelter was easy to come by. Living conditions in Rome's burgeoning slums were abysmal, and most citizens had little hope that conditions would soon improve. In the late republic all political processes—and especially elections—became more and more corrupt, chaotic, and violent. Bread-and-rent riots and campaign demonstrations were intermixed as clever politicians used the ordinary people's rage and misery to further their own political careers.

Since the war against Jugurtha the Roman army had become, for all intents and purposes, an army of mercenaries. The legionaries were being drawn from the poorest citizen classes: sons and grandsons of the displaced farmers who had lost their land to greedy senators. The Roman soldier of the first century B.C. had a much more

tenuous connection to the Roman State than had the soldiers in the time of the Hannibalic War. The old-time Roman soldier had fought for homeland and homestead.
The late Republican soldier fought for pay, because it was
the only job he could get. His prime loyalty was to the
commander who paid him and whose tactical skills kept
him alive, rather than to the state of which he was a citizen and which he had been hired to defend. The late republican soldier's main goal was to use his period of
military service to raise a grubstake that might allow him
to buy a farm—and thus return to the independent existence his ancestors had enjoyed.

The soldier's general disaffection with the senator-dom-
inated government and his desire for a lump sum of cash
were key factors in the outbreak of the Civil Wars that
raged for much of the first century B.C. Marius's lieutenant, Sulla, had taken advantage of the soldiers' loose attachment to republican institutions to seize control of the
Roman government in 82 B.C.: he persuaded the men under his command to help him overthrow the existing government by promising to pay them big bonuses as soon as
the victory had been won. Sulla established himself as
Dictator and used his position to attempt to turn the clock
back. He hoped to put an end to the Civil Wars by in-
stituting a very conservative political order in which a senate stacked with his own partisans was all-powerful. But
Sulla failed to deal with the root problems of highly unequal wealth distribution and so he failed to create a stable
political order. After his death in 78 B.C. the chaotic power
struggles began anew and Sulla's political heirs used the
tools he had forged with deadly efficiency.

The most successful civil warrior of the mid–first century B.C. was Julius Caesar himself. After proving his battlefield skills as a junior officer Caesar was elected consul
(59 B.C.). As consul he employed a network of political
alliances with other powerful senators to gain himself a
long-term command in Gaul. During his nine years campaigning in Gaul, Germany, and Britain (58–50 B.C.) Caesar gained a well-deserved reputation as the republic's

greatest living general. Meanwhile, he developed a special rapport with his troops; they would follow him anywhere, in the secure knowledge that Caesar would lead them to final victory.

Caesar's enemies in the Senate managed to have his Gallic command terminated in 49 B.C., and they recalled Caesar to Rome to face trumped-up legal charges. This meant war: Caesar was not one to put peace above his personal honor. He crossed the Rubicon River into Italy with a small army and won quick victories over his opponents. Led by Caesar's old friend and recent enemy Pompey, most of the senators fled to Greece. Pompey had contacts in the East and friends in the West. He supposed that he could catch Caesar in a pincers movement between Roman armies loyal to himself stationed in Spain and his own forces in Greece. But Caesar made a lightning campaign into Spain that neutralized the western threat to his position. He then pursued Pompey into Greece where the victory at Pharsalus clinched control of the Roman State for Caesar.

After a couple of years of mopping-up operations around the empire, a period during which he confirmed Cleopatra VII as queen of Egypt (and fathered a son by her), Caesar returned to Rome. He refused to have himself declared king, but he was a monarch in all but name—there was not much to choose between king and Dictator for Life. Caesar's blunt manner and unwillingness to play what he saw as an empty game of constitutionality led to anger and frustration among the senators, many of whom Caesar had pardoned. They demanded their traditional prerogatives; when Caesar showed himself unwilling to dance to the intricate patterns of precedence and deference so dear to their hearts, a group of senators formed a conspiracy and assassinated him.

The death of Caesar (March 15, 44 B.C.) left Rome in chaos. Cassius, Brutus, and the other "liberators" had formed no coherent plan for what would come after the Dictator's demise. Apparently they naively supposed that

Rome's business would automatically return to normal: senators running everything and skimming off the cream of the empire; the poor unhappy but disorganized; the soldiers unhappy but loyal to their senatorial commanders. In fact there could be no quick return to normalcy. Not enough Romans had any real stake in a return to the conditions that had pertained before Caesar crossed the Rubicon, conditions that had benefited only elite senators and other wealthy Romans.

TRIUMVIRS

The years following Caesar's assassination are very well documented in the ancient sources, and very complex. A number of powerful men in Rome were each maneuvering to further his own and his friends' interests, and each attempting to do in his enemies. A large contingent of senators hoped vainly for a return to the old order. Antony initially cooperated with them, but he soon realized that he could do better by striking out on his own. The funeral of Caesar, attended by a huge and unruly mob of poor citizens and veterans, demonstrated that the Dictator had been immensely popular with the lower classes in Rome. Antony used the occasion of the funeral speech (made famous by Shakespeare: "I come to bury Caesar, not to praise him") to link himself directly with the fallen Dictator's memory, and to distance himself from most of the senators.

Meanwhile, Octavian had arrived in Rome, at the head of a pick-up army of Caesar's veterans. He had been in school in Greece when he got the news that his adoptive father had been killed. The safe course would have been to continue his studies, but Octavian had immediately taken ship for Italy to claim his legacy. He docked at Brundisium, the main port of the "heel" of Italy. As Octavian rode up the Appian Way toward Rome the rumor spread that the new "Gaius Julius Caesar" had returned to claim his patrimony. Octavian was soon joined by numerous veterans whom Caesar had settled on new-bought farms in southern Italy. These veterans remembered their commander fondly and were more than happy to provide Caesar's son and namesake with a proper entourage. Thus the young heir arrived in Rome with an army (or a group of men who could very soon become an army) at his back, and he was a force to be reckoned with.

Antony and Octavian soon quarreled. Antony saw the young man as a threat to his position as Caesar's logical successor. Octavian was angry because Antony had taken control of Caesar's papers and was withholding payment of Octavian's inheritance. The situation was tense, violence inevitable. The next phase of the Civil Wars began when Antony broke openly with the Senate and took an army to northern Italy to fight one of Marcus Brutus's brothers for control of Gaul and the recruiting grounds of northern Italy. In 43 B.C. the Senate declared Antony a public enemy and dispatched both of the year's consuls against him.

Octavian was still around and the senators figured him for the perfect foil against Antony. They planned, in the words of one of their leaders, to "praise him, use him, and discard him." Despite his youth and lack of experience, Octavian was given the high military rank of propraetor and he marched out with the consular armies at the head of his veteran volunteers. Fortuitously, both consuls were quickly killed in indecisive battles with Antony's forces. Octavian, never one to put himself in harm's way in combat situations, lived—and took command of the entire republican army. He marched back to Rome and was made consul. Although he was less than half the minimum legal age for the consulship the senators were not about to debate the matter with the legions under his command.

The Senate now hoped for a final confrontation between Antony and Octavian. But the two men were survivors, and too clever to exhaust themselves and their forces in a struggle that would benefit only their mutual enemies. A premature war between Antony and Octavian would turn over control of Rome to the Liberator faction. So, rather than fight, Antony and Octavian joined forces. Along with Marcus Aemilius Lepidus, a Roman general who had just arrived from Spain with an army of veterans, Caesar's foremost lieutenant and his adopted son formed a Triumvirate that united the military and political clout of the pro-Caesar faction.

The triumvirs collectively controlled most of the armies of the western empire, and thus they controlled the city of Rome and its government. Their first public act was to initiate a political bloodbath. The triumvirs purged the Senate of all the vocal opponents of Caesar and his friends—beginning with all their own personal enemies. The confiscated estates of the purged were sold to build up the triumvirs' war chest. This cash base was needed to secure triumviral control of the eastern empire. Brutus and Cassius had fled Rome some time before, and they had used their connections in the East to raise a large army. Lepidus was left to look after Italy; Antony and Octavian marched east, to meet and beat the Liberators on the fields of Philippi.

Philippi secured the whole of the empire for the triumvirs, but the question remained: How were they going to administer it? There was no love lost among any of the three; as in the case of Jugurtha and his cousins, a truly cooperative junta was out of the question. Instead, the triumvirs divided the empire into three spheres of influence. Although initially accused by his colleagues of conspiracy, Lepidus was grudgingly given control of the Province of Africa. The bulk of the empire was divided between the two victors of Philippi. Octavian took Italy and most of the western provinces. Antony took all of the East—Greece, Syria, and the Province of Asia—and also kept Gaul as a foothold in the West.

Which of the two competitors got the best deal? Despite the central position of Italy and the importance of the city of Rome, Antony probably felt that he had grabbed the lion's share. The East was rich, populous, and urbanized. There were thousands of veterans settled in colonies throughout the eastern empire, so access to recruiting grounds would be no problem. Furthermore, the East offered the greatest opportunity for glorious feats of arms. With the Gauls beaten, Rome's foremost military challenge was the Parthians of Mesopotamia.

The Parthians were the political heirs of the Achaemenid Persians: an Iranian-speaking military aristocracy that had taken over Mesopotamia from the Greek successors of Alexander. The Parthian horsemen were extremely skilled at mobile desert warfare, and they had successfully resisted Roman imperial thrusts at Mesopotamia. One of Rome's greatest military disasters had been suffered at the hands of the Parthians. Marcus Licinius Crassus, a sometime political ally of Caesar, had led a gigantic legionary army against the Parthians in 54 B.C. Crassus's army was cut to ribbons by the Parthian mounted archers; Crassus himself was killed, most of the army annihilated, and his legionary standards lost. This blow to Rome's military prestige cried out for revenge.

The man who punished the Parthians and added Mesopotamia to the empire would be the hero of the Roman world. Caesar himself had planned a Mesopotamian campaign, but was assassinated before he could launch it. Antony figured to pick up where Caesar had left off. Victory against the Parthians would give Antony the edge he needed when it came time to finish off his rivals. There was a good precedent: Sulla had seized Rome and made himself absolute master of the state after a notable series of victories in the East.

So, as senior partner in the Triumvirate, Antony probably chose the East deliberately, as a wealthy power base that could provide the opportunity for the outstanding victory that would make him Caesar's natural successor in the eyes of the Romans. But in order to fight the Parthians Antony would need a very large army of skilled Roman soldiers. That army must be prepared to fight for several years—beating the Parthians on their own turf would take time. And keeping a large army in the field for a long time meant that Antony needed a great deal of money.

Traditionally Roman commanders raised funds by squeezing the provinces. Antony had extensive provincial territories under his command, and his tax collectors raised a good deal of money from them. But extorting great amounts of cash from an area he intended to use as his long-term base had drawbacks—notably it made the provincials resentful and rebellious. There was the danger of killing the golden egg–laying goose if the squeezing was too harsh. For example, the Liberators had squeezed the East very hard indeed to raise their armies and there had been some ugly incidents. The most extreme case was Xanthus (near the Anatolian southwest coast), whose population had fought Brutus to the end and had committed mass suicide rather than put up with his extortionate demands. When the eastern provincials began to protest the rigor with which Antony's men were raising funds, the triumvir took pause. The last thing Antony needed was a provincial uprising on his hands. Everyone remembered the revolt of 88 B.C. in the Province of Asia (western Anatolia). That uprising, sparked by King Mithridates of Pontus (northern Anatolia), had led to the mass slaughter of tens of thousands of Romans and had taken years of hard fighting to put down.

If one hesitated to squeeze the provincials, there was an alternative means of raising cash: convincing rulers of client states to foot the bill. Unfortunately, though, Antony needed the active cooperation of Judaea and the other client kingdoms of the Near East to provide logistical support for his Parthian-campaign invasion forces; their rulers could hardly be expected to foot the whole bill for Antony's army—not if Antony hoped to keep their loyalty. But Antony knew one ruler of a major eastern client state who was vastly wealthy and whose state was not on the "front line" of the Parthian invasion route. Antony had first met her years ago in Alexandria, during his youthful career as a cavalry commander. Later, when she had visited Rome as Caesar's mistress, the acquaintance was renewed. Rumor had it that she had backed the wrong horse before Philippi, by secretly helping the Liberators.

Now she should be all the more eager to make monetary amends to the victor, the man who had avenged the murder of her former lover. Thus Cleopatra, Queen of Egypt, was summoned to meet Antony the Triumvir at Tarsus in southeastern Anatolia.

CLEOPATRA

In 41 B.C. Cleopatra was twenty-eight years old, the age, according to Antony's biographer Plutarch, "when a woman's beauty is at its most superb and her mind at its most mature." Cleopatra had been queen of Egypt since 51 B.C.; she was an expert at murderous intrigue (she had recently assassinated her consort), the veteran of savage Egyptian civil wars (she once smuggled herself through enemy lines wrapped in an Oriental rug), an astute diplomat, and was fluent in several languages. The queen had needed all of her considerable intelligence, wealth, and charm to steer Egypt on the difficult course between groveling obsequiousness to Rome and the excessive independence that would invite a takeover.

Egypt had always been an attractive prize: the richest piece of real estate in the ancient world because of the great agricultural production made possible by the Nile's annual flooding. Since Egypt's conquest by Alexander the Great, the country had been ruled by a Greco-Macedonian elite. Cleopatra was a worthy descendant and successor to Alexander's general, Ptolemy I, who had declared himself king of Egypt after Alexander's death. For almost three hundred years Ptolemy's descendants had fought to keep Egypt independent. So far they had succeeded; the line of Ptolemies had already outlived all the other major kingdoms founded by Alexander's ambitious generals. Like her royal ancestors, Cleopatra was determined to maintain Egypt's status as an independent power in the eastern Mediterranean. But she had her work cut out for her: many Romans saw wealthy Egypt as an overripe plum

204 THE ANATOMY OF ERROR

that was ready for plucking. As Jugurtha had learned, Rome was very demanding to client rulers.

Faced with Rome's Civil Wars, Cleopatra had realized early on that neutrality was impossible. The Roman victor of each stage of the Civil Wars would see a client's neutrality as treason, and that would be all the excuse he needed to turn Egypt into a Roman province. Cleopatra also confronted the problem of the endless political intrigues in Alexandria; if another Egyptian civil war were to break out, the ruler of Egypt needed to be able to depend on Roman intervention on the right side. Thus, in 48 B.C. Cleopatra had thrown in with Caesar, and had gained his close support. When she had a son by Caesar she named him Ptolemy Caesarion and not merely for sentimental reasons—the boy would be the living insurance of the Dictator of Rome's interest in protecting the queen of Egypt. Caesar's death had been a nasty blow to Cleopatra's plans—it meant she would have to choose another Roman as patron, and in 44–42 B.C. it was tough to guess who would come out on top. Maybe she hedged her bets; this would explain the rumors that she had aided Brutus and Cassius.

After Philippi the situation was a good deal clearer. Antony had emerged as the senior partner in the Triumvirate and he was likely to be the master of the Roman East for the foreseeable future. He wanted to be Caesar; enter Cleopatra, who had an intimate connection to the late great Dictator. And happily for Cleopatra, Antony had a reputation as a man who loved the good life and who was susceptible to feminine charms. Clearly he was the right man to step into Caesar's role as protector of Egypt and thus into the bed of Egypt's queen. When the expected message came, requiring Cleopatra's attendance upon the triumvir at Tarsus, she was ready.

Plutarch describes Cleopatra's arrival at Tarsus:

> She came sailing up the river Cydnus in a barge with a golden deck, its purple sails billowing in the wind, while her rowers caressed the water with sil-

ver oars which dipped in time to the music of the
flute, accompanied by pipes and lutes. Cleopatra
herself reclined beneath a canopy of gold cloth,
dressed in the character of Venus. . . . Antony
awaited the Queen enthroned on his tribunal . . .
and the word spread on every side that Venus
[goddess of love] had come to cavort with Bacchus
[god of wine] for the happiness of Asia.

One thing led to the next: a series of sumptuous dinner
parties was held; Cleopatra was pardoned on the charge
of pro-Liberator treason; Antony agreed to the assassination of Cleopatra's sister, a possible rival for the Egyptian
throne; the decision was made that Antony would spend
the winter of 41–40 b.c. in Alexandria, as Cleopatra's personal guest. They became lovers by that winter and
Cleopatra bore Antony's twins (a boy and a girl) the next
fall.

So began the most famous love story in ancient history.
But it is important to keep in mind that the affair was
grounded in a firm foundation of political pragmatism and
personal self-interest on both sides. Antony needed a reliable non-Roman supply of cash to pay his army;
Cleopatra needed a reliable Roman patron to ensure
Egyptian independence. Antony and Cleopatra were both
seasoned survivors of some of the toughest games of political hardball the world has ever witnessed. There is no
reason to suppose that they did not sincerely respect, ad-
mire, and care for each other, but their love affair sprang
from a recognition of their mutual interest, not from an
uncontrollable adolescent passion.

WARS EAST AND WEST

Antony did not wait around Alexandria for his children to
be born. Indeed it would be several years before he was to
see Cleopatra again. In the meantime he had wars to fight
and diplomatic intrigues to deal with. The Parthians had

stolen a march on Antony by a two-pronged attack on the Roman provinces of Asia and Syria. Meanwhile, barbarian Illyrians had invaded the Province of Macedonia. In Italy serious trouble had broken out between Octavian and Antony's relatives—including Antony's brother, Lucius, and his wife, Fulvia. Like Cleopatra, Fulvia was well connected (she had been married to the civil warriors Clodius and Curio before Antony) and a tough faction fighter (she had personally supervised the mutilation of the corpse of one of Antony's rivals). Fulvia intended to challenge Octavian for the control of Italy. But Antony himself was far from ready for an armed confrontation with his fellow triumvirs. In spring of 40 B.C. Antony left the wars in the East to his lieutenants and returned to Italy to settle matters with his erstwhile political partners.

While Antony was raising troops and money in the East, Octavian had his own troubles in the West. The worst problem he faced immediately after Philippi was settling the Civil War veterans. The triumvirs had disbanded some 30 legions—around 100,000 men. Most of the veterans wanted farms in Italy and that meant that many current occupants had to be displaced. The veterans would accept no excuses from their former commander, and the land confiscations stirred up widespread anger against Caesar's heir. That anger was fanned to outright rebellion by Lucius Antonius and Fulvia, who raised an army and temporarily seized Rome. Octavian fought back, aided by Marcus Agrippa, his main military adviser. Agrippa recaptured Rome, besieged Lucius and Fulvia in northern Italy, and soon starved them out. Had the revolt been inspired by Antony himself? This seems very unlikely, since the triumvir did not show up in Italy until after his relatives had been suppressed by Octavian. More likely Lucius and Fulvia were engaging in the sort of free-lance conspiring that made the late republican period so complex, both for participants and for historians.

When Antony and a small force arrived at Brundisium, troops loyal to Octavian tried to prevent him from coming ashore. Antony was furious; he forced a landing and oc-

cupied southern Italy. It looked as if a renewal of the Civil
Wars was certain. But neither side was ready. A deal was
struck which confirmed the main East-West split between
Octavian and Antony as well as Lepidus's possession of
Africa. To seal the deal Antony now married Octavian's
sister, Octavia (Fulvia had conveniently died in the meantime). Antony and Octavia set up their base in Athens, a
position from which Antony could coordinate the wars
against the Parthians and Illyrians and simultaneously
keep an eye on his brother-in-law.

Meanwhile Octavian had a major military problem on
his hands: Sextus Pompey, last surviving son of Caesar's
old rival, had united the fragmentary opposition to the
triumvirs. Sextus raised a war fleet and seized control of
Sardinia and Sicily. This was serious—Sextus's sea power
and control of the two islands threatened Rome's grain
supply. Without massive and constant imports, much of
the tremendous (about 750,000) urban population of Rome
would soon starve. Grain prices soared as speculators began hoarding against a famine. The situation demanded
decisive military action, but this was not Octavian's strong
suit. A preliminary naval battle ended in a disastrous defeat for the triumviral forces and Sextus Pompey magnilo-
quently proclaimed himself "son of Neptune." Octavian
was faced with the prospect of uncontrollable rioting that
would lose him the faith of upper and lower classes alike.
There was nothing the Roman poor feared more than
grain shortages and nothing the rich feared more than the
poor.

Agrippa pulled Octavian's chestnuts from the fire. A
brilliant commander and, unique for the period, completely loyal and free of individual ambition, Agrippa
raised and trained a fleet. He also arranged a troops-for-
ships exchange with Antony. Octavian now had the
forces and the admiral he needed to beat the self-styled
son of Neptune. After several indecisive naval engagements Sextus staked all on a mass battle off the coast of
Sicily—some 300 warships were engaged on each side
and at the end of the day Agrippa had won a great victory

in the name of "Gaius Julius Caesar." But a complication quickly arose. Lepidus, moving up from Africa, had occupied the western half of Sicily and now, with the support of defectors from Sextus, challenged Octavian for control of Sicily. Faced with this crisis, Octavian showed that even if he was not a heroic battlefield commander, he was nonetheless a brave man. He sneaked into Lepidus's camp and proclaimed his presence to Lepidus's men. He had only the name going for him, but that was enough. Many of Lepidus's men were Caesar's veterans and they flocked to his son's standard. Lepidus, now a general without an army, was stripped of his triumviral powers; the field was left to be contested by only two men.

Octavian was the hero of Italy. By sinking Sextus Pompey he had ensured the food supply of the poor and the security of the rich. The man who had successfully played the roles of "savior of Italy," "guarantor of the grain," and "averter of social revolution" added luster to his image by clearing the Adriatic of pirates and engaging in some showy military campaigns in Dalmatia to Italy's northeast. Meanwhile, in Rome, his lieutenants began a great building program and restored ancient temples. Eastern religious practices were banned in the city. Octavian was already preparing himself for his greatest and most enduring role: "defender of the traditional Roman order."

While Octavian was winning glory in the war against Sextus Pompey, Antony was having a tough time against the Parthians. By 38 B.C. his lieutenants had successfully pushed the Illyrians out of Macedon and the Parthians out of Syria and the Province of Asia, but there had been troubles with client kings—some had actually welcomed the Parthian incursions, perhaps because they distrusted the stability of Rome in the era of the Civil Wars. Antony had hesitated to launch the great crusade against the Parthians; Octavian was not a trustworthy partner and there had been a series of slights and insults. The troops that were supposed to come east in exchange for the ships Antony had dispatched for the war against Sextus Pompey never showed up. In 37 B.C. Antony sent the pregnant Octavia back to Italy, ostensibly for her health. It was high time to initiate the Parthian war that would ensure Antony's reputation as Rome's greatest commander.

Antony moved his base of operations to Syria, where he gathered an army of some 60,000 men. Cleopatra, his all-important paymaster, joined him at the city of Antioch. Antony now acknowledged his children by Cleopatra and used his triumviral authority to extend the queen's domains in the Near East. Viewed in isolation, Antony's favors to Cleopatra in this period could be read as the foolish acts of an infatuated man, but in fact they were part and parcel of a comprehensive reorganization of the eastern client kingdoms. In the spring of 36, while Octavian was moving in on Sextus Pompey, Antony launched his long-delayed invasion of Mesopotamia.

The two-year Parthian campaign was a failure. The terrain itself was very difficult. Antony had chosen a reasonable route for the invasion of Mesopotamia, through the northern client kingdom of Armenia. But the invasion bogged down when, owing to the laxity (or treachery) of the Armenian king, the Parthians were able to destroy Antony's siege train. Without artillery Antony was unable to capture key strongholds and Roman infantry proved unequal to the Parthian cavalry in a mobile war. With the army bogged down in Mesopotamia, Roman logistics began to break down. Antony's forces sustained extensive losses and only his undiminished leadership skills enabled the general to extricate the remainder of his troops and so to avoid a total disaster of the sort suffered previously by Crassus and later by the emperor Julian (Chapter 8). Mesopotamia remained in Parthian hands, although Antony took over Armenia in retaliation for the Armenian king's lackluster support. Antony returned to Egypt where he celebrated a hollow Triumph for his Armenian victory. The campaign had not gained him the heroic stature he had sought. Antony had staked a lot on winning big in Parthia; now he would have to face the consequences of having failed to live up to the expectations he had raised among his countrymen.

A BATTLE OF IMAGES

By 33 B.C. it was increasingly clear that the two remaining triumvirs would soon come to blows, and both prepared for the conflict by launching propaganda campaigns. From Egypt Antony declared Ptolemy Caesarion to be Julius Caesar's legitimate son, and thereby challenged Octavian's right to call himself Caesar's heir. But Octavian had much more promising materials to work with and proved himself to be a master at the art of the political smear.

Octavian sought to portray the power struggle between Antony and himself as a conflict between two antithetical cultures. On the one hand there was Rome, led by Octavian, the defender of the Roman order. In the war against Sextus, in his subsequent military campaigns in Dalmatia, and in his civil improvement programs Octavian had succeeded in casting himself in the role of an old-fashioned Roman leader. He emphasized his own traditionalism by refusing to renew his (or Antony's) triumviral powers when they officially lapsed in 33. The people of Italy were suitably grateful to their defender and in a "spontaneous" gesture of support the communities of Italy swore an oath to support Octavian against Rome's enemies. The oath ceremony had no doubt been carefully stage-managed by Octavian's lieutenants, but the gesture was impressive nonetheless. It provided a powerful *image* of old-fashioned patronage, loyalty, and constitutionality. Octavian was clever enough to realize that the final winner of the Civil Wars would be the man who could project the right image.

Ranged against Rome and the defender of Roman tradition there was (in Octavian's propaganda) the evil of the East. Cleopatra was the perfect foil for Octavian. Roman political culture was starkly patriarchal, and the strong, self-willed, sexually aggressive, ambitious woman was the stuff of Roman men's ugliest nightmares. Not only was

Cleopatra an unsuitable woman, she was an eastern Greek woman. There was a deep strain of xenophobia in the Roman psychological makeup, and that xenophobia tended to focus on the Greek East. The Romans had learned a lot from the Greeks, but they did not like to admit it. Eastern and Greek meant, to traditional Romans, everything that was sneaky, subtle, clever, and incomprehensible. Octavian's propaganda machine mixed misogyny with xenophobia and claimed that Cleopatra planned to overthrow the Republic, make herself Queen of the World, and establish her capital at Rome itself!

In Octavian's propaganda Antony became a pathetic victim, the degenerate love-slave of a malevolent eastern witch. This portrayal of his rival conveniently dealt with the sticky problem of why Octavian was preparing to make war on his old comrade in arms, the trusted lieutenant of Julius Caesar. Because of Cleopatra's nefarious influence, Antony was no longer the good old Antony of Philippi days. He had been corrupted by Cleopatra's deviant eastern ways: she had turned the brave soldier of the Republic into a depraved reprobate. Solid proof was produced to substantiate this slanted portrait: not only had Antony formally divorced his long-suffering and loyal wife Octavia, but his will (left for safekeeping with the Vestal Virgins, and now seized by Octavian) indicated that he hoped to be buried next to Cleopatra! Antony, according to his opponent, had lost his Roman soul. The commander of Rome's armies in the East was an animate zombie controlled by a power-mad sorceress-queen.

The war that Octavian ultimately launched was not officially directed against his old friend Antony, but against Cleopatra, the incarnate evil of the sinister East. It was just the sort of righteous and heroic crusade that Antony had hoped to lead against the Parthians, but Octavian had the advantage of having Antony's demoralized troops instead of the Parthians for opponents. The propaganda had its effect—Octavian's men believed they were fighting what amounted to a holy war and Antony's own men began to believe the story that their commander had somehow become tainted by the eastern wiles of the Greco-Egyptian queen.

Agrippa planned a clever delaying campaign, a strategy that maximized the time available for propaganda to subvert the loyalties of Antony's legions. Antony dared not invade Italy, a move that would fit too perfectly into the scheme of Octavian's Eastern Peril propaganda. So Agrippa was afforded the luxury of choosing the ground on which to fight. In the end it came down to a naval battle—Agrippa's forte—fought in September 31 B.C. off the promontory of Actium on the western coast of Greece. Antony's men, those who were left, did not fight with much will. Agrippa's fleet broke Antony's line, Cleopatra's royal flagship beat a hasty retreat (compare Darius III at Issus, Chapter 4), and resistance soon collapsed. Antony and Cleopatra escaped to Egypt on the flagship but the war was all but over.

Octavian pursued the couple at his leisure. When Octavian arrived in the summer of 30, with an unstoppable army, Antony saw that resistance was futile. He followed Cassius's and Brutus's example and committed suicide. Cleopatra lived long enough to realize that there was no hope of striking a deal with Rome's new absolute master. She denied Octavian her ornamental presence at his triumphal parade when she killed herself with a poisonous asp that had been smuggled into her prison by faithful attendants.

With Cleopatra's death three centuries of Ptolemaic rule came to an end, and Egypt became a Roman province, to be administered under the personal supervision of Octavian. Cleopatra had played her best hand; she had bet her kingdom on Antony's military abilities. The hand was well played; Antony had remained a faithful protector until the end. But the cards she had been dealt were simply not good enough.

THE LESSON

What went wrong for Antony? Clearly he had staked too much on the war against the Parthians, but he had, after all, repulsed their invasion of Roman territory. Many Roman generals in the past had suffered reverses on the field and had yet gone on to defeat their rivals in political faction fights. Why had the Parthian failure proved so fatal? First, we should keep in mind that Julius Caesar had established a new standard: that of the invincible general who always won. Antony hoped to fill Caesar's shoes; thus, he was judged by Caesar's military record. The invasion of Parthia found him wanting. Octavian, on the other hand, did not begin his career with notable military successes. He did not set up impossible expectations as a field commander, and so his battle losses tended to be discounted, and when he (or his lieutenants) won, his victories were regarded as notable.

Furthermore, Antony had chosen as his share of the empire an area that was vastly complex, a region that required the astute use of military force and great diplomatic subtlety. The only big victory to be won in the East was over the Parthians, and even beginning a war with them required a great deal of preliminary negotiation with the client states. These negotiations were time-consuming and did not yield much glory. Antony was equal to the diplomatic challenge. His arrangement of the eastern clients was a masterpiece of negotiation that served Rome's long-term interests well. Octavian understood the extent of Antony's achievement; with the exception of Egypt he left Antony's client network largely intact. But the quiet negotiations that led to long-term gains for Rome did not play very well in the rumor mill that was the late Republic. While Antony's arrangements may have done at least as much to ensure the stability of the empire, Octavian's showy war against Sextus Pompey netted much more gain in terms of public opinion.

But, perhaps more important, Octavian seems to have realized from the beginning that the Triumvirate was simply a mask for an ongoing state of civil war. Antony was evidently fooled by the appearance of amity and the lack of actual combat into believing that no war was being fought. He apparently believed that wars are always hot, and that when one was not engaged in combat, one was at peace. It was Octavian's genius to realize that the decade of overt peace between himself and Antony (42–32 B.C.) could be used to fight a cold war in which the best weapons were symbolic. Octavian used whatever and whoever came to hand to fight that war: his father's name, his opponent's taste in bed partners, his own sister.

Octavian realized, as Antony did not, that the Roman Civil Wars were an extended legitimacy struggle, a competition that would be won by the man who could *appear* to be Rome's natural and legitimate leader. Octavian never made the error of separating illusion and reality in his contest with Antony. In reality, there may have been little to choose between the morals of an Antony and an Octavian. Both men had bloodied their hands in the purge that initiated the Triumvirate. Neither showed much consideration for family members (Octavian was later to use his daughter ruthlessly in furthering his dynastic schemes). Antony was no doubt a libertine who outraged traditional Roman family values by his open affairs with foreign women. But Octavian's private life was in reality no model of old-fashioned virtue. He divorced his first wife on the day she bore their daughter, and forced the divorce of Livia, a nineteen-year-old pregnant mother who had caught his fancy, so he could marry her. Yet by the mid-30s B.C., Octavian had managed to project an image of himself as a sober, proper, old-fashioned Roman patriarch.

Antony scorned the game of image, supposing until too late that the Romans would see through Octavian's facade. He imagined that in the hard-bitten real world of power politics image was just fluff and that manpower, military skill, and personal interest determined all important outcomes. Antony thought that his men would fight for him as long as they were paid and as long as he held out the prospect of fat bonuses. He forgot (as Octavian never did) that beneath their mercenary armor, Roman soldiers remained Romans. They had a very loose attachment to the Roman government indeed, but their attachment to entrenched Roman social values—to structures of patriarchy and attitudes of xenophobia—was undiminished. Octavian played upon the deeply rooted Roman-ness of both his own and Antony's men, and played upon their fears of all that was un-Roman. Octavian convinced his own troops that they were on a crusade to save everything that their culture valued, and convinced a significant portion of Antony's men that a victory for Antony would mean in reality a victory for Cleopatra, and the end of the Roman era.

It is an old but true cliché that winners write the histories. Octavian's propaganda successfully portrayed Antony as destroyed by his fatuous love for an evil woman, and after the victory at Actium this story became part of the permanent historical record. Octavian ruled Rome for a long time and the historians of his age knew how he wanted his opponents depicted. The caricature of "Antony, the fool of love" was picked up by Plutarch, who wrote what became the standard biography. Shakespeare adapted Plutarch's portrait into what became the definitive Antony for modern readers. Antony failed to pay enough attention to the interplay between ideology and image; he was punished for his realism both with his failure at Actium and in a historical record that took his opponent's propaganda at face value. It is the crowning irony of Antony's career that this consummate realist—a fine diplomat and first-rate soldier—has gone down in history as the ultimate romantic.

But, if Antony lost in the short and long runs, he had an ironic biological revenge in the middle term. The "fool of love" hadn't been happily married to Octavia, but still managed to sire two daughters by her. These two became important and fertile members of what developed into the imperial family. The later antics of the notorious emperor Nero—who nearly undid all of Octavian's careful work at empire-building, and whose suicide in A.D. 68 terminated the direct imperial succession from Octavian—might have amused the man who was simultaneously his maternal great-great-grandfather and paternal great-grandfather: that man was none other than Mark Antony himself.

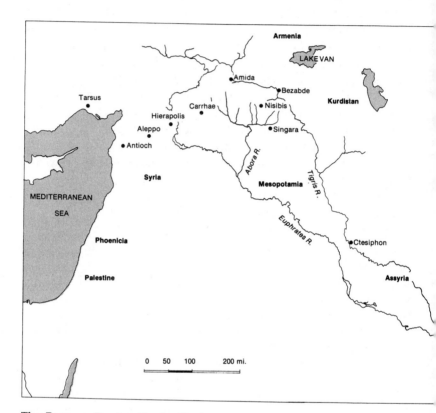

The Romano-Persian Border Region, A.D. 363

Chapter 8

CASPIAN SEA

Iran

PERSIAN GULF

No Second Alexander: Why Julian's Persian Expedition Failed

OCTAVIAN USED HIS VICTORY at Actium wisely. Under the name Augustus (27 B.C.–A.D. 14), as he became known, he founded the system of emperors who would govern the Roman world for centuries. Augustus made his peace with the senatorial elite, with whom he shared power in return for their recognition of the supremacy of Augustus and his heirs. Although he never put the search for military glory behind him completely, he began a process of emphasizing public works, peace, and prosperity, which would continue with great success for the next two centuries. Under the dynasties of Augustus and his successors (27 B.C.–A.D. 180) the Roman world enjoyed the Roman peace. Roman citizenship, Roman law and institutions, and the Latin language (at least in the West) were spread throughout the increasingly well-off Roman provinces.

The situation changed in the late second century A.D. and reached crisis proportions in the third. First came a series of bad emperors and palace coups. Then came invasions by so-called barbarians (mainly Germans and Persians), an epidemic, economic dislocation, wild currency inflation, and the abandonment of many cities. For a while it looked as if the empire would collapse. Order was finally restored and Roman rule reestablished by a series of military reformers in the late third and early fourth centuries, with the emperors Diocletian (285–305) and Constantine (307–337) preeminent among them. These men were no-nonsense and often brutal soldiers who, as emperors, tried to run the empire like an army. They aimed not at sharing power, but at ruling in an authoritarian and imposing fashion. In a sense, the continuing threat of invasion forced their hand, as it also forced them to enlarge and reorganize the army and to build a network of fortifications. To pay for the heavy expense of policing Rome's borders, they raised taxes and tried to supervise the economy, which called for an enlarged bureaucracy. Finally, in order to control the population they wanted a state religion.

Diocletian favored something along the lines of the traditional Roman worship of Jupiter, and he persecuted his major competitor, the growing Christian Church. Constantine, however, reversed course and became a Christian. Perhaps because he admired and wished to make use of the Church's efficient organization, perhaps because of sincere religiosity, he financed an expansion of the Church everywhere in the empire at the expense of paganism. He even established a new, second capital for the Empire in a city untainted by paganism: Constantinople.

Constantine's son and successor, Constantius (337–360), continued to support Christianity and to rule with an iron fist. He was troubled by faction within his own family and with the far more serious threats of Persian invasion in the East and German invasion in Gaul. Under the Sassanid dynasty (founded 227 as a successor-state to the Parthians) the Persians had become a serious military threat, and the Germans were always formidable. The severity of the situation forced Constantius to send his cousin and rival Julian to pacify Gaul while he himself dealt with Persia. Constantius may have feared his cousin's hatred, since Constantius had played a role in the murders of Julian's father and brother. He would have feared Julian even more, however, had he known the extent of Julian's military skill, of his ambition, and of his desire to roll back the tide of Christianity in favor of a revived paganism. By 360, Constantius was dead and Julian was emperor.

HIGH HOPES

On the fifth of March, a sunny day in the year A.D. 363, the Roman emperor Julian, already proclaimed in inscriptions as victor over the Germans, the Alamanni, the Franks, and the Sarmatians, began a quest for another title. Barely thirty-two years old, he was a warrior of vigor. He left Antioch for the East on the Aleppo road and, five days later, reached the rendezvous point for the great army he had called into being—65,000 men strong, its goal was the economic heart of the Persian Empire in southern Iraq. Victory would bring Julian the coveted title of Parthicus or Persicus Maximus. Watching the expedition march by on the roads of Syria (some of them not well paved at all, as Julian complained), an educated man might have gone into symbolic overload as he considered the precedents. Julian was not only defending the frontier: he was following the path that had led to glory for the emperor Trajan, to literary fame for Xenophon and his Ten Thousand, to disaster for Crassus, and, above all, to divinity for Alexander the Great. What Flanders was to the British between 1815 and 1940, what Alsace-Lorraine was to the French after 1870, so the march into Mesopotamia against Persia was to the Romans: the ultimate, mythic field of honor. Nobody knew it better than Julian.

As a young man, Julian had been steeped in the history and mythology of Greece and Rome, and knew perfectly the symbolic meaning of war with Persia. In fact, as the only emperor in history to convert *back* from Christianity to paganism—Julian is infamous in Christendom as Julian the Apostate—he was much more emotionally committed to Greco-Roman tradition than the average Roman leader. He knew the story that even Julius Caesar had cried upon seeing a statue of Alexander the Great, because the statue was a reminder that Persia was the *one* nation that the Romans had not conquered. As for Julian, his own rags-to-riches life story reads like a Greek myth or, better yet, like Gilbert and Sullivan—as long, that is, as one discreetly ignores the corpses. By the age of twenty-nine, Julian had gone from hare to hunter: from house arrest and internal exile, to university in Athens, to appointment as the emperor's second-in-command and generalship of the army of Gaul, to success as the admired conqueror of the German tribes threatening that province, to a successful bid for the purple, to sole rulership of the Roman world. Along the way, he had survived the murders of his father and two brothers, the death (by natural causes) of his mother, the enforced separation from various teachers and mentors, and frequent moves and prolonged isolation.

The fifth of March 363 was a long way from Julian's birth in 332. He had the bad luck to be born into the junior branch of the Roman imperial family during a time of palace struggles. His father, Flavius Constantius, was half brother of the emperor Constantine the Great. Julian's mother, Basilina, came from a great family of Greek Asia Minor, which explains why Julian was raised in a Greek-speaking milieu. In 337, when Constantine died en route to war against Persia, a succession struggle ensued. Julian's father and oldest brother were massacred, probably at the instigation of Julian's cousin, the new emperor, Constantius II. With his mother already dead, Julian was raised by her family in and near Constantinople for the next seven years. Then, in 345, Julian was sent into internal exile on an imperial estate in the interior of Asia Minor; here he was reunited with his older brother, Gallus. These were relatively lonely times for

Julian, but he did make friends with books and with teachers.

The emperor Constantine had converted to Christianity and begun the process of Christianizing the empire. All the members of his extended family were raised as good Christians. In his teenage years of exile, however, Julian began to break secretly with the family's religion. His books of pagan philosophy and theology perhaps gave Julian a way of rebelling against the system that had treated him so brutally. At any rate, the seeds were sown that would later make Julian into the Apostate, the emperor who turned against the Church. Julian kept his religious convictions a secret until he assumed the purple, but when he finally did reveal his paganism, he made things difficult for Christian teachers, and he subsidized pagan sacrifices on a grand scale. Had he lived to a ripe old age rather than dying at thirty-two, Julian might have given the Christian Church a serious run for its money; for every sincere convert to Christianity in the Roman world of the fourth century A.D. there was a courtier who sycophantically mimicked what the emperor did.

All this was still far away in 351, when young Julian was allowed to return to the vicinity of Constantinople, where he continued his studies and the quiet pursuit of paganism, including a secret initiation into the cult of Mithras the Sun God. His mentors ranged from bishops to pagan priests, from philosophers to charlatans, from orators to diviners. They remind us of the paradoxes of his own personality, which ranged from the mystic to the intellectual to the man of action. Julian's brother Gallus favored the active side. Desperately short of relatives, the emperor Constantius now appointed Gallus as Caesar— that is, as his second-in-command—and sent him to govern Antioch. But Gallus proved to be too strong or too brutal, depending on which account one believes; in 354, Constantius had him dismissed and executed. The next year, Julian was granted permission to study at Athens.

There, Julian was present at the very center of the Hellenic intellectual tradition. Athens' renowned philosophers drew students from among both Christians and pagans (the latter preferred to call themselves Hellenes). One of Julian's fellow students was Gregory of Nazianzus, later to become archbishop of Constantinople. Years later, looking back on the apostate-to-be, Gregory saw a man who embodied instability: twitching, jerking, swaying, hysterical, hunched, his eyes wandering and crazy. Fortunately, we have other eyewitness accounts, most notably that of the soldier-historian Ammianus Marcellinus, who admired Julian and saw him in Gaul and Persia. Ammianus's Julian is of middle height, broad and well built, bearded, intelligent-looking, with "fine, flashing eyes." Both sources agree on the prominence of Julian's eyes and nose. Note, too, the beard, a self-conscious and unfashionable mimicking of an earlier period of Roman history. Making allowances for each source's bias and for the difference between Julian the student and Julian the soldier, a composite emerges. The picture we get from these and other sources is of a lively, intense, loquacious, short, and hirsute man—who appeared to the courtier Mamertinus, a man with "eyes brilliant and glinting like stars"; to discontented soldiers, a "talking mole" or "ape in purple." But apes are strong and moles move without being noticed.

As a student, Julian was honing his native intelligence, improving his store of knowledge, and developing valuable skills: self-confidence, rhetorical ability, and discipline. As a philosopher, he prided himself on chastity and asceticism, the latter a quality that would make him a more efficient, if not more endearing soldier. Such skills were soon to be tested. Within a few months, Constantius reluctantly turned to Julian, named him Caesar, and sent him to Gaul (355). The challenge of recurring invasion by federations of German tribes was enormous: for an ambitious man, it was a chance to make or break his name. Julian came to Gaul in 355 as an ex-student; he left in 361 as a conqueror and would-be emperor.

Julian would carry the lessons of Gaul with him into the Persian campaign. He learned the value of Roman discipline over enemy laxity: at the battle of Strasbourg in 357, 13,000 Roman troops smashed a German army several times their number and ended the most dangerous threat to Gaul. He learned the value of frequent expeditions into enemy territory. He learned the importance of his own physical courage in battle. He learned how deep his energy reserves were, how much he could accomplish without sleep, how far he could push. He learned how to address the troops, in Latin rather than his native Greek, and how to inspire them. Above all, he learned to think of himself as a winner.

Julian was an amateur soldier who learned to succeed by challenging the professionals. At Strasbourg, for example, he took the decision to fight on his own, without the advice of his high military counselors. Like many a self-taught and self-made man, he had more than a healthy share of egotism, and a less than impressive willingness to listen to others. Moreover, he was an expert at self-preservation. Having succeeded in pacifying Gaul, he had no intention of sharing his brother's fate. The intellectual-turned-soldier did not have to be pushed too hard by his men before he agreed to accept their acclamation as emperor in 360. The next year he marched east against Constantius, who was trying, without much success, to hold down the Persian front. As a rebel, Julian displayed a knack for speed and decisiveness. For example, he sent a small unit to seize the key fortress of Sirmium (in Yugoslavia); his men succeeded so well that the pro-Constantius commander woke up to the sight of Julian's soldiers around his bed. But Julian never had to fight a major battle; Constantius died, and in late 361, Julian entered Constantinople in peace, to universal acclamation. The survivor, the victim, the alienated native of Constantinople who had been denied his heritage, had finally achieved his revenge.

Domestic politics would not be smooth sailing for the new emperor, however. The trial and execution of some of Constantius's henchmen as well as Julian's efforts to streamline bureaucracy embroiled him in controversy in the capital. Moreover, Constantinople, founded by Constantine as the Christian city par excellence, was the last place for a born-again pagan like Julian. In June 362, therefore, hoping for a friendlier environment, he left for Antioch, capital of Syria.

Julian was thinking big. Not only was Antioch a great center of Greek culture, it was also the logical organizing point of an expedition against Persia. Julian had already made the decision to turn east.

THE PERSIAN CHALLENGE

In 362 and 363, Julian's advisers were by no means agreed on Rome's need to make war on Persia; in fact, most of them opposed the idea. It was true that Persia's King Sapor II had broken the peace treaty of 298, true that he had dueled with Constantius in an inconclusive war for years, true too that he had recently captured the important eastern Roman cities of Amida, Singara, and Bezabde. It was also true that Constantius had attempted to reconquer Bezabde in 360.

But Constantius had failed to retake Bezabde; indeed, Julian had turned on him and marched in rebellion from Gaul while Constantius was distracted in the East. Sapor was an aggressive and dynamic monarch, even by the standards of the warlike Sassanian dynasty; he styled himself not only "king of kings" but "partner of the stars" and "brother of the sun and moon." He had announced to Rome his intention of conquering Armenia and northern Mesopotamia. Yet Sapor had three times tried to take the major Roman fortress of the East, the city of Nisibis, which lay astride the invasion route to Antioch—and three times failed. Moreover, in winter 362–63, Sapor had done an about-face and sent an embassy to the new emperor in Antioch, calling for peace talks. Having failed to invade Roman territory, Sapor was now evidently more worried about Julian invading Persian territory. With Rome's enemy calling for negotiations, there was much to be said for avoiding an unnecessary war.

Perhaps one of Julian's advisers went even further, at least in private, and asked what the point of war against Persia was anyhow. Neither side was strong enough to destroy the other. Persia's recent successes had left it exhausted. Armenia was still a loyal Roman buffer state. The frontier was largely stable. Minor territorial changes might be won, but the existing frontier served nicely as a boundary between the two powers. It ran, roughly speaking, from the Caucasus through Armenia to the confluence of the Euphrates and Khabur rivers, and then south across the desert to the Gulf of Aqaba (roughly, along the eastern borders of modern Turkey, Syria, and Jordan). On the Roman side were the ancient and fertile lands of Syria, Lebanon, Palestine, and Egypt; on the Persian side, the immensely rich Mesopotamian basin. As long as Rome had a generally strong defensive position on the frontier, what difference did a few Persian advances here and there make?

Another adviser might have answered that, strategically, there were two points in favor of war against Persia. First, if recent Persian aggressions were allowed to go unpunished, Persia would only be encouraged to repeat them in the future. Roman gains by treaty would not do; only the clash of arms would teach Persia an effective lesson. Second, there was Armenia, a buffer state between Persia and Rome, and currently a Roman ally, but always ready to flow with the current. "If Armenia perceives a shift in the balance of power toward Persia," our hypothetical Roman strategist might have said, "Rome might well lose Armenia." This kind of argument would have anticipated the "they'll-jump-on-the-other-side's-bandwagon-if-we-don't-act" fear often voiced during the Cold War.

Hence, Julian could argue in favor of a short war with Persia now in order to avoid a long war in the future. He planned to make his point in one summer's campaign: he would start out from Antioch and winter in Tarsus (on Turkey's Mediterranean coast). Nevertheless, Julian's was to be a very ambitious enterprise. He planned to take a large army much deeper into Persian territory than any Roman force had gone in nearly a century.

Because of his great ambitions, Julian came under great criticism for his Persian expedition. Even before his failure, some critics said that Julian had stirred up an unnecessary and potentially disastrous war. One of Julian's highest officials, the prefect of Gaul, wrote him urging against the campaign. Then, there was a steady stream of unfavorable oracles, and these would never have been voiced unless mortals too had their doubts about Julian's plan. Stung by criticism, the emperor found it necessary to reply. When his army first crossed into Persian territory in April, Julian addressed the troops. It is striking that Ammianus has him deal right off with the question of precedent: "I mean to demonstrate to you by multiple examples that this is not, as some scandal-mongers mutter, the first time that Romans have invaded the kingdom of Persia." After describing previous Roman expeditions, Julian offers a justification of his own:

> And whereas these emperors were impelled by ambition to embark on their memorable enterprises, the driving force behind our undertaking is the wretchedness of recently captured cities, the unavenged shades of our slaughtered armies, the immense damage we have suffered, and the loss of our camps. We are all united in our desire to remedy past disasters and to strengthen the Roman state on this flank, so that posterity may have a glorious account to give of us.

Julian thus wraps himself in the Roman battle flag and simultaneously promises sober strategic goals.

It is clear, though, that Julian was thinking not only of grand strategy when he marched against Persia. Both domestic politics and personal psychology played a part in his motivation—as they do, of course, in all leaders' decisions. Ammianus records that Julian was "tired of inactivity and dreamed of trumpets and battles," adding that he coveted the title of Parthicus. Even Ammianus, who confesses to be more of a panegyricist than a historian when it comes to Julian, admits that Julian's ambition was insatiable. We learn, too, that Julian had acquired in Gaul a taste for victory and for enemies making their surrender. Moreover, much of Julian's reputation in Gaul had been built on bold raids into German territory; the mere garrisoning of the Persian frontier was so much less dramatic. After the intrigues and hostilities of Constantinople and Antioch (which had turned out to be an antipagan hornet's nest), warfare was a release.

Finally, we should not underestimate Julian's religiosity or his religious agenda. He was no cynic in his campaign against the Church or in his advocacy of Hellenic philosophy and the traditional Greco-Roman pantheon. Julian was convinced that he was Good, and that his theological enemies were at best misguided. A modern scholar has compared him to Mao or Lenin, and perhaps there was also a touch of Calvin or Savonarola, the ascetic fundamentalists. Julian did not do things by halves, neither in religion nor in war. If Persia was a big enemy, then it ought to be attacked with a big army. Moreover, a victory over Persia by a pagan-led army would be a victory for paganism at home. Julian's prestige would grow upon his triumphant return and earn him the kind of moral capital that would attract Christians back into the ranks of paganism. So he might have imagined as he set out to fight Persia, and who is to say that he was necessarily wrong?

If the relative richness of documentation allows us to probe Julian's psychology (and we must always remember, a probe is not a proof), it is important not to dismiss him as irrational. His motives were mixed, his campaign failed, but he was not merely a politician who used war to solve domestic problems; nor an impulsive youth who was itching for battle; nor a megalomaniac who thought he was Alexander the Great's spiritual heir—or even Alexander's reincarnated soul, as one hostile Church historian accuses Julian of believing. Ideology and personal temperament played an important part in Julian's decision to invade Persia. His failure, nonetheless, does not mean that he was thoughtless or frivolous, nor that he set out with no plan at all. But what was his plan?

STRATEGY OF THE PERSIAN CAMPAIGN

As so often in ancient history, the evidence is tantalizingly incomplete. We know enough about Julian's strategy to form some idea of it, but not quite enough to be certain, especially about several key points. To add to the mystery (and the frustration) the central passage in our best source—the explanation of why Julian turned back from the Persian capital—is missing, the victim no doubt of carelessness on the part of some medieval scribe.

Some historians accuse Julian of not having a clear strategy at all, of simply taking a shot at Persian territory and trusting to luck and his army. This will not do, because Julian was in general careful and meticulous. He may have had the wrong plan, but he certainly had a plan. As he wrote to Libanius in Antioch after the first week of the campaign:

> But as regards the military or political arrangements, you ought, I think, to have been present to observe and pay attention to them yourself. For, as you well know, the matter is too long for a letter, in fact so vast that if one considered it in detail it would not be easy to confine it to a letter even three times as long as this.

Julian had a great deal on his mind during his nine-month stay in Antioch, including both economic and religious policies, but one thing he certainly took care of was training his troops. He paid very close attention to the provisioning of supplies for his invading army. He carefully divided his forces according to a prearranged plan. In fact, if Julian is to be convicted of any failing, it is that his strategy was *too* refined, not that it was thoughtless. Julian had a plan and it might have worked, but it was complex and risky: it relied on many unreliable factors. How like Julian—who was a man of limitless confidence in his ability to ram through his own will, opposition be damned—to come up with such a plan. Julian's self-confidence was his greatest glory and his greatest shortcoming.

An incident from the height of the Persian expedition illustrates this character trait well. The Roman army had reached the Tigris opposite Ctesiphon, but the steep-banked eastern shore of the river was heavily guarded by Persian forces. Julian came up with a tactical plan for crossing: at nightfall, five ships would row across at top speed and establish a beachhead, and the rest of the fleet would immediately follow. Julian's generals unanimously opposed this dangerous tactic. Nevertheless, the emperor insisted on it. When the advance squadron reached the Persian side of the river, they came under heavy attack by firebombs: the flames were visible on the Roman side. Julian, however, saved the day by announcing that this was a prearranged signal of success. A boldfaced lie, but it galvanized the Roman fleet into action. They fought their way onto the other side of the Tigris, routed the Persians in a set battle, and chased them all the way back to the gates of Ctesiphon.

This was Julian's kind of warfare: a lightning shot into enemy territory, devoted troops, a chance for the emperor himself to fight in the thick of things, and, above all, a triumph of one man's intellect and will. The Tigris crossing sums up Julian's self-image: the fiery-eyed razor-sharp intellectual turned steel-willed warrior, trusting no one but himself. This image might have been a recipe for tactical success, but unfortunately, it was inadequate as the strategic basis of an entire campaign.

Julian's strategy had major problems from the start. He could not personally control an army of 45,000 men for six months the way he could control a compact infantry unit in one operation. He certainly could not control the movements of a second Roman army hundreds of miles away under separate commanders, not to mention the Armenian allies with whom they were supposed to link up. Nor could he count on his staff's knowledge of enemy terrain—not given the poor state of military intelligence in antiquity. Finally, he could not count on the Persian army behaving the way he wanted it to behave.

Julian was a brilliant and talented man, but he was equally complex and paradoxical. As a soldier, he was dynamic, courageous, intelligent, and meticulous; but he was also arrogant, stubborn, and caught up in himself. Opposition to a cherished idea made him prickly rather than self-critical. For example, when the Antiochenes responded to his religious and economic policies with passion and ridicule, he called them wicked and vicious and punished them by imposing an anti-Christian martinet as governor. It evidently never occurred to him that *he* might have been in the wrong. When his advisers urged him not to invade Persia, he reacted like Hercules among the Pygmies, as Ammianus puts it sneeringly. It never occurred to him that despite his successes in Gaul, he had a lot to learn about war in the East. Again, Julian did not easily learn from criticism.

Hence, Julian's error can be traced to his belief in two myths: the myth of the expert, whose superior intellect can always come up with the right plan; and the myth of the heroic commander, whose single will can control everything. In Julian's terms, they were the myths embodied in two men: Marcus Aurelius, Rome's most famous philosopher-emperor, and Alexander the Great, the most heroic commander Julian's world knew. Julian had long admired Marcus and, while he had once had his doubts about Alexander, in later years he increasingly identified with Persia's greatest enemy. In modern terms, we might perhaps think of Julian's two errors in terms of the myth of the Schlieffen Plan, Germany's meticulously thought-out blueprint for disaster in World War I, and the myth of Adolf Hitler, the World War I veteran who thought he knew more about strategy than his World War II generals.

The sources agree that Julian's strategy depended on speed, secrecy, and surprise. From Hierapolis (modern Membij, about sixty miles northeast of Aleppo and fifteen miles west of the Euphrates), Julian wrote Libanius: "I dispatched men as wide-awake as I could obtain that they might guard against anyone's leaving here secretly to go to the enemy and inform them that we are on the move." We learn elsewhere that Julian had left Antioch early, at the very beginning of spring—March 5, to be precise—in order to get a jump on the enemy. There was of course no way to hide an army of 65,000 men from Persia's spies, but Julian could keep the enemy guessing about the precise time and route of his expedition. Julian had amassed an enormous fleet, some 1,100 ships, to carry food and siege equipment and to bridge rivers and canals. While Julian sent the fleet southward down the Euphrates, he pushed his army northeastward on to Carrhae (modern Harran) by forced marches, less than a week later. Here Julian's strategy takes on greater shape.

From Carrhae there are two roads into Mesopotamia. The first goes south along the Euphrates; the second goes east along the mountains of Armenia, crosses the Tigris, and then turns south. This second route was the one followed by most invaders, the one the Persians would expect Julian to take. Julian, however, had decided to follow the first route: he would march south, rejoin the Euphrates, and follow it until he reached the canals that crossed over to the Tigris and Ctesiphon.

Part of Julian's strategy was to encourage the false Persian expectation that he would follow the Tigris route. Several stratagems were employed to this end: dummy supply dumps along the road to the Tigris, and a feint in the direction of the Tigris by Julian's army before it wheeled south to the Euphrates. Moreover, Julian detached a large force of 20,000 men under his maternal kinsman Procopius and one Sebastian to march eastward toward the Tigris, though without crossing it. Procopius was a civil servant and diplomat who had been to Ctesiphon; Sebastian had been commander of Egypt. Their army had several tasks. First, it was meant to protect Roman Mesopotamia from Persian invasion; enemy cavalry had been reported in the area. Second, if possible it was to link up with the Armenian king, Arsaces, a Roman ally. Once the link-up was effected, Procopius's army was to march southeast through Kurdistan and ravage it. Third, it was then to march south and reinforce Julian at Ctesiphon.

With luck, Procopius's army would accomplish a fourth task: trick the Persians into pursuing it before they realized that the main invasion force was with Julian along the Euphrates. It looks as if Procopius succeeded: Julian did not encounter the Persian army until he was close to Ctesiphon.

Having taken the Persians off guard, as he hoped, Julian was able to hurry toward his objective. But what precisely was his objective? The ancient sources are vague, so we shall have to reconstruct the answer. There are two possibilities, the Persian winter capital of Ctesiphon and the Persian army. As for the army, Julian would no doubt have been happy to fight the Persians in a set battle, but Sapor would not want to risk his inferior infantry against the Romans. Therefore, Sapor would avoid battle, or in any case choose the most favorable ground for himself. On the other hand, there was plenty of precedent for going after Ctesiphon, which had been captured four times previously by the Romans: by the emperors Trajan (A.D. 116), Avidius Cassius (164), Severus (198), and Carus (283). Capturing Ctesiphon would certainly teach the Persians a lesson, and it would earn Julian the coveted title of Parthicus. The Persian exile Prince Hormisdas, Sapor's brother, was in Julian's entourage. He was a good source of intelligence as well as a suitable pretender to the throne, a pro-Roman king to govern "liberated" Ctesiphon. There was, however, a potential flaw in the plan. Unliberated Ctesiphon had a very favorable natural defensive position, which Sapor had perhaps strengthened further since the Romans had last taken the city.

Julian was no doubt aware of Ctesiphon's defensibility, since Roman officials (including the general Procopius) had visited the city in recent years. Still, when Julian reached the city and held a council of war outside the gates, the opinion of his military advisers was divided. Some reasonable men considered a siege to be a feasible undertaking, but majority opinion was negative. Why were most of his lieutenants now so pessimistic? Was it sensible of Julian ever to have anticipated a successful siege?

Yes, but just barely. Julian had plenty of siege equipment with him. He had taken two heavily fortified Persian cities along his march down the Euphrates, possibly with the help of fifth columns in each. There was a chance that he could repeat his success at Ctesiphon, particularly because when he set out he expected to have several aces up his tunic sleeve: the presence of Prince Hormisdas, the diversion of the main Persian army to the north, and the speed of the Roman army. Julian's plan had been to reach Ctesiphon rapidly, while Sapor was still awaiting the Romans in the north. Then, if all worked out, he could grab Ctesiphon, turn and face Sapor and, with luck, even have the reinforcements of Procopius and the Armenians.

The entire plan, therefore, depended on speed, which in turn required a superbly disciplined army and the rapid capture of enemy strongholds en route. The plan also depended on Procopius's deception. This part worked; although Procopius did not meet Julian in the South, he did at least tie Sapor down for a while. The lightning speed on which Julian had counted, however, was beyond his grasp. He crossed the Khabur River into Persian territory in early April and reached Ctesiphon about eight weeks later on May 27: a distance of over 300 miles in about 60 days, an average of about 5 miles a day. This is slow: compare the estimated average march rate of 15 miles per day in the Macedonian army under Philip and Alexander—or, for that matter, the approximate 10-mile-per-day rate of Julian's army between Hierapolis and Carrhae, back in March.

Julian seems to have underestimated the friction he would encounter, both from the Persians—even without their main army—and from his own men. Persian guerrillas, their raiding Arab allies, and eventually a large Persian army under Sapor's second-in-command harassed the Romans along their march. Worse, valuable time was lost in the siege of two fortified Persian towns near Ctesiphon. Julian was not blind to this problem. At the second siege, he noted that the destruction of the town was urgent and that delay might cost him his more important objectives. The city was eventually taken and the Romans continued their march, but shortly afterward they stopped to besiege a Persian fort, where a group of raiders almost killed Julian.

Another kind of obstacle came from the irrigation canals between the Euphrates and Tigris in the Ctesiphon area: the Persians opened the sluice gates and forced the army to stop and build bridges over the waterlogged ground. In addition, the Persians dammed up the main canal about three miles from the Tigris; clearing it brought on another delay.

A crack army would handle these problems with aplomb, but Julian's army had built-in weaknesses, which meant problems of morale and discipline, which meant more delays. The eastern troops had not entirely shaken off the impression of Persia's recent string of victories, nor had they forgotten their preference for Julian's late rival, Constantius. The percentage of Christians among soldiers was high in the East, and they resented Julian's removal of the cherished Christian symbol from the Roman standards. Julian's Gallic and Gothic veterans were less heavily Christian, but they would have noticed the unfavorable pagan omens that kept piling up. Julian took many different tacks to deal with his troops' morale problems: speeches, sacrifices, booty, prizes for valor, donatives, more speeches when the small size of a donative provoked a near mutiny, and repeatedly throwing himself into the thick of the fighting at great personal risk. The morale problem persisted, but while it troubled and slowed the expedition, it did not destroy the army as a fighting force. The Romans won every battle they fought with the Persians and, even with Julian dead and the Roman army desperately short of food, Sapor was still afraid of Roman prowess.

Winning battles would not open the gates of Ctesiphon, however, and by the time the Romans finally reached that city, they were out of time. To mount a siege would invite an attack on their rear by Sapor, who now knew Julian's whereabouts. Procopius's army might of course show up in Sapor's rear, but that hope was a weak reed to lean on. Therefore, a majority of the Roman war council before Ctesiphon voted for retreat. Julian accepted the disappointing verdict.

The campaign had not been a success, but so far it had not been a disaster, either. The sack of Roman cities had been avenged by the sack of Persian cities. Rich enemy farmland had been ravaged. The Persian army had been outfought and outfoxed. True enough, there would be a domestic political price for Julian to pay and maybe a big one, because he had failed in his main objective. He had overestimated his army's speed, underestimated Persian resistance, and counted on a sophisticated pincers movement whose riskiness should have been apparent all along. Yet error does not necessarily mean disaster. Julian's return from Mesopotamia might only bring down the curtain on Act One of his Persian drama; everything would then depend on how well he played the next act.

This "first act" scenario assumes a safe and easy march home from Ctesiphon. What if the Romans had trouble bringing their army home, however?

FROM ERROR TO DISASTER

By the time he got to Ctesiphon, it was apparent that Julian had made one big mistake—believing that his iron will could cut through all the obstacles to his plan for victory. It was about to become clear that his strategy was based on another mistake—assuming that the enemy would behave the way Julian wished.

The Romans could not march back home the way they had come, along the Euphrates, since they had stripped the country of its food supplies. Nor could they load the ships and bring supplies along the river, since it would require some 20,000 men to tow the ships against the powerful current. The logical choice was to advance along the fertile east bank of the Tigris. The logical choice was also to burn the fleet, since the Romans couldn't use it and they didn't want to risk having it fall into Persian hands. The men were frightened when they saw the ships burn around the beginning of June, though they shouldn't have been; they were frightened, too, when Julian told them where they would be going next, and in this they were right. At his command, the army rapidly marched east of the Tigris and north, with a turn further east into the Persian interior in the offing.

The men were horrified, because they knew that an advance toward Iran would have made sense only if the enemy was in disarray or willing to fight on Roman terms, in a set battle. Unfortunately, the Persians did not cooperate. Instead, they chose a systematic scorched-earth policy and added a touch of psychological warfare, arranging and rearranging their troops in the distance to make it look as if the main Persian army had arrived. Eventually, Julian was forced to admit that his men had been right. Deprived of both supplies and a target, he was forced to break camp on June 16 and head west for the Tigris. Unfortunately for Julian, Sapor had no intention of playing Darius to a second Alexander.

Julian had underestimated the enemy and overestimated the practical workability of his plan. Food quickly became the big issue. Once it reached Ctesiphon, the Roman army needed new supplies of food. The Tigris region was tremendously fertile, but the Persians could torch the fields. Julian had to stop them, produce food from a different source, or get his army back north as quickly as possible. To his credit, Julian had made preparations for new food supplies to be brought by Procopius, Sebastian, and Arsaces. Their armies had followed a policy of strict rationing; in fact, when Julian's troops finally straggled home to Roman territory in July, food was still stored there for them. But that was the problem—the relief forces never brought the food south to Julian's army. When Julian made the tough choice at the beginning of June to leave without taking Ctesiphon, he should have made an even tougher one. Without an assurance that the relief army was coming, the only good choice was to head straight home. To march farther away from his supply base was to court disaster.

Now, two weeks later, Julian finally made that tougher decision and led his army north along the Tigris, but it was already very, very late. He had to face up to a long and difficult journey. While avoiding a decisive battle, the Persians would harass the Romans constantly. They would kill many Romans during the difficult fording of the Tigris, now in flood. Many other Romans would die of starvation. It was a much depleted army that eventually made it back to Roman territory.

As it turned out, it was also an army that had been stabbed in the back by inferior generals. Sapor and the main Persian army finally found the Romans on their march northward. Although the Romans won a tactical victory in a battle on June 22, the Persian army withdrew intact. Persian raiders continued to harass the Romans, killing a few here and there, until finally, on June 26, 363, a Persian raid led to the ultimate casualty: the death of Julian himself.

There is drama, there is mystery, and there is even something pathetic about Julian's death. It was not quite heroic, not quite glorious, and certainly never avenged. Julian received his fatal wound from a spear on the battlefield, but he died with his boots off, as it were, back in his tent. He was not leading a charge against Sapor, but hurrying to shore up his men in a rearguard action. He rode out ahead on horseback and lost contact briefly with his bodyguard. If he hadn't neglected to put on his heavy breastplate, he would probably not have sustained a serious injury. No one knows who threw the spear that killed Julian; among the candidates suggested by contemporaries are a Persian, one of their Arab allies, a disgruntled Roman Christian, a demon, a saint. It hardly matters; dead is dead.

The army chose Julian's successor the next day, a senior officer named Jovian. To add to the problem of the Persian menace, Jovian had little political support among the men, having been pushed through by a minority faction— which may explain why he now all but gave away the store to Persia. To extricate his hungry army from Persian territory, Jovian agreed to harsh terms: the cession of five Roman border provinces east of the Tigris (they had been Persian up until the late third century) and the key fortress of Nisibis, as well as a promise not to protect King Arsaces and his important buffer state of Armenia against the Persians.

A humiliating and harmful treaty, a starving army, an emperor dead, a weakened successor: Julian's invasion of Persia ended up almost as miserably as Athens' invasion of Sicily. It is worth noting, however, that if Julian had lived, things would probably have turned out somewhat better. Unlike Jovian, Julian probably wouldn't have wasted four days in negotiations with Sapor while his troops got ever hungrier. He would probably have driven a harder bargain. Ammianus claims that Sapor was still afraid of the Roman army, and it is certainly true that the Persians had lost every battle. Finally, once safely back on Roman soil, Julian would probably not have honored a treaty made under compulsion; rather, he would have stood and fought. In both making and keeping to the treaty, Jovian intended to preserve his troops for the likely civil war ahead. An idle ambition, as it turned out, since Jovian would die in Asia Minor just the next year, possibly of poison.

One of the new pretenders to the throne was Procopius, co-commander of the diversionary army that failed to come to Julian's aid. This failure was a key contribution to the disaster, and it is hard not to wonder just what went wrong. The Romans under Procopius and Sebastian did meet up with the Armenians under Arsaces, and they did ravage Persian territory in Kurdistan, but they never marched south to help Julian. Ammianus says that Procopius "carried out his orders with loyalty and prudence," so perhaps the problem was Arsaces' disloyalty, as other sources suggest, or perhaps a rivalry between Procopius and Sebastian. In one story, whenever Procopius ordered a march, Sebastian called for a halt, and vice versa, each man seeking popularity with the troops. If we knew precisely what went wrong, we would be in a better position to say whether Julian's strategic plan was a good plan badly executed or simply a bad plan. But in any case, Julian must get a substantial share of the blame for the disaster, for reliance on the second army was his plan and no one else's, and he appointed the commanders personally.

The outcome of Julian's Persian expedition was indeed disastrous. Persia occupied Rome's provinces across the Tigris as well as the fortress-city of Nisibis in Mesopotamia. In short order, Sapor was able to defeat and capture King Arsaces and to incorporate large parts of Armenia into Persia's territory. Until the emperor Anastasius constructed the new fortress of Dara near Nisibis about a hundred and fifty years later, the balance of power along the frontier was greatly in Persia's favor. In other words, Julian's failure turned an imperfect but stable situation into a bad one.

These losses were terrible for Roman morale. Nisibis had survived three Persian sieges and become a symbol of Rome's indomitable will, the embodiment of the "they shall not pass!" mentality. After 363, they passed. Incidentally, that Nisibis was a largely Christian city while Julian, who was assigned the blame for its loss, was a pagan, did not help the state of pagan-Christian relations in the empire.

From 363 it was only fifteen years to the battle of Adrianople (modern Edirne in European Turkey) in 378, when Roman armies were crushed by German invaders: a disastrous turning point in the declining fortunes of the Later Roman Empire. Julian's Persian disaster contributed to the material and moral weaknesses of the army that fought at Adrianople. Moreover, had Julian himself survived, whatever his failures as a strategist, he was a good enough battlefield general to have done much better at Adrianople than the incompetent emperor Valens.

Julian's death brought triumph to the Christians and terror to the pagans. With him gone, the progress of the Church continued with few impediments. Jovian, a Christian himself in spite of his pagan-sounding name, rescinded Julian's anti-Christian legislation. There was a persistent rumor that Julian had been killed by a Christian, that one of his own men had thrown the fatal spear in anger at God's enemy. Whether this story was true or not, the relieved Christian community took Julian's death as a sign from God. Ephrem of Nisibis, a Christian hymnist, put it simply: the Good Lord had delivered Julian to Satan.

The Roman Empire was not peaceful after Julian's death. Julian had been the last emperor from the house of Constantine the Great. Julian's successor, Jovian, reigned for only eight months, to be replaced in 364 by an imperial duo, Valentinian in the West and his younger brother Valens in the East. The next year Procopius, who had gone into hiding after his cousin Julian's death, emerged in Constantinople and raised a serious rebellion. Procopius claimed that, back on the eve of the invasion of Persia, Julian had named him as his heir. He won support from Julian's Gallic troops and pagans, among others, but in the end Procopius was betrayed to Valens and beheaded in 366.

THE LESSON

To put it in a nutshell, Julian failed because he got in over his head. He was a good battlefield commander, a man of physical and moral courage, an inspiring and even beloved leader of the troops, a dynamo of energy. All well and good, but few wars are won without a good strategy—and Julian's strategy was full of flaws. He adopted an intricate and sophisticated strategic plan *without* assuring the requisite support: a firm command structure, a well-disciplined and united army, reliable intelligence and communications, and secure supplies of food, water, and fodder. Above all, Julian underestimated his opponent. As others have noted, what worked against the German tribes would not necessarily work against the Sassanid Persians, the heirs of an ancient and sophisticated military tradition.

All this is not to say that Julian's strategy had no chance whatever of succeeding. Success had been possible. Moreover, had Julian lived, there would have been considerable latitude for him to exercise damage control. The trouble is, success had depended on a number of factors completely outside of Julian's control. Julian unwisely risked a great deal on a war he did not have to fight: Rome's security, his religious and political program, his domestic power base, and the lives of 65,000 Roman soldiers, including his own. He risked and lost. Instead of this high-risk strategy, Julian could have set his sights at a lower and safer level: the capture of a border city or two, the ravaging of Persian Kurdistan. He might even have chosen to negotiate.

Why did Julian make such dangerous choices? For one thing, Julian was a man of action, a devotee of the offensive, a man of ambition, a man with a mission. He thought big: the attempts to turn back the clock on

Christianity and to turn back the clock on Sapor—"Remember the good old days when Romans were pagans and Persians were weak?"—were of a piece. Perhaps a seamless piece: Julian might have thought that the surest way of discrediting Christianity was by proving the power of the pagan gods on the battlefield. By winning a great victory abroad, Julian might inspire moral rearmament at home. In short, ideology seems to have played an important part in Julian's decision to invade Persian territory.

We must also remember Julian's temperament and his power. Julian was a man sure of his abilities to control and to plan. He was both overarrogant and too sensitive to heed sager counsel. And counsel was about all other Romans could give him. As an emperor and a commander beloved by his troops, Julian usually got his own way. In the fourth century A.D., Rome had long since parted company from its republican traditions. The emperor Julian was an autocrat.

In an autocracy, the danger of the visionary military leader who refuses to listen to wise advice is a recurring one. Think of Napoleon or Hitler in Russia. Julian's failure, however, is equally rich in lessons for constitutional governments and democracies. Governments and peoples, too, can be misled by a sense of honor or by ambition or by arrogance into adopting a high-risk strategy or into underestimating the enemy. Consider early twentieth-century France's strategy for war against Germany in World War I. The dream of victory over the hereditary enemy and the doctrine of the offensive hammered out by France's great military minds together led to a disastrous and pointless slaughter of French troops, first in the Vosges Mountains, later in the trenches. Or consider America's involvement in Vietnam. There was precious little conception in the U.S. government of the strength of the will to fight among the North Vietnamese. There was precious little knowledge in the Pentagon of the realities of guerrilla warfare in the jungle. As with Julian, intellectuals and experts thought themselves impervious to the dangers of which others warned.

As long as strategists let their dreams get the better of them, and until governments develop a foolproof method of clamping down on brilliant ideas that are too clever by half, then there will always be Julians to march against Persia.

Conclusions

AMERICA, AND THE MODERN WORLD as a whole, loves a winner. We dread the label of "loser." Failure, in our age, has ceased to be tragic; it has become something that most of us refuse even to contemplate, much less to learn from. This being the case, the reader who has read through this series of case studies in ancient strategic error has already demonstrated a willingness to challenge one of the central tenets of the unexamined paradigm behind much contemporary decision making—a paradigm by no means limited to military policymakers. We hope that simply by having chosen to read this book, therefore, the reader has begun, or furthered, the difficult and rewarding process of coming to "know oneself."

We have argued throughout that knowledge of self and society is the precondition of the sound policy and appropriate strategy that will lead to victories that are worth the winning. The other side of the coin is knowledge of the enemy. The case studies presented here should help the reader to understand his or her enemies, to recognize both their strengths and their weaknesses. But accurate knowledge of self and other may sometimes have another effect as well: it may allow us to see that those we perceived as enemies may not be as much of a threat as they once appeared to be. Many, perhaps all, of the wars discussed here were unnecessary. Each of them entailed the loss of untold lives, and resulted in catastrophic damage to property and social values.

Clausewitz's great insight that war is the continuation of policy by other means, should be tempered by his stark warning: "No one starts a war—or rather, no one in his senses ought to do so—without first being clear in his mind what he intends to achieve by the war and how he intends to conduct it." We would add "and what he and his nation stand to lose in the event of either success or failure." Even in times of emergency when a forceful response might be popular and may seem most natural, before resorting to Clausewitz's "other means" the true strategist will ask himself if the application of military force is the best solution to the policy dilemma facing him. Even if a short-term victory seems assured, the policy gains of using force might be outweighed by the social costs of victory. The wise strategist—the one who knows himself and his enemy, the one who is neither seduced by dreams of success nor afraid to look failure in the face—will realize that every time a nation goes to war it risks making fatal errors. The very wisest will be humble enough to admit that no one can know where all the errors lie.

Still, try as one might to avoid war and its dangers, sometimes war is unavoidable, either because of the justice of a cause or the aggression of an enemy. In those cases, too, when one is constrained to wage war, the lessons of this study may be of use for strategists. Perhaps the simplest way to sum up those lessons is to say that great leaders of the past have often erred because of a failure (which need not mean a lack) of intellect, rather than a failure of talent, energy, or ambition. Most of the subjects we have studied lost the war in spite of winning battles. They lost because they had avoided the painful but necessary process of thinking through and trying to overcome unexamined assumptions, opinions, and prejudices about themselves and about their enemies. Thus, even great warriors like Hannibal or Agesilaus, even brilliant leaders like Alcibiades or Antony, failed because of their strategic illusions. What their examples might offer today's strategist is both humility and determination: victory is not easy, but it is possible if one is willing to think through the most cherished assumptions.

Flexibility, therefore, is one of the keys to successful strategy. Flexibility is also a word to be applied to the lessons of this book. The cases we have studied are neither blueprints nor do they yield simple tags that give quick insight to the busy strategist. It won't hurt the strategist to stop for a minute and ask, "Am I repeating Xerxes' mistakes?" before going on to the thousand other tasks of the day, but it may not help much, either. Rather, the true aim of this book is to encourage a mind-set, a set of intellectual habits that must be incorporated into the continuing and daily process of planning. We hope that the reader goes away convinced of the need to think historically, to compare his or her opinions with those of foreign societies and cultures, to test, question, and reassess the unexamined ideologies behind one's plans. Confidence, to be firm, needs to rest on a foundation of questioning and skepticism. The past is a guide, but it is not a crutch. The strategist engaged in a constant process of rethinking is the one most likely to avoid making disastrous errors.

Further Reading

(*Note:* In the following pages we refer only to works available in English.)

INTRODUCTION

The two great classics of strategy referred to in the introduction are both available in recent editions: Carl von Clausewitz, *On War*, M. Howard and P. Paret, eds. (1976); and Sun Tzu, *The Art of War*, S. B. Griffith, trans. (1980).

Recent introductions to ancient warfare include P. Conolly, *Greece and Rome at War* (1981); A. Ferrill, *The Origins of War* (1985); Y. Garlan, *War in the Ancient World*, J. Lloyd, trans. (1975); J. H. Hackett, ed., *An Illustrated History of War in the Ancient World* (1989); R. Humble, *Warfare in the Ancient World* (1980); J. Warry, *Warfare in the Classical World* (1980); and V. D. Hanson, *The Western Way of War* (1989).

On Vietnam, see S. Karnow, *Vietnam, A History* (1983); and B. Tuchman, *The March of Folly, From Troy to Vietnam* (1984). On Munich and American policy in the Cold War, see J. L. Gaddis, *Strategies of Containment, A Critical Appraisal of Postwar American National Security Policy* (1982).

CHAPTER 1: XERXES OF PERSIA

By far the most important ancient source for Xerxes' war against the Greeks is the *Histories* of the Greek writer Herodotus. Known as the "Father of History," Herodotus wrote around the middle of the fifth century B.C. Herodotus states in his introduction that he wanted to explain the origins of the animosities between the powers of Asia and the Greeks, and so in addition to a detailed narrative of the war itself, he spends a good deal of time discussing background issues, including a fascinating discussion of the western provinces of the Persian Empire. Many translations of Herodotus are available; the one by A. de Selincourt in the Penguin series is very readable. The standard commentary on Herodotus, W. W. How and J. Wells, *A Commentary on Herodotus*, 2 vols. (1912, repr. 1957), is somewhat out of date, but still useful. Later Greek writers provide some anecdotal detail about figures in the war; notable is Plutarch's Life of Themistocles. For an early dramatized account of the war, see Aeschylus's tragedy *The Persians*. We have very little in the way of literary sources from the Persian side.

Partly as a result of the nature of our sources, and partly because of the "western" bias of much modern historiography, modern histories of Xerxes' war are usually told from a Greek point of view. N. G. L. Hammond, *A History of Greece to 322 B.C.*, 3rd ed. (1986), is a fine introduction to Greek history, and emphasizes the military operations of the Greco-Persian wars. See also O. Murray, *Early Greece* (1980); and V. Ehrenberg, *From Solon to Socrates* (1968). Good accounts of the war, written for the general reader, include P. Green, *Xerxes at Salamis* (1970), a lively, opinionated, almost novelistic book; and E. Bradford, *The Battle for the West: Thermopylae* (1980). For readers wanting more depth and detail, A. R. Burn, *Persia and the Greeks: The Defense of the West ca. 546–478 B.C.*, 2nd ed. (1984), is a well-written and well-documented discussion. Another good scholarly, if more narrowly focused, treatment of the war is C. Hignett, *Xerxes' Invasion of Greece* (1963), a narrative of the period 480–479 B.C.

Among other more specialized studies, G. B. Grundy, *The Great Persian War and Its Preliminaries* (1901), is still valuable, especially for topographical issues; on topography see also W. K. Pritchett's ongoing series of *Studies in Ancient Greek Topography*, 6 vols. to date (1965–). While there is no biography of Xerxes available for the general reader, A. Podlecki, *The Life of Themistocles* (1975), provides a biographical treatment of one of the major Greek figures of the war.

H. Bengtson, ed., *The Greeks and the Persians from the Sixth to the Fourth Centuries* (1968), contains a series of background studies, which deal with both parties to the conflict. For a detailed narrative history of the Persian Empire, based on Greek literary sources and Persian-era documentary sources, along with a discussion of the war from an overtly pro-Persian perspective, see A. T. Olmstead, *History of the Persian Empire* (1948).

CHAPTER 2: THE ALCIBIADES SYNDROME

The study of the Alcibiades syndrome begins with Thucydides, whose *Peloponnesian War*—the longest and most thorough ancient account, and a brilliant study of war, politics, and character—is indispensable. For an excellent and detailed scholarly commentary, see the five-volume *Historical Commentary on Thucydides*, ed. A. W. Gomme, A. Andrewes, and K. J. Dover (1966–81). The second most important ancient source is Plutarch's Life of Alcibiades. Although Plutarch lived hundreds of years later and although some of his details are questionable, he was in general a good and careful scholar. One might then turn to Xenophon's *Hellenica*—a somewhat pedestrian book, but it does take up the narrative in 411 at the point where Thucydides' history breaks off abruptly (Thucydides died after the war's end but before he could finish writing). The story of the war is also told in the *Universal History* of

Diodorus of Sicily, Books 12 and 13. Diodorus lived some 350 years after the war, but he drew his information (sometimes carefully, sometimes not) from the near-contemporary Ephorus, and is therefore a valuable source. Plutarch provides valuable biographical information in other Lives too, including those of Pericles, Nicias, Lysander and, to a lesser extent, Themistocles, Cimon, and Aristides. Aristophanes provides vivid if exaggerated pictures of the home front in his comedies *Acharnians, Peace, Lysistrata, Birds,* and *Frogs,* and occasionally refers to Alcibiades. Literary vignettes of Alcibiades, which may or may not be true to life, appear in several of Plato's dialogues, including *Alcibiades I* and *II* and the *Symposium.* Aristotle, or at least one of his students, discusses constitutional changes and offers a hostile account of Cleon in his *Constitution of Athens.*

Modern scholarship relies heavily on these literary sources, while also drawing information from epigraphy: the hundreds of contemporary inscriptions, many discovered only in this century, that provide much useful information about the period. Many relevant inscriptions can be found in translation in C. W. Fornara, ed., *Archaic Times to the End of the Peloponnesian War* (1977). Archaeology and the study of Greek topography have also made valuable contributions to our knowledge. A good example of this approach is W. K. Pritchett, *Studies in Ancient Greek Topography. Vol. 2: Battlefields* (1969).

For modern studies, one might begin with Thucydides and then turn to D. Kagan's excellent four-volume series on the history of the Peloponnesian War (*The Outbreak of the Peloponnesian War* [1969], *The Archidamian War* [1974], *The Peace of Nicias and the Sicilian Expedition* [1981], and *The Fall of the Athenian Empire* [1987]). There are many original and penetrating insights and some controversial theories in G. E. M. de Ste. Croix, *Origins of the Peloponnesian War* (1969). Two recent books on Alcibiades are W. M. Ellis, *Alcibiades* (1989), and S. Forde, *The Ambition to Rule: Alcibiades and the Politics of Imperialism in Thucydides* (1989); P. Brunt's "Thucydides and Alcibiades," *Revue des études grecques* 65 (1952), 59–96, remains fascinating. A lucid introduction to Thucydides as text is W. R. Connor, *Thucydides* (1984).

Some essays on individual points of strategy and tactics are: P. Brunt, "Spartan Policy and Strategy in the Archidamian War," *Phoenix* 19 (1965); T. Kelly, "Thucydides and Spartan Strategy in the Archidamian War," *American Historical Review* 87 (1982); A. Andrewes, "Notion and Kyzikos: The Sources Compared," *Journal of Hellenic Studies* 102 (1982); J. Ober, *Fortress Attica, Defense of the Athenian Land Frontier, 404–322 B.C.* (1985), chap. 3; B. S. Strauss, "Aegospotami Reexamined," *American Journal of Philology* 104 (1983); and the same author's "Tactics and Topography of Aegospotami," *American Journal of Philology* 109 (1988).

On the social history of the Peloponnesian War, see B. S. Strauss, *Athens After the Peloponnesian War: Class, Faction, and Policy 403–386 B.C.* (1986), chs. 2–3. For a general introduction to ancient Greek history, see N. G. L. Hammond, *History of Ancient Greece*, 3rd ed. (1986). For the relevance of Thucydides to modern international relations, see R. N. Lebow and B. S. Strauss, eds., *Hegemonic Rivalry from Thucydides to the Nuclear Age* (1990).

CHAPTER 3: LYSANDER AND AGESILAUS

No ancient writer is as authoritative about the Spartan hegemony as Thucydides is about the Peloponnesian War. The logical, if not fully satisfactory starting point is Xenophon. Although an Athenian, Xenophon served in the Spartan army, at times under Agesilaus's command, and settled for some years in the Peloponnesos as a Spartan pensioner. Three of his numerous writings cover the subject of this chapter: the *Hellenica* (available in a Penguin edition as *The History of My Times*), a memoir of mainly Spartan history from 411 to 362; the *Agesilaos*, an encomium of king; and the *Constitution of the Lacedaemonians*, a mixture of factual description, myth, praise, and criticism. All three are highly colored by a general pro-Spartan bias and anti-Theban hatred, interlaced with occasional but penetrating criticisms of Sparta. More balanced are Plutarch's Lives of Lysander, Agesilaus, and Pelopidas; unfortunately his Life of Epaminondas has not survived (see Further Reading for Chapter 2 for more comments on Plutarch). Plutarch also wrote a Life of Lycurgus, which liberally mixes myth and fact, and collected Sayings of Spartans and Sayings of Spartan Women—many, alas, spurious. (Penguin's *Plutarch on Sparta*, R. Talbert, ed., contains Plutarch's Lives of Lycurgus and the third-century kings Agis and Cleomenes, his Sayings of Spartans and of Spartan Women, and Xenophon's Constitution, as well as useful introductions and notes.) The fragmentary Oxyrhynchus historian (available, along with other important contemporary documents, in P. Harding, ed., *From the End of the Peloponnesian War to the Battle of Ipsus* [1985]), offers a fascinating but biased discussion of the outbreak of the Corinthian War. Another valuable if tendentious source is Diodorus of Sicily, who discusses this period in books 14 and 15 of his *Universal History* (see Further Reading for Chapter 2 for more comments on Diodorus). Aristotle offers a fundamental and devastating critique of Sparta's failure in his *Politics*, especially 1269a–1271b. See also Polybius's *Histories*, Book 6, paras. 10, 48–9. Herodotus's *Histories* is important for Sparta before 430 B.C.

The best brief introduction to Sparta is W. G. Forrest, *A History of Sparta 950–192 B.C.* (1980) or, for more of an institutional approach, M. I. Finley, "Sparta and Spartan Society" in Finley, *Economy and Society in Ancient Greece* (1983) or the less recent H. Michell, *Sparta* (1952). Other recent introductions are L. F. Fitzhardinge, *The Spartans* (1980); J. T. Hooker, *The Ancient Spartans* (1980); and A. Powell, *Athens and Sparta: Constructing Greek Political and Social History from 478 B.C.* (1988), especially good on Sparta's manipulation of symbols. Further details on Spartan society, with a mixture of historical, archaeological, and anthropological evidence, can be found in P. A. Cartledge, *Sparta and Lakonia: A Regional History c. 1300–362 B.C.* (1979).

For a thorough discussion of Sparta in the period 404–360, see Cartledge's magisterial *Agesilaos and the Crisis of Sparta* (1987), which we have frequently drawn on. C. D. Hamilton employs a more traditional military-political approach to the subject in his *Sparta's Bitter Victories: Politics and Diplomacy in the Corinthian War* (1979), as does J. Buckler in *The Theban Hegemony, 371–362 B.C.* (1980). On the military history of the period, see J. K. Anderson, *Military Theory and Practice in the Age of Xenophon* (1970). On the Spartan army, see J. F. Lazenby, *The Spartan Army* (1983). On Sparto-Persian relations, see D. M. Lewis, *Sparta and Persia* (1977). For a revisionist interpretation of Leuctra see V. Hanson, "Epameinondas, the Battle of Leuctra (371 B.C.) and the 'Revolution' in Greek Battle Tactics," *Classical Antiquity* 7 (1988), 190–207.

On the image of Sparta in antiquity see E. N. Tigerstedt, *The Legend of Sparta in Classical Antiquity*, 3 vols. (1964–78); on Sparta's image in later years, see E. Rawson, *The Spartan Tradition in European Thought* (1980).

CHAPTER 4: DARIUS III OF PERSIA

While the modern literature on Alexander and Macedon is vast, that on Darius and Persia is limited—no surprise, considering the ancient sources. We are completely dependent on Greek and Macedonian writers (and their Roman followers) for the details of Darius's deliberations and policies: needless to say, these sources are highly biased, and every statement in them requires critical evaluation. Useful information about Persian history comes from art and architecture and from the valuable inscriptions at the royal palaces and monuments, but virtually all of these considerably antedate Darius's rule. Darius's coins and a relief from his unfinished tomb present stylized likenesses. Baked clay tablets from Persepolis and Mesopotamia, though much earlier, are nonetheless instructive. For the evidence, see I. Gershevitch, ed., *Cambridge History of Iran. Vol. 2: The Median and Achaemenid Periods* (1985), especially chs. 10 and 11, 17 and 18.

For the Greek literary evidence on Persia down to the late fifth century, see Further Reading for Chapter 1. On fourth-century Persia, see Xenophon, especially his *Anabasis*, and the snippets left of the writings of Ctesias. See J. M. Cook, *The Persian Empire* (1983), ch. 2, for a discussion of the sources. Cook's book is probably the best brief general introduction to this period of Persian Achaemenid history; for other books on Persia see Further Reading for Chapter 1. E. Badian discusses fourth-century Persia (as well as Alexander's campaign) in "Alexander in Iran," in I. Gershevitch, ed., *Cambridge History of Iran*, vol. 2, 420–501. On Greco-Persian relations, see A. R. Burn, "Persia and the Greeks," in I. Gershevitch, ed., *Cambridge History of Iran*, vol. 2, 292–391.

None of the works of the several Greek and Macedonian authors who wrote about Alexander in the fourth century B.C. have survived, except as quoted in later Greek and Latin literature; several ancient histories of Alexander, all written hundreds of years later, are extant. The best is Arrian's *Expedition of Alexander* (ca. A.D. 150). Much useful information survives in Book 17 of Diodorus of Sicily's *Universal History* (ca. 20 B.C.). The Roman Quintus Curtius Rufus (first century A.D.) adds a heavy dose of moralizing and myth to the facts in his *History of Alexander;* Plutarch's Life of Alexander (second century A.D.) is briefer but somewhat more reliable. Perhaps the least useful is Justin, a second-century A.D. Roman writer who abbreviates the book of Trogus, a Romanized Gaul writing at about the time of Christ.

The best modern introduction to Alexander is R. L. Fox's *Alexander the Great* (1973). Fox gives Darius a much fairer shake than most writers, and is an excellent stylist as well. For a shorter introduction (Fox is over 500 pages long), try J. R. Hamilton, *Alexander the Great* (1973). U. Wilcken's *Alexander the Great* (1967), though older, is also useful.

J. Keegan, the military historian, provides a good appreciation of Alexander's leadership in a chapter of *The Mask of Command* (1987). The military historian J. F. C. Fuller offers a longer analysis of issues of generalship, especially in the set-piece battles, in *The Generalship of Alexander the Great* (1960). Logistics and supply are discussed incisively by D. Engels, *Alexander the Great and the Logistics of the Macedonian Army* (1978).

CHAPTER 5: HANNIBAL VERSUS ROME

The most important ancient source for the early part of the war (down to Cannae) is the third book of the *Histories* of Polybius, a Greek aristocrat who wrote a history of Rome's rise to power in the mid–second century B.C. During the time he was writing his history, Polybius was a (rather privileged) prisoner of war in Rome and he writes from an overtly pro-Roman perspective. He attempted, however, to be as fair as possible to the Carthaginian side. Regrettably, much of his text is lost to us; the surviving sections are available in a good translation by E. Schuckburgh (1980). For a commentary, see F. W. Walbank, *A Historical Commentary on Polibius*, vol. 1 (1957). More chauvinistically pro-Roman is Livy, who wrote a massive and highly colored Roman history in the mid–first century B.C. Livy's history includes a detailed discussion of the Punic Wars (Books 21–30). Livy used Polybius's history as the basis of his own account, and is the best surviving narrative history of the war against Hannibal for the years 215–202. The relevant books of Livy's histories are available in a Penguin edition. Among other ancient sources for the war are Plutarch's Lives of Marcellus, Cato the Elder, and Fabius Maximus (a good Penguin edition is available).

There are many modern accounts of the war. B. Caven, *The Punic Wars* (1980) is a good narrative history with usable maps. T. A. Dorey and D. R. Dudly, *Rome Against Carthage* (1972) is lively and anecdotal. More detailed, fully documented, with good maps and a glossary of Latin terms is J. F. Lazenby, *Hannibal's War: A Military History of the Second Punic War* (1978). The much-discussed issue of Hannibal's route over the Alps is the subject of D. Proctor, *Hannibal's March in History* (1971).

The two greatest generals of the war (and especially Hannibal) have often been treated biographically. For popular accounts of the Carthaginian's career, see H. Lamb, *Hannibal: One Man Against Rome* (1958); L. Cottrell, *Hannibal, Enemy of Rome* (1960); or G. de Beer, *Hannibal: Challenging Rome's Supremacy* (1969), which has nice photographs. For Scipio Africanus, see the almost hagiographic biography by B. H. Liddell Hart, *A Greater Than Napoleon: Scipio Africanus* (1930), which emphasizes strategic and tactical issues; or the two important studies by H. H. Scullard, *Scipio Africanus and the Second Punic War* (1930) and *Scipio Africanus: Soldier and Politician* (1970).

Background information on Rome in the period of the early to middle republic can be found in H. H. Scullard, *A History of the Roman World, 753–146 B.C.*, 4th ed. (1980); and R. M. Errinton, *The Dawn of Empire: Rome's Rise to World Empire* (1972), which covers the period 264–146. A. J. Toynbee, *Hannibal's Legacy: The Hannibalic War's Effects on Roman Life*, 2 vols. (1965), is a monumental study by a great historian. Toynbee contrasts the situation in Rome and Italy before the First Punic War with the situation after the end of the Second. For detailed accounts of various factors in Rome's victory, see P. A. Brunt, *Italian Manpower, 225 B.C.–A.D. 14* (1971), for demographics; H. H. Scullard, *Roman Politics, 220–150 B.C.*, 2nd ed. (1973), for political affairs; and J. H. Thiel, *A History of Roman Sea-Power Before the Second Punic War* (1954), for the Roman fleet. For the Roman army, see the studies cited in Further Reading for Chapter 6; on war elephants, see H. H. Scullard, *The Elephant in the Greek and Roman World* (1974).

Despite the recent intensive archaeological exploration of the ancient city of Carthage, much remains obscure about Carthaginian history. But for surveys of what is known, see B. H. Warmington, *Carthage* (1964); and G. Picard, *The Life and Death of Carthage* (1968).

CHAPTER 6: JUGURTHA VERSUS ROME

The Roman war against Jugurtha did not generate a large specialist literature in antiquity and has been largely ignored by modern military historians. By far the most important ancient account of the war is Sallust, *The Jugurthine War*, an account written by a historian of the mid–first century B.C. who wrote with a strongly pro-Roman and moralistic bent. The Penguin edition of Sallust's works has useful introductory material on the Roman army, Roman politics, and Numidian history. For a detailed commentary on Sallust's account, as well as a chronology of the war and an introduction to Rome's Numidian policy, see G. M. Paul, *A Historical Commentary on Sallust's 'Bellum Jugurthinum'* (1984). Among secondary ancient sources for the war, see Plutarch, Lives of Marius and Sulla (Penguin edition). The Greek and Latin authors Valerius Maximus, Florus, and Diodorus of Sicily refer to the war in passing; their works can be found in the Loeb Classical Library editions.

For an excellent introduction to Roman history in this period, see H. H. Scullard, *From the Gracchi to Nero*, 5th ed. (1982). For the events of the Third Punic War, see D. Armstrong, *The Reluctant Warriors* (1966), a lively narrative account, though written in a Cold War idiom and explicitly identifying Carthage with the United States. Some of the most useful background material is to be found in discussions of Roman imperialism, which is the subject of a fierce ongoing scholarly debate. See E. Badian, *Foreign Clientelae, 264–70 B.C.* (1958); *Roman Imperialism in the Late Republic*, 2nd ed. (1968); and W. V. Harris, *War and Imperialism in Republican Rome, 327–70 B.C.*, corrected ed. (1985).

The war against Jugurtha was intimately involved with Rome's social and political history in the period of the late republic. For the political background, see E. S. Gruen, *Roman Politics and the Criminal Courts, 149–78* B.C. (1968). For the social background, A. Toynbee, *Hannibal's Legacy*, vol. 2 (see Further Reading for Chapter 5); P. A. Brunt, *Social Conflicts in the Roman Republic* (1971); K. Hopkins, *Conquerors and Slaves* (1978). Relevant biographies of Roman figures include A. Astin, *Scipio Aemilianus* (1967); P. A. Kildahl, *Caius Marius* (1968); and T. R. Carney, *A Biography of C. Marius* (1970).

The Roman army and the reforms of Marius are important elements in the story of Jugurtha. See F. E. Adcock, *The Roman Art of War Under the Republic* (1940, repr. 1963); H. M. D. Parker, *The Roman Legions*, 2nd ed. (1958); R. E. Smith, *Service in the Post-Marian Roman Army* (1958); and M. J. V. Bell, "Tactical Reform in the Roman Republican Army," *Historia* 14 (1965), 404–22.

CHAPTER 7: MARK ANTONY

Despite its romantic associations, the story of Antony's failure has tended to be eclipsed by the success stories of Julius Caesar and Octavian/Augustus. The most readable ancient account is Plutarch's Life of Antony (available in a Penguin edition). Written in the second century A.D., but based on contemporary documents, Plutarch's Life, like all other ancient sources, is tinged with Octavian's successful propaganda. For a commentary, see C. B. R. Pelling (ed.), *Plutarch, Life of Antony* (1988). Other important ancient sources include Plutarch's Lives of Brutus, Cicero, and Julius Caesar; and Suetonius, Lives of Julius Caesar and Augustus (in *The Twelve Caesars*, available in a Penguin edition). Cicero's *Letters* (his very revealing personal correspondence) and *Philippics* (speeches directed against Antony) are both available in Loeb editions. The best ancient narrative account of the period is Appian, *The Civil Wars* (in Loeb edition).

Among modern discussions of the war, see J. M. Carter, *The Battle of Actium: The Rise and Triumph of Augustus*

Caesar (1970; despite its title, Antony is treated quite sympathetically). For accounts of the decisive battle, see W. W. Tarn, "The Battle of Actium," *Journal of Roman Studies* 21 (1931), 173–199; and G. W. Richardson, "Actium," *Journal of Roman Studies* 27 (1937), 153–164. For Antony's life, see E. Huzar, *Mark Antony: A Biography* (1978, repr. 1986). The difficult task of writing a biography of Octavian has often been attempted. See G. P. Barker, *Augustus: The Golden Age of Rome* (1937) for a readable popular account; J. Buchanan, *Augustus* (1937), for a more detailed narrative treatment; and A. H. M. Jones, *Augustus* (1970), for an assessment of Augustus's long-term policy goals. For biographies of other major players in the drama: H. Volkmann, *Cleopatra: A Study in Politics and Propaganda*, trans. T. J. Cadoux (1978), which points out the difficulty of understanding the real Cleopatra; M. Reinhold, *Marcus Agrippa* (1933); and F. A. Wright, *Marcus Agrippa: Organizer of Victory* (1937), a well-written popular account, though less fully documented than Reinhold's; D. L. Stockton, *Cicero: A Political Biography* (1971); and M. Hadas, *Sextus Pompey* (1930, repr. 1966).

The question of Antony's failure is intimately bound up with the issue of the "crisis of the Roman Republic." H. H. Scullard, *From the Gracchi to Nero*, 5th ed. (1982), is a good introduction. R. Syme, *The Roman Revolution* (1939), is still among the most important discussions. For more recent trends in scholarship, see P. A. Brunt, *The Fall of the Roman Republic and Related Essays* (1988).

CHAPTER 8: NO SECOND ALEXANDER

By the standards of evidence in ancient history, we know a great deal about the emperor Julian. Only a few of the Caesars have left us their own writings, but Julian's letters, speeches, treatises, pamphlets, and epigrams fill three volumes in the Loeb Classical Library. The fullest ancient account of his reign appears in the history of Ammianus Marcellinus (see W. Hamilton, trans., *Ammianus*

Marcellinus, *The Later Roman Empire (A.D. 354–378)* [1986]). Speeches addressed to or on the subject of Julian by the orator Libanius of Antioch, a friend of the emperor, are collected and translated in Loeb editions. Three important ancient documents in translation—a court panegyric addressed to Julian, a Christian homily against Julian, and a Christian Syriac hymn commemorating Julian's death—are collected with excellent commentary and notes in S. N. C. Lieu, ed., *The Emperor Julian, Panegyric and Polemic* (1986).

While there are still many unanswered questions about Julian's Persian expedition, recent scholarship has made major contributions. Several short but astute biographies of Julian have appeared in recent years, including G. W. Bowersock, *Julian the Apostate* (1978); R. Browning, *The Emperor Julian* (1976); and C. Head, *The Emperor Julian* (1976). Julian's intellectual world is examined in P. Athanassiadi-Fowden, *Julian and Hellenism, An Intellectual Biography* (1981).

A. Ferrill devotes a brief but incisive chapter to Julian in his *The Fall of the Roman Empire, The Military Explanation* (1986). R. T. Ridley offers a thoughtful analysis in "Notes on Julian's Persian Expedition (363)," *Historia* 22 (1973), 317–26, as does W. E. Kaegi in "Constantine's and Julian's Strategies of Strategic Surprise Against the Persians," *Athenaeum* n.s. 59 (1981), 209–13. N. J. E. Austin raises interesting questions about Ammianus's role in Julian's expedition in his *Ammianus on Warfare: An Investigation into Ammianus's Military Knowledge* (1979). See also G. A. Crump, *Ammianus Marcellinus as a Military Historian* (1975).

For the history of the period more generally, see P. Brown's impressionistic and provocative *The World of Late Antiquity, A.D. 150–750* (1971); or the more thorough A. H. M. Jones, *The Later Roman Empire, 284–604*, 2 vols. (1964). On Christianity, see R. MacMullen, *Christianizing the Roman Empire* (1984).

Index

Achaemenid Persians, 201

Achilles, 49–50

Achilles fantasy, 50

Actium, battle of (Roman Civil Wars), 212, 215, 217

Adherbal, 173, 175–179

Adrianople, battle of, 240

Aegospotami (Peloponnesian War), 69–70, 72, 77

Affair of the Herms, 62

Agamemnon, 93

Agesilaus, 77–79, 81, 86, 88, 90–101, 117

Agoge system in Sparta, 81–83, 90

Agrippa, Marcus, 206–208, 212

Ahuramazda, Divine Lord of Light and Truth, 23

Alcibiades, 47, 50, 59–64, 66–67, 69–72, 88, 112

Alcibiades syndrome, 50–73, 87

Alexander the Great, 93, 104–131, 133, 203, 219, 230

Alexander the Great and the Logistics of the Macedonian Army (Engels), 4

Alps, Hannibal's crossing of the, 143–144

Ammianus Marcellinus, 222, 226–227, 230, 238–239

Amphipolis, battle for (Peloponnesian War), 56–58

Amyntas, 125

Anastasius, 239

Ancient military failures, reasons to study, 8–13

Antiochus III, 157, 163–164
Antonius, Lucius, 206
Antonius, Marcus (Mark Antony), 191–215
Appeasement vs. resolve, 10–12
Archeologists and military history, 4
Archidamian War, 51–52
Archidamus, King of Sparta, 51
Arginusae, battle of (Peloponnesian War), 67–69
Aristophanes, 50
Aristotle, 84, 87, 100
Arrian, 123
Arsaces, 232, 237–239
Art of War, The (Sun Tzu), 6
Artaxerxes II, 110
Artaxerxes III, 111–112, 115
Artaxerxes IV, 112
Artemisium, battle of (Greek and Persian War), 37–38
Assyrian Empire, 20–21
Ataturk, 106
Athens
    Greek and Persian War and, 18, 24–26, 29–32, 36, 38–40
    Peloponnesian War and, 45–73, 75
    post Peloponnesian War, 87–89, 95, 97
    See also Greece
Atossa (Cyrus's daughter), 22, 31
Attalus III, 174
Augustus, Emperor (Octavian), 191, 193–195, 198–200, 206–208, 210–215, 217
Aulis, Agesilaus's sacrifice at, 92–93, 97
Aulus Albinus, 182–183
Avidius Cassius, 232

Babylon, conquest of by the Persians, 21, 42
Baebius, 181
Bagoas the eunuch, 111–112
Basilina (mother of Julian), 220
Behistun inscription, Darius's autobiography in, 22–23
Bestia, Lucius Calpurnius, 179–182
Bocchus (king of Mauretania), 184–186
Bomilcar, 184
Brasidas, 56–57, 72

Bronze Age of Greece, 17
Brundisium, Mark Antony's landing at, 206–207
Brutus, Marcus Junius, 191–193, 197, 200, 202, 204

Caesar, Julius, 189–199, 204, 213
Cambyses, 22, 24
Cannae, battle of (Second Punic War), 5, 135, 137, 146–148, 151, 154–155, 163
Cartagena, 136–137, 153, 156
Carthage and the Punic Wars, 134–161, 163, 170–172
Carus, 232
Casilinum, Capanian fort of, 149
Cassius, Gaius, 191–193, 197, 200, 204
Catapults, use of by Greco-Romans, 5
Cavalry, role of in Greco-Roman warfare, 5
Chaeronea, battle of, 104, 115, 119
Charidemus, 124–125
Christian Church, persecution of, 218. See also Julian, Emperor (the Apostate)
Cirta, siege of and massacre at (Jugurthine War), 178–179, 185, 187
Civil Wars (Rome), 166, 186–187, 190–215
Clausewitz, Carl von, 2–3, 41, 107, 117, 187, 246
Cleombrotus, 98
Cleon, 51, 54–57
Cleopatra VII, 197, 202–205, 209–212, 215
Clodius, 206
Codomannus. See Darius III
Constantine the Great, Emperor, 218, 220–221
Constantinople, establishment of, 218, 224
Constantius, Emperor, 218–224, 234
Constantius, Flavius, 220
Corinthian War, 88–89, 94–95, 97, 110
Coronea, battle of (Corinthian War), 92, 97
Crassus, Marcus Licinius, 201, 209, 219
Ctesiphon, Julian's campaign against, 229, 231–237
Cunaxa, battle of, 112
Curio, 206
Curtius, 122, 127
Cyrus, King of Persia, 21–22, 24, 31, 42–43
Cyrus, Prince of Persia, 86, 88, 112
Cyzicus, battle of, 117

Dardanelles, whipping of by Xerxes, 33, 36
Darius I, 22–23, 26, 29, 31, 109
Darius III (Codomannus), 104–131
Dark Age of Greece, 17
Datis, 29–31
David, 50
Delian League, 45–46
Delphi, oracle at, 35, 38
Demosthenes, 115–116
Diocletian, Emperor, 218
Diodorus of Sicily, 117, 123–124

Egypt, under Cleopatra, 197, 202–205, 209–212
Engels, Donald, 4
Epaminondas, 97–99, 119
Ephesos, battle of, 116–117
Ephrem of Nisibis, 240
Esther, Book of, 105

Fabian strategy, 148–149, 156, 184
Fabius Maximus, 146, 148–150
Face of Battle, The (Keegan), 4
Failures, reasons to study, 8–13
Flaminius, Gaius, 145–146
Flexibility, as key to strategy, 247
Four Hundred (Athenian oligarchy), 66
France. See Gaul and the Gauls
Frogs, The (Aristophanes), 50
Fulvia (wife of Lucius Antonius), 206

Gallus (Julian's brother), 220–221
Gaugamela, battle of, 107–108, 120, 127–128, 130
Gaul and the Gauls
    Caesar's wars in, 189–190, 196–197
    Julian's campaign to pacify, 218, 222–223, 227
    Punic Wars and, 134, 141, 144, 151, 153, 159
Granicus River, battle of, 107, 109, 119–121
Greece
    Bronze Age of, 17
    Hellenistic era after Alexander the Great, 133–134
    Macedonian Wars and, 163–164, 168

Greece *(cont.)*
  Mithradates and, 190
  operational tactics of, 4–6
  Peloponnesian War, 45–73, 75–79, 100, 110, 112
  Persia and (Greek Wars), 17–43
  Punic Wars and, 152
  relations with Persian Empire post Peloponnesian War, 75–76, 88,
    93–95, 100, 109–110, 114–118, 121–122, 130
  Spartan imperial policy after the Peloponnesian War, 75–101
  World War I and, 106
Gregory of Nazianzius (archbishop of Constantinople), 222

Haliartus, battle of, 85–86
Halicarnassos, battle for, 121–122
Hamilcar Barca, 135–136, 139
Hannibal vs. Rome, 5, 133–161, 163, 169–170
Hanson, Victor, 4
Hasdrubal (brother of Hannibal), 153
Hasdrubal (uncle of Hannibal), 136–137
Hellenistic era after Alexander the Great, 133–134
Hellespoont straits, whipping of by Xerxes, 33, 36
Henry V, 50
Heracleides, 113
Herms, Affair of the, 62
Herodotus, 32
Hiempsal, 173, 175
Hippias, 25, 29–31
History of the Jugurthine War (Sallust), 166
Hitler, Adolf, 231, 242
Homer, 17
Hormisdas, Prince of Persia, 232–233
Hundred Years' War, 106

Ideology and strategy, 6–9
Iliad (Homer), 17, 49
Infantry, role of in Greco-Roman warfare, 4–5
Iono-Decelean War, 52, 65
Isocrates, 110
Issus, battle of, 107, 119–120, 124–126, 130
Italy. *See* Roman Empire

Joan of Arc, 106
Jovian, 238–240
Jugurtha and the Jugurthine War, 6, 163–187, 204
Julian, Emperor (the Apostate), 209, 218–243

Keegan, John, 4
Kennedy, John F., 50
King's Peace, 94–96, 110

Lamachus, General (Sicilian Expedition), 61–62, 64
Lepidus, Marcus Aemilius, 200, 207–208
Leuctra campaign, 79, 84, 98–99, 101
Libanius, Julian's letters to, 228, 231
Life of Lycurgus (Plutarch), 81
Livia (wife of Octavian), 214
Livy, 136, 138
Lycurgus, laws of, 79–85, 87, 90, 96, 100
Lysander, 68–70, 72, 75, 77–79, 81, 85–90, 92, 95, 99, 101, 114
Lysandria, 86

Macedon
   Alexander the Great and, 104–131, 133
   cavalry use by, 5
   Romans and (Macedonian Wars), 152, 163–164, 168
Magnesia, battle of, 164
Mago, 153–156
Mamertinus, 222
Mantinea, battle of (Peloponnesian War), 59–60
Marathon, battle of (Greek and Persian War), 29–32
Marcellus, 152
Marcus Aurelius, 230
Marius, Gaius, 164–167, 184–186, 189–190, 196
Marx, Karl, 81
Masinissa, 170–173
Massiva, 182
Medes, 21, 24
Melos, battle for (Peloponnesian War), 59
Memmius, Gaius, 180–181
Memnon of Rhodes, 105, 111, 116–123, 130
Mentor of Rhodes, 111
Metaurus, battle of (Second Punic War), 153

Metellus, 183–185
Micipsa, 171–174, 176
Military failures, reasons to study, 8–13
Mithradates of Pontus, 190, 202
Munich model of appeasement, 11–12
Muthul, battle at (Jugurthine War), 184
Mycenaean world of Greece, 17

Napoleon, 242
Naval tactics, classical, 5–6
Nazis, 106
Nero, Claudius, 153
Nero, emperor of Rome, 215
New Carthage, 136–137, 153, 156
Nicias, 51, 57–62, 64–65
Notium, battle of (Peloponnesian War), 67
Numidians
   and Hannibal, 145, 154, 157, 170
   and Rome (Jugurthine War), 163–187, 189

Octavia (wife of Mark Antony), 207, 209, 211, 215
Octavianus, Gaius Julius Caesar (Octavian), 191, 193–195, 198–200,
      206–208, 210–215, 217
Odyssey (Homer), 17
Olympias (wife of Philip II), 104, 116
On War (Clausewitz), 2, 187
Operational tactics, 4–6
Orontes, 111
Ottoman Empire and World War I, 106

Paradigms for strategic decision making 7–9, 245
Parsifal, 50
Parthians
   campaigns of Mark Antony against the, 201–202, 205–206,
      208–210, 212–213
   cavalry use by the, 5
Pasargadae, Cyrus's grave in, 22
Peace of Nicias, 51, 58–60
Pelopidas, 97–98
Peloponnesian War, 45–73, 75–79, 100, 110, 112
Pergamum, 164, 174

Pericles, 46–47, 50–54, 59
Pericles (son of the great Pericles), 68
Perseus (son of Philip V), 164
Persian Empire
  Achaemenid Persians, 201
  Darius III and, 103–131
  early history of, 20–23
  Greek Wars and, 17–43
  Peloponnesian War and, 48, 65–68, 70, 72
  post Peloponnesian War, 75–76, 88, 93–95, 100
  role of king in, 22–23, 31, 42
  Sassanid dynasty, war with Rome (Julian), 218–243
Pharsalus, Caesar's victory at, 191, 193, 197
Philip of Macedon, 5
Philip II of Macedon, 93, 104, 111–112, 114–116, 118
Philip V, 152, 163
Philippi, battle of (Roman Civil Wars), 190–195, 200, 202
Pisastratus, 25
Plato, 81
Plutarch, 59, 81, 84, 123, 203–205, 215
Policy and strategy, 2–4
Polis system of government in Greece, 17–18
Polybius, 136, 138, 147, 154, 164
Pompey, Gnaeus, 191–192, 197
Procopius, 232–233, 235, 237, 239–241
Projectile barrage, role of in Greco-Roman warfare, 4–5
Ptolemy I, 203
Ptolemy Caesarion, 204, 210
Punic Wars, 134–161, 163, 169–171
Pylos, battle for (Peloponnesian War), 56, 58, 60
Pyrrhus, 155

Resolve, use of military force to demonstrate, 10–12
Rock of Behistun, 22–23
Roman Empire
  Caesar and, 189–199, 220
  emperors of, 217–243
  growth of and the Punic Wars, 133–161, 163–164
  Jugurthine War and, 165, 167, 170–187
  Julian and, 218–243
  late Republic (post Jugurthine War), 189, 195–198

Roman Empire (cont.)
  Mark Antony and, 191–215
  operational tactics of, 4–6
  Punic Wars, after the, 163–164, 167–170
Rubicon, Caesar's crossing of the, 197

Sacred Band (Theban infantry), 97–98
Saguntum, 142–143, 150
Salamis, Battle of, 18–20, 38–40
Sallust, 166, 172–173, 175–176, 178, 181
Sapor II, 224–225, 232–233, 235–239
Sardis, battle for (Greek and Persian War), 28
Sassanid dynasty (Persia), 218–243
Satraps' Revolts, 110–111
Schlieffen Plan, myth of the, 231
Scipio Aemilianus, 172–173, 181
Scipio Africanus, Cornelius, 144, 149, 152–154, 156–157, 170
Scipio, Cornelius, 144
Scythians, 27
Sebastian, 232, 237, 239
Sempronius, Tiberius, 144–145, 160
Severus, 232
Sextus Pompey, 207–210, 213
Sicilian Expedition, (Peloponnesian War), 50–51, 60–65, 70
Sicily, battles for
  Peloponnesian War, 50–51, 60–65, 70
  Second Punic War, 152
Sirmium, Julian's capture of, 223
Spain
  Carthaginian domination of, 136–137, 141–142, 144, 150
  Roman domination of, 167–169, 172
Sparta
  Greek and Persian War and, 18, 24–26, 28, 35, 37–38
  imperial policy after the Peloponnesian War, 75–79, 83–101
  Macedonian battles with, 123–124
  Peloponnesian War and, 45–73, 75, 100
  social and political system of, 79–85
  See also Greece
Spurius Albinus, 182
Stalin, Josef, 106
Strasbourg, battle of (Julian), 223

Strategy and policy, 2–4; and ideology, 7–9
Sulla, 185–186, 189, 196, 201
Sun Tzu, 6–7, 112
Syracuse, battles for
  Peloponnesian War, 50–51, 60–65, 70
  Second Punic War, 152

Tactics, operational, 4–6
Tarentum, Roman destruction of, 150
Tarquin the Proud, 191
Technology, role of in war, 10
Ten Thousand, Xenophon and his, 219
Themistocles, 19, 39–40, 42
Thermopylae, battle for (Greek and Persian War), 35–38
Thucydides, 48–49, 54, 57–59, 62, 65, 72
Timaia (Queen of Sparta), 66
Tissaphernes, 112
Tragedy, classical, 91
Trajan, Emperor, 219, 232
Trasimene, battle of (Second Punic War), 146, 154
Trebia, battle of (Second Punic War), 145, 154, 160
Triumvirate (following Caesar's death), 198–215
Trojan War, 93
Truceless War, 139, 141
Tuchman, Barbara, 12–13
Tyre, battle for, 126–127

Valens, 240–241
Valentinian, 240
Vietnam, America's involvement in, 10–12, 242–243

Western Way of War, The (Hanson), 4
World War I, 106, 242
World War II, 106, 231

Xanthus, mass suicide in, 202
Xenophon, 219
Xerxes, 18–20, 31–43

Zama, battle of (Second Punic War), 157, 170, 184
Zarathustra, 23